JERUSALEM
PRAYER TEAM
✡

"Pray for the Peace of Jerusalem..."
www.jerusalemprayerteam.org

DR. MICHAEL D. EVANS

#1 *NEW YORK TIMES* BESTSELLING AUTHOR

MIKE EVANS

STAND WITH ISRAEL

FRIENDS OF ZION

TIMEWORTHY
BOOKS

P.O. BOX 30000, PHOENIX, AZ 85046

Design: Peter Gloege | LOOK Design Studio

Hardcover: 978-1-62961-018-4
Paperback: 978-1-62961-019-1
   Canada: 978-1-62961-020-7

Unless otherwise indicated, all scripture quotations are taken from The New King James Version of the Bible. Copyright© 1979, 1980, 1982, 1983, 1984 by Thomas Nelson, Inc. Publishers. Used by permission.

Scripture quotations marked NIV are taken from The Holy Bible: New International Version® NIV®. Copyright © 1973, 1978, 1984 by International Bible Society. Used by permission of Zondervan Publishing House. All rights reserved.

Scripture quotations marked NLT are taken from the New Living Translation, copyright © 1996, 2004 by Tyndale Charitable Trust. Used by permission of Tyndale House Publishers.

Scripture quotations marked ESV are taken from The Holy Bible, English Standard Version. Containing the Old and New Testaments. J. I. Packer, ed. Wheaton, Illinois: Crossway Bibles (a division of Good News Publishers), 2001.

This book is dedicated to
the six million Jewish men, women and children
who were murdered in Nazi death camps
during the Holocaust, and to the survivors—
living memorials of courage, resolve and resilience.
We echo their heartfelt cry of "Never Again!"

Psalm 122

I was glad when they said to me,
"Let us go to the house of the Lord."
And now here we are,
standing inside your gates, O Jerusalem.
Jerusalem is a well-built city;
its seamless walls cannot be breached.
All the tribes of Israel—the Lord's people—
make their pilgrimage here.
They come to give thanks to the name of the Lord,
as the law requires of Israel.
Here stand the thrones where judgment is given,
the thrones of the dynasty of David.

Pray for peace in Jerusalem.
May all who love this city prosper.
O Jerusalem, may there be peace within your walls
and prosperity in your palaces.
For the sake of my family and friends, I will say,
"May you have peace."
*For the sake of the house of the L*ORD *our God,*
I will seek what is best for you, O Jerusalem. (NLT)

GOD'S CALL AND CHARGE

A t the lowest point in my life as a Christian and a minister, I thought God was through with me. My father's rejection had eaten at me like acid. For over five years, I had given him half my paycheck to cover his house and car payments. He had never uttered a thank you for my sacrifice. As a result, I had become depressed, was experiencing tachycardia (an abnormally fast heart rate), and at the same time, was battling a heredity condition in the dystonia family (a neurological disorder that causes involuntary movement of the head and neck).

As I sat on our back steps one morning, I reached for my Bible and opened it only to read God's words of assurance: *"Do not remember the former things, nor consider the things of old. Behold I will do a new thing, now it shall spring forth; shall you not know it? I will even make a road in the wilderness and rivers in the desert,"* (Isaiah 43:18, NKJV.)

WOW! God was promising to do a new thing. He was speaking to me through the Word—affirming me as His child. The presence of God filled my being!

That scripture became my constant companion. I posted it in my car, in my office, on the mirror in my bathroom, and on the refrigerator door. I made it into a card and put it in my wallet. I thought about it, meditated on it, and prayed it day after day. A sign inside the door of my office read, "God is closer than you think; greater than you think; more committed than you think." I still had no idea how huge was my discovery.

I preached on the following Sunday morning, but instead of going home to my wife, Carolyn, to announce my retirement from the ministry, I shocked her with: "I'm going to Israel! I'm going to meet with Prime Minister Begin. God is telling me to go."

"Honey, are you absolutely certain this is God leading you?" Carolyn wondered. "You don't know the prime minister. Did you get an invitation from somebody to go?"

"No, but God said, 'Go,' and I can't run *from* God. I want to run *to* God." I was convinced it would happen.

I flew to New York and took a room at the Plaza Hotel to pray. The following morning as I sat in the hotel, reading my Bible, God again gave me a scripture He had given me before: *"But those who wait on the LORD Shall renew their strength; They shall mount up with wings like eagles, They shall run and not be weary, They shall walk and not faint,"* (Isaiah 40:31, NKJV.)

I sent a wire to the prime minister's office asking for a meeting and advised where I would be staying. I didn't know why he would even want to see me, an unknown Christian. I was not well-known as a Zionist, nor was I akin to Dr. Billy Graham, but I was going to do what God had directed me to do.

Several days later, I set off for the airport and an encounter that would become the focus of my life and ministry. After a long and tiring flight, I checked in to the hotel in Jerusalem and began to pray. For a week I stayed in my hotel room fasting and praying.

One morning the phone rang shrilly. A voice on the other end said, "This is Yehiel Kadashai, Prime Minister Begin's personal secretary. Is this Mike Evans? The prime minister would like to meet with you. Are you available to meet this afternoon?"

My heart stood still. I stammered, "Yes, what time should I come?"

Mr. Kadashai confirmed a time, and I dropped the handset back in the cradle. My knees turned to jelly and I dropped to the side of the bed. I was going to meet the prime minister of Israel! God had honored His promise to me.

A week after my arrival, I found myself in Menachem Begin's office. The prime minister was a small man, but with a commanding presence. We shook hands and he invited me to sit. I started the conversation with, "Hello, how are you?" Then he talked for thirty minutes, which was good because I was speechless! Four times during our conversation he asked, "Why did you come?" The silence stretched between us. Finally, he asked again, "Do you know why you came?"

"No." I quietly responded. "I just know that God sent me."

"God sent you, but He didn't tell you why?"

"No, He didn't tell me why."

He called for his secretary to come into his office.

"Nearly eight thousand miles, Kadashai, to meet with me, and he says nothing except God sent him. Kadashai, shake his hand. We have found an honest man! He believes God sent him, but he admits he doesn't know why."

Then he turned to me and asked, "When God tells you why, will you come back and tell me?" I agreed to his request.

The following morning, God gave me the answer to deliver to Prime Minister Begin. I called his secretary and arranged to meet with him again. As I walked into his office later that day, he held out his hand and asked, "So, why did you come?"

"To build a bridge," I blurted out.

"Oh, I see—a bridge? What kind of bridge? Like the Brooklyn Bridge in New York City?"

"No, Mr. Prime Minister, a bridge of love." It suddenly became clear to me what the "new thing" was that God was going to do in my life. "A bridge between Christians in America and Jews in Israel," I smiled.

"I like that," Mr. Begin said. "I will help you build that bridge."

The next morning following my devotions, I picked up the *Jerusalem Post* and read the story of Jonathan Netanyahu. Suddenly the Spirit of God spoke to me as I looked at the Word of God: *"And you shall love the Lord your God with all your heart, with all your soul, with all your mind, and with all your strength. This is the first commandment,"* (Mark 12:30, NKJV.) I felt strongly that I was to go to the home of Benzion Netanyahu and offer my condolences on the anniversary of the death of his son Jonathan. He had been the lone casualty during the raid to rescue Jewish hostages being held in Entebbe, Uganda.[1] I had no idea what might happen when I arrived, but God had paved the way before me. The elder Mr. Netanyahu was a considerate host. He greeted me graciously and invited me into his home. He pointed to an overstuffed chair. "Come in, have a seat. Would you like tea?"

After our tea had been served, I said, "Mr. Netanyahu, I saw a picture of you standing on the tarmac when your son's body was flown home from Uganda. It had to have been the worst day of your life, yet you held your head high. It was your eyes that captivated me. They were filled with the pain of a father who had tragically lost his son."

Benzion's eyes brimmed with tears. "That was, indeed, the worst day of my life."

Just then a door opened and a young man walked into the room. About thirty years old, he was dressed in a suit and carried himself with purpose. He glanced at me and shyly smiled. "I heard your American accent and wondered who was visiting today."

Benzion gestured with his right hand, "This is my son Benjamin."

We shook hands, and Benjamin asked, "What brings you to our home?"

"I was just telling your father I came to offer my condolences on the anniversary of the death of Jonathan."

Benjamin took a seat on the arm of a nearby chair, and I sat down again. "You were intrigued by the story about Jonathan?"

"I wanted you to know that you are not alone," I continued. "You do not face the loss of your son and brother alone. You have friends who stand with you. I think God wanted me to come here and tell you that, and so I have come."

As Benjamin looked into my eyes, pain at the loss of his brother was palpable. I stood slowly, put my hand on Benjamin's shoulder, and said, "You loved your brother Jonathan as the Jonathan of old loved his friend David. From the ashes of your despair will come strength from God."

The sound of my voice seemed as if it were coming from far off, but the words kept rolling off my lips like water cascading over the rocks. "Yet unlike Jonathan of old, who died in battle defending his country, you will accede to the seat of power. One day you will become the prime minister of Israel, not once but twice. And the second time will be the most crucial in Israel's history. May I pray with you?"

Benjamin acquiesced, and I reached in my pocket for a small vial of oil I had purchased earlier that day. I anointed his head with oil. As my voice trailed off, I suddenly felt weak, as if delivering those words had drained all my energy. As I sank down into a chair, I ran my hand over my face and it was wet with tears.

Benjamin nodded and stood. "Lucky for you, we do not live in ancient times. You know what happened to the prophet whose words did not come true. We shall see if these words are genuine. But I must tell you, Mr. Evans, I have no interest in politics. I am going into business."

I nodded. "Yes, but I am not afraid to be held accountable for the words God has given me." I pushed up from the chair. "Gentlemen, I appreciate your hospitality in allowing me into your home."

"Come. I will walk you to the door," Benjamin offered.

The next day, I again met with Prime Minister Begin and told him of my encounter with the Netanyahu family. I said, "I met the prime minister of Israel yesterday."

He chuckled and said, "No, you met me two days ago."

"No, I met the man who will someday be prime minister of Israel twice." I told him of the prophecy that Benjamin would be prime minister of Israel, and asked Mr. Begin if he would give the young man a post in his government.

Begin nodded. "Benzion Netanyahu's son? He is a fine young man. But he withdrew from public life after the death of his brother." He thought a moment longer and then stood. "My friend, I am glad to have this time with you." He came from behind the desk and embraced me. "I hope we can enjoy many more times like this."

The following day Benjamin was offered the position of Deputy Chief of Mission at the Israeli Embassy in Washington, D.C. It was, indeed, the beginning of his political career that in 2013 found him serving a second time as prime minister of Israel.

It was the start of a God-ordained friendship with Mr. Begin and a relationship with Israel that would redefine the rest of my life. My good friend Ben Armstrong, executive director of the National Religious Broadcasters, wrote of my relationship with the prime minister, "Mr. Begin genuinely loved Mike Evans. He was his friend."

It was also the beginning of my association with Dr. Reuven Hecht, one of the prime minister's advisors, and Isser Harel, the director of Mossad, Israel's intelligence agency.

On September 30, 1980, Harel invited Reuven and me to dinner at his home. It was my introduction to the vagaries of terrorism. As we enjoyed our meal and talked of various terrorist attacks targeting Jews, I asked Harel, "Will terrorism ever come to America?"

Harel leaned back in his chair. "America is developing a tolerance for terrorism. The United States has the power to fight terrorism, but not the will; the terrorists have the will, but not the power. Yet, I fear it will come in time."

Intrigued by his answer, I asked, "Where will it come?"

He thought for a moment. "New York is the symbol of your freedom and capitalism. It's likely they will strike there first at your tallest building, because it is a symbol of your strength and power."

Harel paused. "As I said, terrorists have the will, but not the power. All of that could change in time. Oil buys more than tents. You in the West kill a fly and rejoice. In the Middle East, we kill one, and a hundred flies come to the funeral."

Twelve years later, terrorists launched their first attack on the World Trade Center. Harel's ideas quickly took on the tenor of the prophetic. Unsuccessful in their attempt to bring the high-rise buildings to the ground, a second attempt was made. On September 11, 2001, the worst terrorist attack ever on American soil rocked both New York City, the financial center of the United States, and Washington, DC, its seat of government. Like Pearl Harbor, it would be a day of infamy never to be forgotten.

The following year, with the assistance of then-Prime Minister Ehud Olmert, I launched the Jerusalem Prayer Team. Today Team members own a five-story building in the heart of Jerusalem in a prominent location overlooking Independence Park and within walking distance to the Old City.

It will house a museum dedicated to the heroes and history of those who have helped the Jewish people resettle in their homeland. The museum will provide interactive displays and areas for research, as well as a bond between those Christian Zionists who have aided Israel through the years with the Jewish people. The vision of the Jerusalem Prayer Team is to have a place where the achievements of dedicated men and women can be shared with thousands of visitors yearly. For decades, sympathetic Gentiles from around the world have joined Jewish people in the trenches. With each succeeding battle for existence, new Christian Zionists have sprung up to stand with the Children of Israel in their battle to survive. Those are the men and women the new Museum of Christian Zionism will spotlight—those who have staunchly supported the Jewish people before, during, and after the formation of the State of Israel.

Today my heart is overflowing with gratitude to God as the dream He placed in my spirit more than thirty years ago has become a reality. When the contract for the purchase of the building that will house the Jerusalem World Center—within walking distance of the Temple Mount in Jerusalem—was signed, I was reminded once again that every promise from God is certain and sure, no matter how long we have to wait for it. Abraham waited for the promised birth of Isaac for some twenty-five years, but in God's perfect timing, the son of promise was born.

When I first met with Prime Minister Menachem Begin more than thirty years ago and we agreed to work together to build a bridge between Christians and Jews, part of that dream was to have a permanent presence in the Holy City. Now we are moving forward with this beautiful facility to minister to the Jewish people and to you.

Through the years, I've been asked repeatedly why Christians should support Israel. I've written this book in an attempt to clarify the biblically-based reasons why, together, we should support the Jewish people in their God-given land.

STAND WITH ISRAEL

There are numerous reasons why, as Christians, you and I should stand with Israel in these last days. In the pages of this book, we will explore many of them. Below are just five of the imperatives for championing God's Chosen People:

1. God promises to bless those who bless Israel and curse him who curses Israel. (Genesis 12:3.)

This verse was God's promise to Abraham forevermore. Jehovah would bless those men who chose to bestow compassion and benevolence upon His people. This was not just an Old Testament command; the New Testament gives several examples of God's generosity to Gentiles who aided the Jewish people—Cornelius in Acts 10, the Centurion in Luke 7, and Julius in Acts 27, the centurion who was charged with delivering Paul to Rome. When the ship on which they sailed ran aground near Malta, he saved Paul from certain death at the hands of the other soldiers onboard. Each of these men, and many others, aided the Jewish people, as have a myriad of others down through the ages and even today.

2. God has raised up intercessors to pray for the Jewish people.

In Numbers we are instructed how to pray for the Children of Israel:

> *The Lord bless you and keep you; the Lord make his face shine on you and be gracious to you; the Lord turn his face toward you and give you peace,* (Numbers 6:24-26, NIV.)

When we pray for Jerusalem we are saying, "Maranatha, come Messiah!" The Messiah is indeed coming to Jerusalem! That is something on which both Jews and Christians agree.

3. God has called us to be watchmen on the walls—caretakers of the House of Israel. Isaiah 62:6-7 (NIV) records:

> *I have posted watchmen on your walls, Jerusalem; they will never be silent day or night. You who call on the Lord, give yourselves no rest, and give him no rest till he establishes Jerusalem and makes her the praise of the earth.*

As Believers, we assume the name of Christ and serve the God of Abraham, Isaac, and Jacob and find strength. We heed the warnings of the prophets Isaiah, Jeremiah, Ezekiel, Daniel, Hosea, and Joel and find direction. We sing the Psalms of King David and find hope. The mention of Jerusalem, our spiritual city, quickens our hearts. We stand with our Jewish brothers and sisters in the battle against anti-Semitism and the threat of terrorism and reap the blessings of God.

4. God's word says we are to comfort the House of Israel.
(Isaiah 40:1-2.)

As Christians, we are not engaged in terrorist attacks *against* our enemies; we are intent upon doing God's work on Earth *for* Him. We are strong advocates for the State of Israel—defenders of God's Word and His children, supporting programs to provide food, clothing, housing, and more for Jews who have returned to Israel

5. Jesus' final message to His disciples in Matthew 25:40 (NIV) contains our instructions:

> *The King will reply, "Truly I tell you, whatever you did for one of the least of these brothers and sisters of mine, you did for me."*

Not once did Jesus deny His Jewish heritage. The Bible tells us that Mary and Joseph observed the ordinances for the birth of a baby—He was circumcised on the eighth day; He observed the feasts of the Jews; He wore the tallit, the prayer shawl, when He prayed. He honored His brethren, and you and I are to do the same. For centuries the Jewish people have seen only the harshness of those who profess to be Christians, yet practice anti-Semitism. The time has come for you and me to practice loving acts of humanity toward the descendants of Abraham, Isaac, and Jacob.

> *Then the King will say to those on his right, 'Come, you who are blessed by my Father; take your inheritance, the kingdom prepared for you since the creation of the*

world. For I was hungry and you gave me something to eat, I was thirsty and you gave me something to drink, I was a stranger and you invited me in, I needed clothes and you clothed me, I was sick and you looked after me, I was in prison and you came to visit me,' (Matthew 25:34-36, NIV.)

CHAPTER ONE

ISRAEL IS GOD'S DREAM

"The Lord said to Abram after Lot had parted from him,
"Look around from where you are, to the north and south,
to the east and west. All the land that you see
I will give to you and your offspring forever.
I will make your offspring like the dust of the earth,
so that if anyone could count the dust, then your
offspring could be counted. Go, walk through the length
and breadth of the land, for I am giving it to you."

(GENESIS 13:14-17, NIV)

Israel is a tiny country with a population of less than 8 million and a land mass comparable to the state of New Jersey—the fifth smallest state in the US. It is 290 miles in length and only 85 miles wide. Israel's role on the world stage should seemingly be relatively minor, yet hardly a day goes by when events in or concerning Israel do not dominate international headlines. What many today seem to overlook is that Israel didn't just rise from the rocky land of Palestine in 1948; it has been in existence for centuries although known by different names.

Columnist Charles Krauthammer wrote of the land:

Israel is the very embodiment of Jewish continuity:
It is the only nation on earth that inhabits the same

land, bears the same name, speaks the same language, and worships the same God that it did 3,000 years ago. You dig the soil and you find pottery from Davidic times, coins from Bar Kokhba, and 2,000-year-old scrolls written in a script remarkably like the one that today advertises ice cream at the corner candy store.[2]

Until the days of the Roman conquest, Israel had existed as an independent country. After the diaspora (dispersion) in 70 AD and 135 AD, a strong Jewish presence was still evident in the land. Seven hundred years ago, the Ottoman Empire gained control over the region and remained in power until World War I.

When looking at other nations in close proximity to Israel, it is apparent that Israel has always been surrounded by Johnny-come-lately enemies. The Kingdom of Saudi Arabia rose from the sands of the desert in 1913; Lebanon was formed in 1920; Iraq in 1932; Syria in 1941; the Hashemite Kingdom of Jordan in 1946, and Kuwait in 1961.

Of the claims of a so-called Palestinian State, Journalist Rockwell Lazarus wrote:

> There has never been a civilization or a nation referred to as "Palestine" and the very notion of a "Palestinian Arab nation" having ancient attachments to the Holy Land going back to time immemorial is one of the biggest hoaxes ever perpetrated upon the world! There is not, nor has there ever been, a distinct "Palestinian" culture or language. Further, there has never been a Palestinian state governed BY Arab Palestinians in history, nor was there ever a serious Arab-Palestinian national movement until 1964...three

years BEFORE the Arabs of "Palestine" lost the "West Bank" and Gaza as a result of losing the 1967 Six-Day War (which the Arabs started).[3]

During World War I, Ottoman Empire Sultan and Caliph of Islam Mehmed V chose to side with Germany and was conquered by Great Britain. In a stunning, yet anti-climactic upset of the Turks, British Field Marshal Edmund Allenby marched into Jerusalem without his troops firing a single shot.

With the Turks and Germans having fled the city, the residents of Jerusalem were left to fend for themselves in the face of what they thought would be Allenby's impending attack. They could not know that Allenby, a religious man, was unwilling to inflict damage on the Holy City. He consulted with the War Office and with King George V about how to take Jerusalem. His sovereign counseled him to make it a matter of prayer. Presumably he did just that, and ultimately decided to drop leaflets on the city from an airplane. They addressed the absent Turkish authorities and invited the people to surrender. The Arab who penned Allenby's instructions wrote the general's name incorrectly. The leaflet was therefore signed, not "Allenby," but "Allah Bey" which means son of Allah.

The Turks, having seen few if any aircraft, were frightened to see them overhead with leaflets raining from the heavens. According to one account:

> General Allenby gave orders before the victorious advance and gave instructions that "on no account is any risk to be run in bringing the city of Jerusalem or its immediate surroundings within the area of operations." General Allenby was familiar with the

Scriptures, and he would therefore see fit to protect a dedicated city. He had taken the Bible with him from England for the campaign. Eventually, when the time came to attack and occupy the city, Allenby sent six bombers over it armed with leaflets. The leaflets were to call on the city to "surrender" and the bombs carried were in case of emergency.[4]

Jerusalem's civilian mayor, Haj Amin Nashashibi, decided to accept Allenby's offer. He borrowed a white sheet from an American missionary and walked outside the city through the Jaffa Gate toward the southwest. He assumed that was the direction from which the main body of troops would come. To help assure their safety, he and his associates took the cowardly action of surrounding themselves with a small group of boys before and behind them.

Not far down the road the entourage encountered two British scouts, Sergeants Hurcomb and Sedgwick of the London Regiment. With hand signals, the mayor made his intentions of surrender clear to the two men. Within hours British troops marched into the city. The Jews, the largest segment of the population, had heard of the Balfour Declaration. The arrival of these troops signified to them the seriousness of the Declaration to give them a national homeland.

Arabs were cheering too. They were familiar with the exploits of Lawrence of Arabia[5] and the way in which he represented British support for the Arab desire for national independence. Of course, the Christians cheered with the knowledge that Jerusalem's Holy Sites were no longer under Muslim domination.

The six bombers sent to drop leaflets continued circling outside the city. Sighted below was a battery of Turkish artillery manned by gunners about to target the Holy City. The bombers dropped the remainder of their payload on the emplacement. Panicked, the Turks fled. It was as if the prophet Isaiah had seen it all beforehand when he wrote in Isaiah 31:5, NKJV:

> *"Like birds flying about,*
> *so will the Lord of hosts defend Jerusalem.*
> *Defending, He will also deliver it;*
> *Passing over, He will preserve it."*

The objects passing over could easily have been vultures to destroy; but that was not God's purpose. Yahweh's commitment was to save and preserve Israel and His children.

Two days later, on December 11, Allenby arrived at the Jaffa Gate to mark the beginning of the new regime. A fierce Turkish counterattack on November 25 had slowed progress into the Judean Hills from Jaffa, and his troops had fought hard to reach Jerusalem. Allenby dismounted, reached for the visor of his cap, and removed it. Humbly he entered the Holy City on foot as the bells of various churches and the clock tower rang out a joyous welcome. The British, under Field Marshall Edmund Allenby, had ended the Ottoman rule over Palestine.

Once inside, Allenby mounted the steps of the Turkish citadel and read a proclamation assuring the city's inhabitants that the rights of the religious communities would be preserved and their various shrines scrupulously protected. He also gave formal greetings to the chief rabbis, the mufti, the Latin and Orthodox patriarchs, and other religious leaders.

An official report revealed that:

From 2 to 7 that morning the Turks streamed

through and out of the city, which echoed for the last time their shuffling tramp. On this same day, 2,082 years before, another race of conquerors, equally detested, were looking their last on the city which they could not hold; and inasmuch as the liberation of Jerusalem in 1917 will probably ameliorate the lot of the Jews more than that of any other community in Palestine, it was fitting that the flight of the Turks should have coincided with the national festival of the Hanukah.[6]

The "war to end all wars" ended in 1918, but the armistice lasted only until Adolf Hitler rose to power in Germany. In September 1939, Hitler ordered his troops to invade Poland in a land-grab attempt to enlarge Germany. French and British leaders issued an ultimatum to the determined Nazi Führer—withdraw or suffer the consequences. Ignoring the demand, Hitler began his march across Europe while both Great Britain and France declared war against the German Reich. It was not until after the attack on Hawaii's Pearl Harbor in December 1941 that America joined the Allies and entered the war both in the Pacific and in Europe. (It was not until 1959 that Hawaii became a state.) After six long and bloody years of battle that would leave six million Jews dead in Nazi concentration camps, Germany surrendered unconditionally in 1945.

At the end of the conflict, Britain found itself in control of Palestine with a growing dilemma: How to walk the tightrope between world opinion and the Arabs. After the horror of the Holocaust, the world increasingly demanded a return to their homeland in Palestine—thought to be a place of safety for the Jews. Arabs in the region were adamantly opposed to the move. Greatly frustrated by the situation, the British announced in February 1947 that control of Palestine would be ceded to the United Nations.

In November 1947, the UN offered a plan for partition that would divide the region into an Arab state and a Jewish state, calling for British troops to leave Palestine by August 1948. The Jews welcomed the proposal; the Arabs scorned it. The British were suspicious, and because of their skepticism, little was done to prepare the region for their upcoming departure from Palestine. Some British leaders felt it would be impossible for a Jewish state to flourish in the face of such hostility from the Arabs.

In the interim, Jewish leaders moved forward with plans for statehood. A provisional government was established under David Ben-Gurion in March 1948. Two months later, on May 14, 1948, as Egyptian fighter-bombers soared overhead and British troops readied for departure, Ben-Gurion and his political partners gathered at the museum in Tel Aviv:

> At 16:00 [4:00 PM], Ben-Gurion opened the ceremony by banging his gavel on the table, prompting a spontaneous rendition of Hatikvah, soon to be Israel's national anthem, from the 250 guests.[7]

The very day after Israel's rebirth as an independent nation, she was attacked by her much larger Arab neighbors, who supported the Palestinians. Only through the grace and protection of God was Israel able to survive. Again and again over the years this tiny island of freedom has suffered assaults and attacks from evil men dedicated to the annihilation of the Jewish people.

Today Israel is more isolated than ever. Security is a constant struggle as all of Israel's neighbors either actively oppose her or at least harbor those who do. Since the reuniting of the city of Jerusalem, there have been nearly 10,000 terrorist attacks in the Bible land. There have been more suicide bombings in the city of Jerusalem than in any other city in the world.

As my dear friend Prime Minister Benjamin Netanyahu has repeatedly pointed out, the contention is not about a Palestinian state, the division of Jerusalem, settlements, checkpoints, security fences, or borders. The issue is Israel's very right to exist as a nation. Most of the Arab world still refuses to accept this simple proposition.

Not only do they think Israel has no right to exist as a *state*, but they think the Jewish *people* have no right to survive. The opposition of the Arab countries to Israel's national aspirations has always been tied to the Muslim world's ultimate resistance to the right of the Jewish people to exist at all. Peaceful co-existence has never been the goal of the Arabs. Even having Jews living in other lands is not an option for fanatical Islamics and modern-day Neo-Nazis. The real goal has been the abnegation, and in its worst and most absolute form, the very extermination, of the Jewish race itself.

This is why Palestinian children are taught to hate and kill Jews from their first breath and why the Islamic world throws parties in the streets every time Jewish blood is shed. This is why in radical Islamic theology the successful homicidal maiming and murder of Jews represents the highest aspiration many Palestinian mothers have for their children.

Anti-Israeli sentiment has in fact become the new anti-Semitism. It makes Israel the new "collective Jew" which justifies assault on individual Jews as the extension of the state. This hatred—not any other issue—is the true source of murder and terrorism.

Author George Gilder wrote of today's version of the Hitler youth movement:

Today Hitler's rants have morphed into a global program of religious education and military ideology sustained by Arab and Iranian oil money. The hundreds of thousands Brown Shirts in Germany have become millions of frothing jihadi youths similarly inculcated with anti-Semitic hatred and a lust for violence. Leading politicians in Iran, Egypt, Syria, Malaysia, Venezuela, and other nations, and jihadi imams and mullahs around the globe have declared their resolve to destroy Israel....Anti-Semites have the moral support of much of the UN bureaucracy, including its "human rights" apparatus, which is chiefly devoted to anti-Semitic [agitation propaganda.]...The UN Secretary General has called for a global boycott of Israel for its efforts to defend itself against new campaigns of extermination. ...Scores of nations, representing 1.8 billion Muslims, have endorsed jihad.[8]

The terror wars that Israel fights in the twenty-first century are not against a particular Arab nation. Rather, the conflict is against an unpredictable and often unidentifiable band of terrorists with the ability and mobility to shift from country to country almost at will. They seem invisible, striking without warning. The attacks are meant to instill fear and trepidation among the Jewish populace. This is one of the many reasons the US alliance with Israel is a necessity. The US learned a harsh lesson on September 11, 2001: If terrorism is not contained in the Middle East, there will be more attacks in the West.

Author David Naggar wrote:

As for Israel, one either sees or does not see that

Israel is on the front line of a war that pits the advancement of humankind against barbarism. One either sees or does not see that the fight in Afghanistan is the same as the fight in Iraq, and the same as the fight in Yemen and Somalia. The Jihadists are using the whole global boxing ring. They are not confining the fight to the battlegrounds we dictate. Like the game whack-a-mole, if the seekers of liberty and human advancement seem to be gaining the upper hand in one part of the world, Jihadists will simply fold their tents at night and surface in another part of the world in the morning.[9]

The spiritual door was opened for an attack against the US, primarily *because* the policy of the government has been to make demands and pressure the Israelis not to retaliate in a significant way against terrorist strikes launched against them.

Since its independence in 1948, Israel has fought five wars: The War for Independence (1948-49); the 1956 war—the Sinai campaign; the Six-Day War in 1967; and the Yom Kippur War in 1973, and the Lebanon War in 2006. In all five cases, Israel was attacked. It was never the aggressor. It won all five wars against impossible odds. Yet amazingly enough, most of the world views tiny, democratic Israel as the threat to peace rather than the homicidal, terror-producing powers that surround her.

In October 2009, less than six months after assuming office, President Barack Obama flew to Cairo to deliver a major speech (See Appendix A) designed to impress the Muslim world. In his speech, the president designated Israel as the "second major source of tension" in the Middle East—following fanatical Muslim terrorists. At the same time, he stated unequivocally that the United States would not turn a blind eye to the desire of the Palestinians for statehood. It seems that Mr. Obama was then, and still is, dedicated to the proposition of a fifty-fourth Muslim nation. With the creation of a Palestinian state, Israel would be even further isolated—an island in a sea of fanatical Muslim countries.

The friendship between America and Israel has been of the utmost importance to a succession of presidents since Harry Truman, the first world leader to endorse the new nation. In recent years, nations such as the United States of America, Canada, and Great Britain that have long stood with Israel have moved away from their traditional support. We do so at our own peril because we are standing at a prophetic crossroads—one that will determine the future of our world. We must not fail to do our part to fight and win the battle for Israel's survival.

CHAPTER TWO

THE BLESSINGS AND CURSES OF GOD

"The LORD shall bless thee out of Zion: and thou shalt see the good of Jerusalem all the days of thy life,"

(PSALM 128:5, KJV).

I n Zechariah 2:8, God warns of the danger of offending Israel:

> *For thus says the Lord of hosts: "He sent Me after glory, to the nations which plunder you; for he who touches you touches the apple of His eye."*

Earlier in Genesis 12:1-3, God had assured Abraham that those who blessed Israel would be blessed, and anyone who cursed Israel would be cursed. These three scriptures alone should be sufficient warning as to why we area called to support Israel:

> *The Lord had said to Abram, "Go from your country, your people and your father's household to the land I will show you. "I will make you into a great nation, and*

I will bless you; I will make your name great, and you will be a blessing. I will bless those who bless you, and whoever curses you I will curse; and all peoples on earth will be blessed through you," (NIV.)

Hebrew writer Israel Matzav wrote about blessing and cursing:

One need not be a Jew or Christian or even believe in God to appreciate that this verse is as accurate a prediction as humanity has ever been given by the ancient world. The Jewish people have suffered longer and more horribly than any other living people. But they are still around. Its historic enemies are all gone. Those that cursed the Jews were indeed cursed.... Those who curse the Jews still seem to be cursed. The most benighted civilization today is the Arab world. One could make a plausible case that the Arab world's preoccupation with Jew-hatred and destroying Israel is a decisive factor in its failure to progress. The day the Arab world makes peace with the existence of the tiny Jewish state in its midst, the Arab world will begin its ascent. The converse is what worries tens of millions of Americans—the day America abandons Israel; America will begin its descent.[10]

In October 1991 during the Madrid Peace Conference, I stood gazing at the ceiling in the grand Hall of Columns in the Royal Palace in Madrid. It was ornately embellished with the images of false gods: Apollo, Aurora, Zephyrus, Ceres, Bacchus, Diana, Pan and Galatea. The beautiful interior was all glitter and no substance, a disguise for its actual purpose: the place where even more land-for-peace would be demanded of the Jews. From their lofty perch, these counterfeit gods looked down on the official proceedings to elicit a counterfeit peace. Like the apostle Paul at Mars Hill, I found myself praying to the One True God while under that canopy of idolatry. How ironic that Israel had been forced there, of all places, for an international peace conference—to Spain, where one-third of the Jewish population of its day had been massacred during the Inquisition. Representatives of nation after nation mounted the podium to insult and accuse Israel, and to demand that her leaders relinquish the majority of her land.

I can still hear their voices reverberating through the marble halls: "We will accept your land in exchange for peace." What they were really saying was: "This is a stick-up. Give me all your land and you won't get hurt—much." Muggings usually happen on the streets of major cities, and the Madrid Peace Conference, by any measure, was an international mugging. And the world was the silent majority too intimidated to report the crime to the police. Most of the nations represented pretended not to see the gun pointed at Israel's head.

I looked on as US President George H.W. Bush opened the Conference. Israel had been banned from joining the Desert Storm coalition because anti-Semitic Arab countries were incensed at the thought of Jews fighting alongside Muslims. President Bush had also asked Israel not to retaliate when bombarded by thirty-eight SCUD missile attacks. President Yitzhak Shamir honored his request.

At the end of the Peace Conference, Israel was "rewarded" with the freeze of a $10 billion dollar loan guarantee, money needed to provide housing for Russian Jewish refugees. Syria was awarded billions of dollars by the US. It was subsequently spent on the purchase of North Korean missiles to be used against Israel. Many of those missiles filtered into the hands of Hezbollah terrorists in Lebanon and have since been launched into Israeli towns and villages in various attacks on its northern cities.

As President Bush was opening the conference at the Royal Palace in Madrid, the Perfect Storm (the one made famous by the movie) swirled in the north Atlantic. It created the largest waves ever recorded in that region. The storm traveled 1,000 miles "east to west" (as opposed to the normal west to east pattern) to crash onto the eastern coast of the United States; sending 35 foot waves crashing into the Kennebunkport Maine home of the Bush family. This was one of the worst storms in American history and one of the top ten in insurance claims. Thirteen people died as a direct result of the storm, and property damage totaled over $200 million.

Furthermore, when the Madrid Conference was moved to Washington, D.C., for a resumption of the land-for-peace talks, Hurricane Andrew struck Florida. It wreaked havoc; causing an estimated $30 billion in damages, leaving 180,000 Americans homeless, and securing a spot on the top ten list of the largest disasters in American history.

The Prophet Daniel wrote in chapter 11, verse 32:

> *But the people who know their God shall be strong,*
> *and carry out great exploits,* (Daniel 11:32, NKJV).

The nations that ransacked, burned, leveled, and tried to obliterate the Jewish people are today rife with devastation. We have only to examine history to ascertain that the remnants of those once-great empires are now dust and ashes. Time after time since the beginning of her existence, nations have come against Israel. Yet, like the Phoenix, she has risen from the ashes each time. Not one ruler who ordered the destruction of Jerusalem long survived.

Nebuchadnezzar conquered Jerusalem in 586 BC and was doomed to live as a beast of the field for seven terrifying years. He was restored to sanity when he recognized the God of the Israelites.[11] His kingdom of Babylon was conquered by Cyrus the Great.

In 332 BC Alexander the Great captured Jerusalem. His empire fragmented after his death and the followers of Ptolemy in Egypt and then the Seleucids of Syria ruled over Jerusalem. The Jews, horrified by the desecration of the Temple under the Seleucid ruler, Antiochus IV, staged a revolt and regained independence under the Hasmonean Dynasty. It lasted one hundred years, until Pompey established Roman rule in the city. The Holy Roman Empire collapsed after the Temple was destroyed and Jerusalem was leveled.

The British, who ruled over Palestine and Jerusalem following World War I, could once brag that the sun never set on the British Empire. Indeed, one-fifth of the world's population was then under its rule. However, after turning away Jews from both Britain and Palestine when they fled Hitler's gas chambers, and after arming Arabs to fight against them in Palestine, the empire quickly began to disintegrate. Great Britain today is comprised of just fourteen territories, consisting of a number of islands. Gone are the days when the empire stretched from India to Canada and from Australia to Africa.

In 1939, Winston Churchill stood before Parliament in London and countered efforts to renounce support for a Jewish homeland. In his speech, he praised the work of those already in Palestine and then damned those who had come against the Jews already in the land:

> They [the Jews] have made the desert bloom... started a score of thriving industries...founded a great city on the barren shore...harnessed the Jordan and

spread its electricity throughout the land...So far from being persecuted, the Arabs have crowded into the country and multiplied till their population has increased more...We are now asked to submit—and this is what rankles most with me—to an agitation which is fed with foreign money and ceaselessly inflamed by Nazi and Fascist propaganda.[12]

Today little has changed; there are still many whose only agenda is to force the Jews from Israel—or annihilate them, if at all possible.

Yet, Jerusalem and Israel stand today as a testimony to the determination and courage of the Jewish people. The burning question is: Does America stand with or against Jerusalem and the nation of Israel?

Israel is the key to America's survival. Would September 11th have happened if America had stood with Israel over the years, rather than weakening her by rewarding terrorists like Arafat and his successor, Mahmoud Abbas? The English Poet Alfred Lord Tennyson wrote: "More things are wrought by prayer than this world dreams of."[13] What might have been prevented had US support for Israel been unwavering; had the churches in America banded together to pray for the peace of Jerusalem; had chosen to bless Israel?

Rather than offer support, a signal has been sent to would-be terrorists that crime pays, that America is weak. Twenty-two years ago, Israel stood up to the nations of the world by attacking Iraq's *Osirak* nuclear reactor for which she was condemned by many nations, including the US. Ultimately, Israel's courageous act may have saved millions of American lives, not only on September 11th, but in the months of war in Iraq that followed.

In 1980, I did an interview with Isser Harel, head of Mossad,

Israeli intelligence, from 1952-1963. *The Jerusalem Post* published an article based on that interview—"America the Target,"—on September 30, 2001 (See Appendix B). It will help you understand the seriousness of the matter. I was so convinced Harel was right, that in 1999, I wrote a novel called *The Jerusalem Scroll* in which Osama bin Laden would obtain a nuclear bomb from the Russian mafia and attempt to blow up New York City and Los Angeles. Bin Laden would attempt both; but thank God, he never gained possession of a nuclear bomb. The United States has been blessed beyond measure, and I believe it is because she has been the world's least anti-Semitic country.

An amazing Scripture in the Bible is found in Luke 7:5 (KJV)*: "For he loveth our Nation, and hath built us a synagogue."* The Jewish Elders made an appeal to Jesus to come to Capernaum to the house of Cornelius, a Gentile, to heal a servant who was close to death. The Jews said to Jesus, "He deserves a blessing because he has been a blessing. He has performed some wonderful deeds of compassion for our people."

A similar story is found in Acts 10. A Gentile in Caesarea was selected by God to receive the Gospel. Why? The answer is given repeatedly in the book of Acts:

> *A devout man [Cornelius] and one who feared God with all his household, who gave alms generously to the people, and prayed to God always,* (Acts 10:2, NKJV.)

Who were the people to whom Cornelius gave these alms? They were the Jews!

> *...Your prayers and your alms have come up for a memorial before God,* (Acts 10:4, NKJV.)

...your prayer has been heard, and your alms are remembered in the sight of God, (Acts 10:31, NKJV.)

Three times in the same chapter, a godly Gentile expressed his unconditional love for the Jewish people in a practical way. Then Cornelius was divinely selected by God to be the first head of a Gentile household to receive the Gospel, and the first to receive the outpouring of the Holy Spirit.

Why Christians should wholeheartedly support the Jewish people and their beloved country, Israel, may be considered by some to be a selfish reason in some respects, but a valid one nonetheless. After promising Abraham that He would make his offspring a great nation, the God of Israel pledged that He would *"bless those who bless you"* (Genesis 12:3, NKJV). We have already seen that God's eternal covenant was passed down through Isaac, Jacob, and the 12 tribes of Israel. This means that the blessing promised by the God of Israel would come to those who particularly bless the Jewish people.

How can we bless the Jews? There are many ways this can be done. One of the most important and obvious ways is to support their God-given right to live in their biblical Promised Land, especially in their eternal capital city, Jerusalem. The sad fact is that many governments, international organizations, Muslim groups and even some Christians do not acknowledge that divine right. For Christians, this non-biblical stand weakens our testimony, weakens the nation of Israel, weakens the United States, and puts our nation in harm's way.

In a conference on Israel, author Joel Rosenberg said:

> There is a danger to our country if we abandon Israel, if we turn on Israel. We are in enough trouble fiscally, but more importantly morally and spiritually.

This is not a good time to add the abandonment, rejection, betrayal of Israel to our national sins.[14]

Failure or refusal to support the Jews and their right to reside
in their ancient homeland can cause us to miss the blessings of God.
It can, however, do much more than that; it also places us in danger
of being cursed by our Creator. God Himself warns humanity of this
danger.

By contesting the right of Jews to live in their covenant land, and
thereby going against God's Holy Word, many are opening themselves up to be cursed! Therefore, anyone who seeks the blessings
bestowed by our Heavenly Father should make sure they are obeying
His command to bless His special covenant people.

The Church must never lose sight of the fact that the Lord and
Savior we serve, Jesus Christ, was born a Jew. He is the offspring of
Abraham, Isaac, and King David. Christians need only look at the
genealogies provided in Matthew and Luke. God included them in
the Bible for a reason, not so we could just hurry through them or
skip over them. Jesus is our King because he is David's heir to the
throne. New Testament scriptures only reaffirm God's promises to
Israel throughout the Old Testament.

The Liberal Left media has painted a picture of the Palestinians
as the underdogs—deprived of their land. Nothing could be further
from the truth. Israel has more right to the land than any of its Arab
neighbors, having received the grant first from God in a covenant
with Abraham, and regaining the land in 1947 through the United
Nations. When one looks deeply into the situation between Israel
and the Palestinians, it soon becomes obvious that the goal is not for
a state, it is to drive Israel from the land altogether.

A singular truth is that wealthy Arab nations have turned away from the Palestinians, refusing to offer them refuge. Why? Perhaps the refusal is based on Jordan's experience with refugees—insurrection and civil war at the hands of PLO terrorists and threats on the life of King Hussein. Added to that are the questions: What other reason would Arab countries have to blame and target Israel? Would the Palestinians even want the land if not for the Jews?

The great Master of the Universe reveals that our personal, family, and national welfare is closely related to how we treat the Jewish people. God not only promised to reward individuals for blessing His covenant Jewish people, but He also pledged in the same Scripture to bless families, and by extension, entire nations: *"And in you all the families of the earth shall be blessed,"*(Genesis 12:3, NKJV.) Should anyone need any other reason to support the contemporary offspring of Abraham, Isaac, and Jacob, especially in their brave endeavors to establish a thriving modern state within their biblically-designated ancestral borders?

Bulgarian pastor George Bakalav wrote of God's very special covenant with Abraham:

> Prior to Abraham, God had relationship with number of other saints such as Job and Noah. However, God promised Abraham two specific things He never promised anyone else: the land of Canaan would become the land of Israel and Abraham will have a special heir born of his own flesh and blood. This heir of Abraham would be later recognized also as an heir of David, the promised Messiah, the Savior and the ruler of the world. Thus Abraham becomes the father of the Jewish people. The land of Israel, which at that

time was occupied by the Canaanites, is given to Abraham and his decedents as part of this covenant.[15]

As we have seen, both the Old and New Testaments make abundantly clear that Christians must support Israel in every possible way. This does not mean that the Israeli people and their government are perfect. Far from it: They are fallen human beings like everyone else on Earth, in desperate need of salvation. (See II Chronicles 7:14.) Bible prophets, including the Apostle Paul, foretold that the restored Jewish remnant in the Lord's land would mourn over their sins in the Last Days and be grafted back into their own sacred tree.

While working, and praying for all Israel, we must wholeheartedly support what the sovereign Lord is doing in returning His covenant people to their God-given land. In doing so, we will be blessed as they are blessed. Best of all, we will please our heavenly Father by obeying His revealed will on a matter that is clearly close to His heart:

> Thus says the Lord: "Against all My evil neighbors who touch the inheritance which I have caused My people Israel to inherit—behold, I will pluck them out of their land and pluck out the house of Judah from among them," (Jeremiah 12:14, NKJV.)

When we refuse to pray for the Jewish people, we are saying simply, "God, I know better than you. I will not obey Your Word." God's Word says, *I have written my name there* [in Jerusalem]...." Almighty God has promised to dwell with them in the land (Zechariah 2:10). God will determine blessings or curses on nations depending on how they treat Israel.

When God promised to bless Abraham and his descendants, He meant it! A friend in Israel sent me these amazing facts as an indication of how God has blessed His people:

» Israel has the highest density of tech start-ups in the world.

» Israel's companies attract more venture capital per person than any other nation.

» Israel has more companies listed on NASDAQ than Europe, Japan, Korea, India and China—combined!

» Israel has twice the number of engineers per capita than the US.

» Israel has the highest Research and Development spending per GDP in the world.
God keeps His promises and blesses His people!

Additional scripture readings:

*Now the LORD had said unto Abram, Get thee out of thy country, and from thy kindred, and from thy father's house, unto a land that I will shew thee: And I will make of thee a great nation, and I will bless thee, and make thy name great; and thou shalt be a blessing: **And I will bless them that bless thee, and curse him that curseth thee: and in thee shall all families of the earth be blessed,*** (Emphasis mine, Genesis 12:1-3, KJV.)

And the LORD said unto Abram, after that Lot was separated from him, Lift up now thine eyes, and look from the place where thou art northward, and southward, and eastward, and westward: **For all the land which thou seest, to thee will I give it, and to thy seed for ever.** *And I will make thy seed as the dust of the earth: so that if a man can number the dust of the earth, then shall thy seed also be numbered. Arise, walk through the land in the length of it and in the breadth of it; for I will give it unto thee. Then Abram removed his tent, and came and dwelt in the plain of Mamre, which is in Hebron, and built there an altar unto the LORD,* (Emphasis mine, Genesis 13:14-18, KJV.)

As for me, behold, my covenant is with thee, and thou shalt be a father of many nations. Neither shall thy name any more be called Abram, but thy name shall be Abraham; for a father of many nations have I made thee. And I will make thee exceeding fruitful, and I will make nations of thee, and kings shall come out of thee. And I will establish my covenant between me and thee and thy seed after thee in their generations for an everlasting covenant, to be a God unto thee, and to thy seed after thee. And I will give unto thee, and to thy seed after thee, the land wherein thou art a stranger, all the land of Canaan, for an everlasting possession; and I will be their God, (Genesis 17:4-8, KJV.)

And the angel of the LORD called unto Abraham out of heaven the second time, And said, By myself have I sworn, saith the LORD, for because thou hast done this thing, and hast not withheld thy son, thine only son: That in blessing I will bless thee, and in multiplying I will multiply thy seed as the stars of the heaven, and as the sand which is upon the sea shore; and thy seed shall possess the gate of his enemies; And in thy seed shall all the nations of the earth be blessed; because thou hast obeyed my voice, (Genesis 22:15-18, KJV.)

And there was a famine in the land, beside the first famine that was in the days of Abraham. And Isaac went unto Abimelech king of the Philistines unto Gerar. And the LORD appeared unto him, and said, Go not down into Egypt; dwell in the land which I shall tell thee of: Sojourn in this land, and I will be with thee, and will bless thee; for unto thee, and unto thy seed, I will give all these countries, and I will perform the oath which I sware unto Abraham thy father; And I will make thy seed to multiply as the stars of heaven, and will give unto thy seed all these countries; and in thy seed shall all the nations of the earth be blessed; Because that Abraham obeyed my voice, and kept my charge, my commandments, my statutes, and my laws, (Genesis 26:1-5, KJV.)

CHAPTER THREE

JERUSALEM, THE HEART AND SOUL OF THE EARTH

*"Yet I have chosen Jerusalem, that
My name may be there..."*

(2 CHRONICLES 6:6, NKJV.)

Alll expressions of Divine love still hold true for Israel today; none have been canceled. Israel—the Promised Land, Holy Land, Land of Canaan—is, and always will be, the apple of God's eye (Zechariah 2:8). She remains God's joy and delight, His royal diadem (Isaiah 62:3), His firstborn, His Chosen One, His beloved (Jeremiah 2:2, Hosea 11:1). Indeed, He says of His people, *"For they shall be like the jewels of a crown,"* (Zechariah 9:16.)

Israel is not simply a long, narrow strip of land on the Mediterranean Sea; it represents part of a Divine land grant—from God to the descendants of Abraham, Isaac, and Jacob.

On that day the Lord made a covenant with Abram and said, "To your descendants I give this land, from the Wadi of Egypt to the great river, the Euphrates—the land of the Kenites, Kenizzites, Kadmonites,

Hittites, Perizzites, Rephaites, Amorites, Canaanites, Girgashites and Jebusites," (Genesis 15:18, NIV.)

It was a gift from Jehovah, and the ownership of Israel's land is non-negotiable. In March 2002, Senator James Inhofe (R-OK) addressed the issue of Israel's right to her land:

> Every new archeological dig supports the fact that the Jews have had a presence in Israel for 3,000 years - coins, cities, pottery, other cultural artifacts The Jew's claim predates the claim of any other people in the region. The ancient Philistines are extinct as are other ancient peoples. They do not have the unbroken line the Israelis have. Ownership is and will be in the hands of God's Chosen People—forever.[16]

There are a myriad of scriptures to support the rights of the Jewish people to the land:

It is God's land and His prerogative to determine ownership:

> *The land shall not be sold permanently, for the land is Mine...* (Leviticus 25:23, NKJV.)

> *Rejoice, O Gentiles, with His people...He will provide atonement for His land and His people,* (Deuteronomy 32:43, NKJV.)

> *For a nation has come up against My land...* (Joel 1:6, NKJV.) *Then the Lord will be zealous for His land...* (Joel 2:18, NKJV.)

God determines the consequences of what happens when people violate His covenant:

> *...I will uproot them from My land which I have given them...* (2 Chronicles 7:20, NKJV.)

> *Lord, You have been favorable to Your land; You have brought back the captivity of Jacob. You have forgiven the iniquity of Your people; You have covered all their sin,* (Psalm 85:1-2, NKJV.)

> *I brought you into a bountiful country...but when you entered, you defiled my land and made my heritage an abomination,* (Jeremiah 2:7, NKJV.)

> *I will gather all nations, and bring them down to the Valley of Jehoshaphat; and I will enter into judgment with them there on account of My people, My heritage Israel, Whom they have scattered among the nations; they have also divided up My land,* (Joel 3:1, NKJV.)

God speaks of the End Times and those who come against Israel:

> *You will come up against My people Israel...I will bring you against My land, so that the nations may know Me, when I am hallowed in you...* (Ezekiel 38:16, NKJV.)

God will save His people, Israel:

> *"The Lord their God will save them in that day, as the*

flock of His people, for they shall be like the jewels of a crown, lifted like a banner over His land..." (Zechariah 9:16, NKJV.)

God has committed the land to Abraham and his offspring forever:

"I will establish my covenant as an everlasting covenant between me and you and your descendants after you for the generations to come, to be your God and the God of your descendants after you. The whole land of Canaan, where you now reside as a foreigner, I will give as an everlasting possession to you and your descendants after you; and I will be their God," (Genesis 17:7-8, NKJV.)

"With a little wrath I hid My face from you...but My kindness shall not depart from you, nor shall My covenant of peace be removed..." (Isaiah 54:8-10, NKJV.)

The loss of governance by Israel through sin and dispersion has not altered God's commitment to make it theirs forever. (Read Ezekiel 37:1-28.)

When you sign your name to a check, you represent that you possess the amount indicated on that check. God wrote His Name in Jerusalem, and He has the power and authority to possess what His name represents.

On July 30, 1980, the Israeli Knesset voted to affirm a united Jerusalem as the capital of the State of Israel. Shortly afterward, I had the privilege of talking with the man who had become my dear friend, Prime Minister Menachem Begin. We discussed the vastness of the territory held by Israel's enemies. For instance, at that time:

> » Arab dictators controlled 13,486,861 square kilometers in the Middle East, and Israel controlled 20,770 (Palestinefacts.org).

> » The population of Israel was roughly 7.8 million, compared to the population of 300 million living in the surrounding Arab countries.

> » The odds against Israel are decidedly skewed. The Arab nations demanding a Palestinian state are represented by 21 separate countries.[17]

Several arguments abound as to why the Palestinian Authority continues to reject any and all offers of a Palestinian State as did Yasser Arafat in 2000 and as Mahmoud Abbas has continued to do. Formal statehood would limit the ability of the PLO and Hamas in Gaza to commit acts of terrorism. The same applies to Hezbollah in Lebanon. The organization continues to play a lesser role in the government of that country. Were the leaders of Hezbollah to gain full control within Lebanon's borders—which they could do at any time— the first rocket launched toward Israel from the confines of Lebanon would result in the immediate demise of that country. Controlling Lebanon would reduce the ability of Hezbollah members to attack the nation of Israel. Playing a lesser role in government gives them a license to terrorize Lebanon's neighbor.

This was a lesson learned when Gaza achieved pseudo-statehood.

It became easier for Israel to retaliate when attacked. For the PA to achieve statehood would be a catastrophic move: It would lose the "victim" status which it has enjoyed for decades, and would lose sizeable donations from US, EU, and Arab backers. Would that those organizations, including the UN and Russia come to understand that the Palestinians do not want a state. It would rob them of the cover they now enjoy when it comes to terroristic acts against the Jewish people in Israel. It is obvious, when at some point in each round of negotiations the Palestinians in a huff pick up their marbles and go home.

To this day, the same countries trying to foist a Palestinian state off on Israel do not recognize Jerusalem as the capital of Israel. In my discussion with Prime Minister Begin, I asked, "How can this lack of recognition be possible when so many people in America and the world believe the Bible?" Mr. Begin just smiled that enigmatic smile of his, but offered no answer. As we talked, I told him about a publication that had come into my possession from the Egyptian state information service, "Jerusalem, an Arab City." It had been printed by *al-Ahram* press in Cairo. The book stated on page eight, "Jerusalem was invaded by Christian Arabs in the year 90 BC and remained under their domination until it was occupied by the Romans in the first century AD."[18]

Of course, both of us were well aware that the Arab world's claim to Jerusalem is based on misinformation. How could a state publication declare a right to Jerusalem based on the presumption that Christian Arabs had invaded Jerusalem 90 years *before* the birth of Christ? It is this type of propaganda that floods the Arab world feeding and fueling the hatred for the Jewish people.

The prime minister answered my question before I had time to formulate another:

Being a student of the Bible, you know that almost 3,000 years ago King David united the Kingdoms of Judea and Israel. He transferred the seat of power from Hebron to Jerusalem, where he ruled for 33 years. He wanted to build the Temple on Mount Moriah, where Abraham was to offer his son, Isaac, as a sacrifice.

David petitioned God to be allowed to build a home for Him in Jerusalem. God answered, *"You have shed much blood and have made great wars; you shall not build a house for My name, because you have shed much blood on the earth in My sight,"* (I Chronicles 22:8.)

God promised David a son who would follow after him as king and would build the Temple. Since then, Jerusalem has been the capital of the Jewish state... one of the oldest capital cities in the world.

The Prime Minister was aware there are detractors who refuse to recognize Israel, much less Jerusalem as its capital city:

We came to Camp David to make peace with Egypt and one of your statesmen told met that the government of the United States did not recognize Jerusalem as the capital of Israel. I answered, "Whether you recognize or don't recognize it, Jerusalem is the capital of the State of Israel."

After the Six-Day War, the eastern part of Jerusalem was liberated from Jordanian occupation. For 19 years we couldn't go to the Western Wall to pray. That was the only time since the [second] Temple had been destroyed by the Romans. Under all other regimes we were free to go to the Western Wall to pray, but the Jordanians didn't allow us passage, in breach of the arms agreement.

The Olive Mountain Cemetery in which our greatest sages have been buried for centuries was completely desecrated. Monuments were destroyed and turned into floors of places which are unmentionable. I will not even use the names [latrines]. All of our synagogues were destroyed...the Jewish Quarter, which was centuries old was leveled.

Under our jurisdiction, we reconsecrated the Olive Mountain Cemetery and everyone has access to the Holy Shrines—the Holy Sepulcher, the Church of the Nativity. A Muslim goes to the mosque to pray in absolute safety.

Here in Jerusalem is the government, the Parliament, the president, the Supreme Court. Whoever says, either on behalf of a great power or of a small country, "We can't recognize Jerusalem as the capital of Israel," my reply is always the same: "Excuse me, sir, but we don't recognize your non-recognition."

The prime minister's comments brought to mind something Moshe Dayan said during his address to the 34th General Assembly of the United Nations in September 1979:

Jerusalem has known many foreign rulers during the course of its long history, but none of them regarded it as their capital. Only the Jewish people have always maintained it as the sole center of its national and spiritual life. For thousands of years Jews have prayed daily for their return to Jerusalem, and for the past century and a half, Jerusalem has had a continuous and uninterrupted Jewish majority. [19]

Jerusalem is the symbol of all that Israel represents in our world. Teddy Kollek, Jerusalem's first mayor wrote:

> Jerusalem, this beautiful, golden city, is the heart and soul of the Jewish people. One cannot live without a heart and soul. If you want one single word to symbolize all of Jewish history, that word is Jerusalem.[20]

Out of the long negotiations to establish a Jewish homeland a friendship grew between Dr. Chaim Weizmann, a Jewish statesman, and Lord Balfour, the British foreign secretary. Balfour was unable to understand why the Jews were insisting they would only accept Palestine as their permanent homeland. One day Lord Balfour asked Dr. Weizmann for an explanation. "Mr. Balfour, let's suppose I propose that you replace London with Paris, would you accept?"

A surprised Balfour responded, "But, London is ours!"

Replied Weizmann, "Jerusalem was ours when London was still a swampland."[21]

The very name of the Holy City evokes a stirring in the heart and soul. It has been called by many names: City of God, City of David, Zion, the City of the Great King, Ariel (Lion of God), Moriah (chosen of the Lord). But only one name resonates down through the centuries—Jerusalem! David's city!

A world map drawn in 1581 has Jerusalem at its very center with the then-known continents of the world surrounding it. It resembles a ship's propeller with the shaft in the center being Jerusalem.

Another analogy is of Jerusalem as the navel of the earth. Its history can be summed up in one word—troubled! Lying as it does between the rival empires of Egypt to the south and Syria to the north, both striving for dominance in the region, Israel has constantly been trampled by the opposing armies. She has been conquered at various times by the Canaanites, Jebusites, Babylonians, Assyrians, Persians, Romans, Byzantines, Arabs, Crusaders, Ottomans, and the British. While her origins are lost in the hazy mists of antiquity, archaeological evidence of human habitation goes back some 4,000 years. Jerusalem is first mentioned in Joshua 10:1.

We read there that Adoni-Zedek was the king of Jerusalem and fought unsuccessfully against Joshua. The Israelites first occupied Jerusalem during the days of the Judges (1:21), but did not completely inhabit the city until 1049 BC when David wrested it from the Jebusites and declared it the capital city of the Jewish people.

In *Jerusalem, Sacred City of Mankind*, Teddy Kollek and Moshe Pearlman wrote:

> The history of Jerusalem from earliest times is the history of man, a history of war and peace, of greatness and misery, of splendor and squalor, of lofty wisdom and of blood flowing in the gutters. But the golden thread, the consistent theme running through that history, is the unshakeable association of the Jewish people with the city.
>
> The story of this association is repeatedly interrupted by a succession of conquerors—Egyptians, Assyrians, Babylonians, Persians, Seleucids, Romans, Moslem Arabs, Seljuks, Crusaders, Saracens, Mamelukes, and Ottomans. Yet throughout the three

thousand years since David made it the seat of Israel's authority, the spiritual attachment of the Jews to Jerusalem has remained unbroken. It is a unique attachment.[22]

When the Jews were driven from their land at various times, wherever they found themselves in exile, they faced toward Jerusalem when praying. After Nebuchadnezzar signed a decree making it illegal to pray to anyone except him, Daniel 6:10 says:

> *Now when Daniel knew that the writing was signed, he went home. And in his upper room, with his windows open toward Jerusalem, he knelt down on his knees three times that day, and prayed and gave thanks before his God, as was his custom since early days,* (NKJV.)

Jewish synagogues faced Jerusalem. When a Jew built a house part of a wall was left unfinished to symbolize that it was only a temporary dwelling—until he could return to his permanent home, Jerusalem. Even today the traditional smashing of a glass during a wedding ceremony has its roots in the Temple in Jerusalem. This act of remembering the loss of the center of Jewish festivities during the marriage feast sets *"Jerusalem above [their] highest joy,"* (Psalm 137:6, KJV.)

CHAPTER FOUR

JERUSALEM'S SPIRITUAL SIGNIFICANCE

*Break forth together into singing, you waste
places of Jerusalem; for the LORD has comforted
his people, he has redeemed Jerusalem,*

(ISAIAH 52:9, RSV.)

When compared with the great cities of the world, Jerusalem is small in size and population. It lies alongside no great river as do London, Paris, and Rome. It boasts no port, no key industries, no mineral wealth or even an adequate water supply. The city doesn't stand on a major thoroughfare connected to the rest of the world. Why then is Jerusalem the naval of the earth, the shaft that propels the world ever forward?

The answer can only be found in its spiritual significance. Jerusalem is the home of two of the world's monotheistic faiths—Judaism and Christianity, and is claimed by a third—Islam. Biblical prophets proclaimed that from Jerusalem the Word of the Lord would go out to the world—a Word, which would change the moral standards of all mankind:

For out of Zion shall go the law, and the word of the
LORD from Jerusalem, (Isaiah 2:3, ESV.)

The spiritual stature of Jerusalem is echoed in its physical situation; it sits atop the Judean hills high above the surrounding countryside. Traveling to Jerusalem is always spoken of as "going up to Jerusalem." Those who leave the City of God are said to go down—in perhaps more than just the physical sense.

When viewing the history of Jerusalem as a whole, no other city has suffered as has David's City. At times the city has been overrun by violent assailants. It is recorded in Jeremiah that the city would surrender after suffering the horrors of starvation—and be reduced to cannibalism (Jeremiah 19).

While Christian and Muslim claims to Jerusalem came much later, the story of the Jews in Jerusalem began three millennia ago, and has never ceased. The link of the Jewish people has been historical, religious, cultural, physical, and fundamental. It has never been voluntarily broken; any absence of the Jews from their beloved city has been the result of foreign persecution and expulsion. To the Jews alone belongs David's City, the City of God.

For the Jewish people whose cry for centuries has been, "Next year Jerusalem," it is more than a location on the map, it is not just a tourist Mecca where one can visit various holy sites; Jerusalem *is* holy. It is the essence of that for which Jews have hoped and prayed and cried and died. It is their God-given land.

The God who cannot lie made a vow to His people:

The LORD had said to David and to Solomon his son,
"In this house and in Jerusalem, which I have chosen

out of all the tribes of Israel, I will put My name for-ever," (2 Kings 21:7).

Israel is *God's* Dream; the title deed belongs to Him. It is His to bestow on whomever He will—and He has given the right of occupation to the Jewish people. When God made His eternal promises to Israel, there was no United Nations, no United States, no Russia, no European Union, and no Arab League; there were only pagan nations to challenge this dream, to challenge God and His Word. Today, those same pagan voices are challenging the right of the Jews to occupy a unified Jerusalem.

When you and I as Christians are apathetic toward God's divine plan or His eternal purpose, it means that we are rejecting our Lord's divine assignment to the Church. God's prophetic time clock has been set on Jerusalem time throughout history, and the spotlight of heaven remains shining upon the Jews as His Chosen People. It began with them, and it will end with them.

We embrace the name of Christ and serve the God of Abraham, Isaac, and Jacob and find strength. We heed the warnings of the prophets Isaiah, Jeremiah, Ezekiel, Daniel, Hosea, and Joel and find direction. We sing the Psalms of King David and find hope. The mention of Jerusalem quickens our hearts, for it is our spiritual city. We join our Jewish brothers and sisters in their fight against anti-Semitism and the threat of terrorism and reap the blessings of God.

God's plan is an eternal one! As Christians, we cannot afford to neglect our responsibility to stand with the House of Israel. It is as important as it is to believe the promises of God. As Christians, we are the engrafted vine; we bow before a Jewish Messiah; and what we do matters in the light of eternity.

Jerusalem is the only city for which God commands us to pray.

When you pray for Jerusalem as instructed in Psalm 122:6, you are not praying for stones or dirt, you are praying for revival (2 Chronicles 7:14), and for the Lord's return. Also, you are joining our Lord, the Good Samaritan, in His ministry of love and comfort to the suffering House of Israel:

> *"Inasmuch as you did it to one of the least of these My brethren, you did it to Me"* (Matthew 25:40, NKJV.)

This is our divine commission.

King David explained precisely why God Almighty has commanded us to pray for the peace of Jerusalem, and has commanded a blessing upon us for doing so. The revelation is found in Psalm 122:8: *"For the sake of my brethren and companions, I will now say, 'Peace be within you.'"* God is telling us to pray for the peace of the inhabitants of Jerusalem. David felt that prayer needed to be offered up for all of his brothers, and friends who lived there. Prayer needs to be offered today for the Children of Israel and for peace for those who reside there from the over 120 nations of the world. It is the city most targeted by terrorists, simply because of hatred for the Jewish people and the significance of Jerusalem to them. It has drawn the Jewish people of the world like a prophetic magnet—those who have prayed, "Next year in Jerusalem."

In Psalm 122:9, David's revelation says, *"Because of the house of the LORD our God I will seek your good."* When we pray for the peace of Jerusalem, we are ultimately praying for Satan to be bound. In Isaiah 14, Satan said he would battle God from the Temple of the Lord, on the sides of the north:

> *For you have said in your heart: 'I will ascend into*

heaven, I will exalt my throne above the stars of God; I will also sit on the mount of the congregation On the farthest sides of the north; (Isaiah 14:13.)

When we pray for the peace of Jerusalem, we are praying for those who live there, and we are praying for the Messiah to come. The prophecies of the Bible point to the Temple of the Lord as the key flashpoint that will bring the nations of the world to Jerusalem, and result in the battle that will end Satan's reign over the earth for all eternity. It will spell his final defeat!

In 691 A.D., Islamic adherents of the Umayyad dynasty began a campaign to "exalt and glorify"[23] the city of Jerusalem. Umayyad Caliph Abd al-Malik built the Dome of the Rock over the Foundation Stone, the Holy of Holies. It was thought to have been erected in direct competition with Christianity. The edifice still stands today. Islam later attributed another event to the Foundation Stone: the binding of the son of Abraham the "Hanif," the first Monotheist. As the Koran does not explicitly mention the name Isaac, commentators on the Koran have erroneously identified the son bound by Abraham as Ishmael. Thus Islam teaches that the title deed to Jerusalem and the Temple Mount and all of Israel belongs to the Arabs—not the Jews.

In fact, Mohammed never set foot in Jerusalem, nor is the city mentioned by name in the Koran. His only connection to Jerusalem is through his dream or vision where he found himself in a "temple that is most remote" (Koran, Sura). It was not until the 7th Century that Muslim adherents identified the "temple most remote" as a mosque in Jerusalem (perhaps for political reasons). The truth remains that this site on which now stands the Dome of the Rock, and is sacred to Jews as the Temple site, will be the basis for the battle of the ages that will one day be fought.

There is a divine reason the Church was born in Zion. All roads lead to Jerusalem, Judea, and Samaria. The world is hopeless, not knowing what to do. Heaven and Earth met in Jerusalem, and will, when Messiah returns, meet there again. The destiny of America and the world is linked to Jerusalem. It is the epicenter of spiritual warfare and affects the entire world.

Jerusalem, Judea, and Samaria are the battle zones. It is no accident that the Great Commission is directed toward these prophetic areas:

> *But ye shall receive power, after that the Holy Ghost is come upon you: and ye shall be witnesses unto me both in Jerusalem, and in all Judaea, and in Samaria, and unto the uttermost part of the earth,* (Acts 1:8, KJV.)

If Christians are not salt and light, then the Great Commission will become the Great Omission!

If our Lord and Savior reached out in compassion to Israel, and made prayer for her His highest priority, do we dare make it our lowest? There is a direct correlation between the power that Heaven promised for the Church at its birth in Jerusalem, and the Church's obedience to be a witness in Jerusalem, Judea, and Samaria. The Church cannot, and must not, ignore Christ's eternal mission for her, and at the same time, expect power from on high. If His disciples' obedience was directly related to a power surge from Heaven and the birth of the Church, can disobedience empower the Church and lift her heavenward to fulfill her final mission?

Another significant reason why Christians should rejoice in Israel's physical restoration and strongly support her continued existence in the Middle East is the prophesied future of her ancient and modern capital city, Jerusalem. Holy Writ reveals that Zion is to be the very seat of the Messiah's earthly reign. The nations on earth will come up to visit Jerusalem when Jesus rules from the Holy City as King of Kings and Lord of Lords!

It is evident from Scripture that the Sovereign Lord of Creation has chosen the city of Jerusalem as His earthly capital. This decision was made by the very same God who promised to restore His covenanted Jewish people to the sacred city and surrounding land in the last days before the Second Coming. How can Christians look for and welcome Jesus' prophesied return, and not rejoice in and actively defend the Jewish return that was foretold to at least partially precede it?

God described the details and boundaries of the land in Genesis 15:18-21, NKJV:

> On the same day the Lord made a covenant with Abram, saying: 'To your descendants I have given this land, from the river of Egypt to the great river, the River Euphrates."

This was a royal land grant, perpetual and unconditional:

> Also I give to you and your descendants after you the land in which you are a stranger, all the land of Canaan, as an everlasting possession; and I will be their God, (Genesis 17:8, NKJV.)
> ...the land on which you lie I will give to you and your descendants, (Genesis 28:13, NKJV.)

God has never revoked Abraham's title deed to the land; nor has

He given it to anyone else. The spot where God confirmed His covenant is an area north of Jerusalem between Bethel and Ai. It is in the heart of what is called the West Bank, or Judea and Samaria. (The United Nations refers to this as "occupied territory," and demands that Israel relinquish it.) An inalienable right is one that cannot be given away. The Bible declares this to be so in Genesis 25:23. The people were forbidden to sell the land because, *"The land must not be sold permanently, because the land is mine and you are but aliens and my tenants,"*(NKJV.)

Jerusalem is the only city God claims as His own; it is called the City of God and the Holy City in Scripture. He declared to Solomon in 2 Chronicles 33:7:

> *In this house and in Jerusalem, which I have chosen*
> *out of all the tribes of Israel, I will put my Name forever,*
> (NKJV.)

At the Middle East peace conference convened at the Royal Palace in Madrid, I was the first person to speak after Secretary of State James Baker concluded his remarks. I asked two questions: Why can't America recognize Jerusalem as Israel's capital? Secondly, we are moving a military presence into the Arab world for security. Why can't we have a military presence in Israel to help its security? It has suffered so greatly, and has especially paid a dear price during the Persian Gulf War. Baker was incensed by my remarks and said he refused to be entangled in a fruitless debate and that the status of Jerusalem should be determined by negotiations.

To this day, America has refused to recognize Jerusalem as Israel's capital. This is a grave mistake. I have shouted the words of Prime Minister Menachem Begin as a warning from the White

House in Washington to the Royal Palace in Madrid as I rebuked world leaders with his words, "God does not recognize America's non-recognition position!"

Additional Scripture Readings:

> *Arise, shine; for thy light is come, and the glory of the LORD is risen upon thee. For, behold, the darkness shall cover the earth, and gross darkness the people: but the LORD shall arise upon thee, and his glory shall be seen upon thee. And the Gentiles shall come to thy light, and kings to the brightness of thy rising,* (Isaiah 60:1-3, KJV.)

> *And many nations shall come and say, 'Come, and let us go up to the mountain of the Lord, To the house of the God of Jacob; He will teach us His ways, And we shall walk in His paths.' For out of Zion shall go forth the law, And the word of the Lord from Jerusalem,* (Isaiah 2:3, NKJV.)

> *Look upon Zion, the city of our appointed feasts; Your eyes will see Jerusalem, a quiet home; A tabernacle that will not be taken down; Not one of its stakes will ever be removed, Nor will any of its cords be broken,* (Isaiah 33:20, NKJV.)

> *Thus says the Lord, "I will return to Zion, And will dwell in the midst of Jerusalem. Jerusalem shall be called the City of Truth, The Mountain of the Lord of hosts, The Holy Mountain,"* (Zechariah 8:3, NKJV.)

I will not give sleep to mine eyes, Or slumber to mine eyelids, Until I find out a place for the LORD, an habitation for the Mighty One of Jacob...For Your servant David's sake, Do not turn away the face of Your Anointed...For the LORD has chosen Zion; He has desired it for His dwelling place. "This is my resting place forever; Here I will dwell, for I have desired it," (Psalm 132:4-5, 10, 13-14, NKJV.)

Moreover I will appoint a place for My people Israel, and will plant them, that they may dwell in a place of their own, and **MOVE NO MORE***; nor shall the children of wickedness oppress them anymore, as previously,* (2 Samuel 7:10, Emphasis mine, NKJV.)

He will set up a banner for the nations, And will assemble the outcasts of Israel, And gather together the dispersed of Judah From the four corners of the earth, (Isaiah 11:12, NKJV.)

The Lord also will roar from Zion, And utter His voice from Jerusalem; The heavens and earth will shake; But the Lord will be a shelter for His people, And the strength of the children of Israel, (Joel 3:16, NKJV.)

Those who trust in the Lord Are like Mount Zion, Which cannot be moved, but abides forever. As the mountains surround Jerusalem, So the Lord surrounds His people From this time forth and forever, (Psalm 125:1-2, NKJV.)

Then I, John, saw the holy city, New Jerusalem, coming down out of heaven from God, prepared as a bride adorned for her husband, (Revelation 21:2, NKJV.)

For thus says the Lord of hosts: "He sent Me after glory, to the nations which plunder you; for he who touches you touches the apple of His eye, (Zechariah 2:8, NKJV.)

"For I," says the Lord, "will be a wall of fire all around her, and I will be the glory in her midst," (Zechariah 2:5.)

This is the word of the LORD concerning Israel. The LORD, who stretches out the heavens, who lays the foundation of the earth, and who forms the spirit of man within him, declares: "I am going to make Jerusalem a cup that sends all the surrounding peoples reeling. Judah will be besieged as well as Jerusalem. On that day, when all the nations of the earth are gathered against her, I will make Jerusalem an immovable rock for all the nations. All who try to move it will injure themselves. On that day I will strike every horse with panic and its rider with madness," declares the LORD. "I will keep a watchful eye over the house of Judah, but I will blind all the horses of the nations. Then the leaders of Judah will say in their hearts, 'The people of Jerusalem are strong, because the LORD Almighty is their God.' "On that day I will make the leaders of Judah like a firepot in a woodpile, like a flaming torch among sheaves. They will consume right and left all the surrounding peoples, but Jerusalem will remain intact in her place," (Zechariah12:1-6, NIV.)

In the last days the mountain of the LORD's temple will be established as chief among the mountains; it will be raised above the hills, and all nations will stream to it. Many peoples will come and say, "Come, let us go up to the mountain of the LORD, to the house of the God of Jacob. He will teach us his ways, so that we may walk in his paths." The law will go out from Zion, the word of the LORD from Jerusalem. He will judge between the nations and will settle disputes for many peoples. They will beat their swords into plowshares and their spears into pruning hooks. Nation will not take up sword against nation, nor will they train for war anymore, (Isaiah 2:2-4, NIV.)

CHAPTER FIVE

GOD'S WORD IS IMMUTABLE

For out of Zion shall go forth the law,

And the word of the Lord from Jerusalem,

(ISAIAH 2:3, NASB.)

The survival of the Jews is a fulfillment of biblical prophecy. Had the Jews not survived, God's Word would not be true! Throughout the Bible God has made eternal promises to the people of Israel, some of which He has yet to fulfill.

God made a covenant with the Children of Israel and deeded the land to Abraham, Isaac, and Jacob through their descendants—not through Ishmael and his descendants. His covenant promise cannot be broken—not by captivity in other nations, not by war, not by repeated cycles of iniquity and penitence. Ultimately His chosen ones returned to their land of promise—not because of mandates issued by other countries or the United Nations. It is God's covenant promise fulfilled.

Yet, throughout the centuries, a remnant—God's precious seed—remained in the Promised Land. That you and I live today to see the scattered Jews brought back and restored to their covenant land should be a matter of both wonder and worship for a God who keeps His promises—always:

> ...for the LORD is good and his gracious love stands forever. His faithfulness remains from generation to generation, (Psalm 100:5, ISV.)

The return of the Jews to the Promised Land following World War II required the Christian Church to take a closer look at the Abrahamic covenant because of the revulsion of the Holocaust. It was a combination of the return and the awfulness of what had been done to the Jewish people in the concentration camps that dealt a death blow to anti-Semitism in many, but sadly, not in all churches.

Now Christians are forced to either believe the entire Bible, or none of it. Israel is the fulfillment of biblical prophecy. To purposefully close our eyes to the cries of His people is like willfully and disdainfully ignoring God's instructions in His Word. The fact that the Jewish people exist is a miracle. The rebirth of the Nation of Israel is a miracle. The restoration of the Hebrew language is a miracle, as are the return of the Jewish people to their homeland, and the reunification of Jerusalem.

You either embrace Israel or you oppose Israel. One cannot straddle the fence; it's just that simple. Why do we as Christians aid Israel? Because God affirms Israel in His Word. I have heard some Christians say disdainfully, "I will not support the Jews in Israel. They are sinners, and the nation is a sinful one." How easily we forget all the mercy God has shown to a sinful United States to whom He made not one direct promise. How can we sing, "God Bless America," when this nation leads the world in having killed a number approaching 60 million babies by abortion since Roe vs. Wade became law—and then curse Israel with a self-righteous attitude? When you do the math, that is approximately the number of total casualties of the Holocaust and World War II combined. Given that Germany faced judgment for its actions in the war, how, then shall the United States escape judgment? Will turning away from Israel be the straw that breaks the camel's back? And if yes, what then awaits America?

True, some Jews are guilty of the same sins as other secular Western nations—abortion, homosexuality, murder, adultery, and more. However, the promises of God given to the Children of Israel through the Old Testament prophets were unconditional. Fulfillment of His prophetical edicts is not reliant upon their belief, submission, or uprightness; it is entirely dependent on God's supreme power and His unchangeable resolve (Isaiah 2:2-5). He promised that after His people were returned to Israel, He would be revealed to them:

> *Therefore say: This is what the Sovereign Lord says: "Although I sent them far away among the nations and scattered them among the countries, yet for a little while I have been a sanctuary for them in the countries where they have gone." Therefore say: "This is what the Sovereign Lord says: 'I will gather you from the nations and bring you back from the countries where you have been scattered, and I will give you back the land of Israel again.' "They will return to it and remove all its vile images and detestable idols. I will give them an undivided heart and put a new spirit in them; I will remove from them their heart of stone and give them a heart of flesh. Then they will follow my decrees and be careful to*

keep my laws. They will be my people, and I will be their
God," Jeremiah 11:1-20, NIV.)

It is our responsibility as Christians to pray with and for the Jewish people. Those who stand in opposition to Israel are not merely anti-Semitic. The battle is not simply a physical one; it is spiritual. The powers behind it can only be defeated through intercessory prayer and through love for those God loves.

John, the brother of Jesus Christ, wrote:

If someone says, "I love God," and hates his brother, he
is a liar; for the one who does not love his brother whom
he has seen, cannot love God whom he has not seen, (I
John 4:20, RSV.)

To summarize the 66 books of the Bible in one word, you only have to say "Israel." The Bible begins with and ends with Israel. There is no word used more. There are no promises given to any people more than to Israel. Israel's very existence demonstrates the faithfulness of God, the inspiration and infallibility of the Bible, and the sovereignty of God.

There is a doctrine in vogue spawned by Hell, which teaches that the Church has replaced Israel in the plans and heart of God. This doctrine is known alternately as replacement theology, progressive dispensationalism, or supersessionism. The early Church did not teach this; its roots date back to the European Church. The doctrine states that the Church has supplanted Israel in God's plan for the ages, and that the Jews have been rejected; that they have been blinded for having crucified Christ. These followers believe Israel failed God and as a result was replaced by the Church. It teaches that the Church is a spiritual Israel and that Jerusalem is any town in which there is a church.

The prevailing view among those espousing supersessionism—that the Church has replaced God's Chosen People—is vastly different from the theology taught in the New Testament. The Church is totally divergent from Israel—the two are not interchangeable. The Church was born on the day of Pentecost; Israel was born of God's covenant with Abraham.

For centuries the evils of replacement theology have resembled a cancer within the Body of Christ. The claim that the Jews rejected Christ, therefore all the promises of Abraham were bestowed on the Church and all the curses fell upon Israel is a patent error. In recent years, Evangelical Christians have worked diligently to dispel that lie.

How do you know if your own church believes in replacement theology or supersessionism? Simply put, if the Church does not support Israel or the Jewish people, there is a strong possibility that it is because of this doctrine. Many churches will not acknowledge 1) that they teach this philosophy, and 2) that it is even believed. Israel is the litmus test.

In the first place, replacement theology rejects the concept that the promises God made to Israel are for this present hour; instead, that they were cancelled at Calvary. That as a result, these promises now fall to the Church, which replaces Israel. The absurdity of this theology is that if Christian leaders believe God ended His promises to the Jewish people, they must also believe He might revoke His promises to them as well!

What exactly do these supersessionists believe?

> » They tend to be anti-Israel, and therefore do
> not honor Israel.

» They tend to be pro-Palestinian.

» They marginalize Christians who support Israel, even with humanitarian issues.

Obviously, these theologians have abandoned the apostle Paul's teaching to the Romans. He wrote:

> *I say then, has God cast away His people? Certainly not! For I also am an Israelite, of the seed of Abraham, of the tribe of Benjamin. God has not cast away His people whom He foreknew. Or do you not know what the Scripture says of Elijah, how he pleads with God against Israel?* (Romans 11:1-2, NKJV.)

Replacement theology was first developed by Justin Martyr (circa 100-165 AD) and Irenaeus of Lyon (circa 130-200 AD.) It was widely accepted within the Church by the fourth century. It has led to a great deal of persecution of Jews by Christians. Although the Catholic Church officially reversed its stance on replacement theology in the twentieth century, many conservative Protestant groups still believe in this doctrine.

A statement issued by the Dallas Theological Seminary, a leading center of study reads:

> Dispensationalists see a clear distinction between God's program for Israel and God's program for the Church. God is not finished with Israel. The Church didn't take Israel's place.[24]

To believe that God broke His covenant with Israel is heresy. You would have to accuse God Almighty of being a promise breaker! Do you believe God broke His covenant with Abraham, Isaac, or Jacob, and that He would break His covenant with you?

When the Church tries to replace Israel:

>> Arrogance and egotism replace love and compassion.

>> It becomes boastful and complacent.

>> Both Israel and the Jewish people are diminished.

>> Anti-Semitism becomes rampant.

>> Bible prophecies lose their importance and fulfillment is often overlooked.

>> The Old Testament loses its significance and substance. The Bible of the early Church was not the New Testament, but rather the Hebrew Scriptures.

Sadly, the Church failed from its inception to realize the importance of those truths. Had that not been the case, the anti-Semitism that has plagued it for centuries might have been circumvented. Instead, the Church has been infected with the cancer of replacement theology—a very real violation of the Word of God. It has often made the Church a repository of hatred rather than love as it should have been for the past 2000 years.

In Numbers 23:19, ESV, we are told of God's infallibility:

God is not man, that he should lie, or a son of man,

*that he should change his mind. Has he said, and will
he not do it? Or has he spoken, and will he not fulfill it?*

Hebrews 6:18 tells us it is *impossible* for God to lie; and Titus 1:2 states flatly that God *cannot* lie.

If a God who does not and cannot lie made a covenant with the Jewish people, He *will* keep His word.

Additional Scripture Reading:

> *He remembers His covenant forever, The word which
> He commanded, for a thousand generations, The cov-
> enant which He made with Abraham, And His oath to
> Isaac, And confirmed it to Jacob for a statute, To Israel
> as an everlasting covenant, Saying, "To you I will give
> the land of Canaan As the allotment of your inheri-
> tance," (Psalm 105:8-11, NKJV.)*

> *I say then, has God cast away His people? Certainly
> not! For I also am an Israelite, of the seed of Abraham, of
> the tribe of Benjamin. God has not cast away His people
> whom He foreknew...,* (Romans 11:1-2, NKJV.)

> *In the last days the mountain of the Lord's temple will
> be established as the highest of the mountains; it will be
> exalted above the hills, and all nations will stream to it.
> Many peoples will come and say, "Come, let us go up to
> the mountain of the Lord, to the temple of the God of
> Jacob. He will teach us his ways, so that we may walk in
> his paths." The law will go out from Zion, the word of the
> Lord from Jerusalem. He will judge between the nations*

and will settle disputes for many peoples. They will beat their swords into plowshares and their spears into pruning hooks. Nation will not take up sword against nation, nor will they train for war anymore. Come, descendants of Jacob, let us walk in the light of the Lord, (Isaiah 2:2-5, NIV.)

"So then, the days are coming," declares the Lord, "when people will no longer say, 'As surely as the Lord lives, who brought the Israelites up out of Egypt,' but they will say, 'As surely as the Lord lives, who brought the descendants of Israel up out of the land of the north and out of all the countries where he had banished them.' Then they will live in their own land," (Jeremiah 23:7-8, NIV.)

Therefore say: "This is what the Sovereign Lord says: 'Although I sent them far away among the nations and scattered them among the countries, yet for a little while I have been a sanctuary for them in the countries where they have gone.' Therefore say: "This is what the Sovereign Lord says: 'I will gather you from the nations and bring you back from the countries where you have been scattered, and I will give you back the land of Israel again.' "They will return to it and remove all its vile images and detestable idols. I will give them an undivided heart and put a new spirit in them; I will remove from them their heart of stone and give them a heart of flesh. Then they will follow my decrees and be careful to keep my laws. They will be my people, and I will be their God," (Ezekiel 11:16-20, NIV.)

"The days are coming," declares the Lord, "when the reaper will be overtaken by the plowman and the planter by the one treading grapes. New wine will drip from the mountains and flow from all the hills, and I will bring my people Israel back from exile. *"They will rebuild the ruined cities and live in them. They will plant vineyards and drink their wine; they will make gardens and eat their fruit. I will plant Israel in their own land, never again to be uprooted from the land I have given them,"* says the Lord your God, (Amos 9:13-15, NIV.)

The word of the Lord Almighty came to me. This is what the Lord Almighty says: "I am very jealous for Zion; I am burning with jealousy for her." This is what the Lord says: "I will return to Zion and dwell in Jerusalem. Then Jerusalem will be called the Faithful City, and the mountain of the Lord Almighty will be called the Holy Mountain." This is what the Lord Almighty says: "Once again men and women of ripe old age will sit in the streets of Jerusalem, each of them with cane in hand because of their age. The city streets will be filled with boys and girls playing there." This is what the Lord Almighty says: "It may seem marvelous to the remnant of this people at that time, but will it seem marvelous to me?" declares the Lord Almighty. This is what the Lord Almighty says: "I will save my people from the countries of the east and the west. I will bring them back to live in

Jerusalem; they will be my people, and I will be faithful and righteous to them as their God," (Zechariah 8:1-8, NIV.)

CHAPTER SIX

SALVATION
IS OF THE JEWS

*"The LORD lives; and blessed be my rock, and
exalted be my God, the rock of my salvation...*

(II SAMUEL 22:47, RSV)

A nother compelling reason for Christians everywhere to
enthusiastically defend the Jewish people and their modern
reborn state is this: Our eternal salvation has come through the
agency of the Jews. The physical descendants of Jacob wrote all
but a small portion of the world's bestselling book: The Bible. The
Bible says:

> *For if the Gentiles have shared in the Jews' spiritual
> blessings, they owe it to the Jews to share with them
> their material blessings,* (Romans 15:27, NIV.)

Christians owe a debt of eternal gratitude to the Jewish people
for their contributions that gave birth to our faith. As Christians, we
are indebted to the lineage of the Jewish people for our Lord and

Savior Jesus Christ and to the conservation of the Holy Scriptures. Following are only a few of the things the Jewish people have given to Christianity:

> » The Word of God
>
> » The Messiah
>
> » The Patriarchs
>
> » The Apostles
>
> » The Disciples

Both the *Tanakh* (Jewish Bible) and the Christian New Testament disclose that of all the nations on the earth only one was ordained by God to be saved: Israel. The Messiah was to be born in Bethlehem, be taken to Egypt for His preservation, grow up in Nazareth, ride into Jerusalem on the foal of an ass, and there stand in judgment. He then gave His life freely for the sins of all mankind.

I have heard it said, "The reason I don't support Israel is because the Jews crucified Christ. They are under judgment because they rejected God's Word." The truth is that although men were the instruments of death, no one forced Christ to die. John 10:17 tells us that Christ willingly gave His life:

> *"Therefore My Father loves Me, because I lay down My life that I may take it again. No one takes it from Me, but I lay it down of Myself. I have power to lay it down, and I have power to take it again,"* (John 10:17-18, NASV.)

Dr. Billy Graham wrote:

Jesus actually had avoided capture or death at the hands of His enemies on several occasions, but as He approached Jerusalem for the last time He knew His work was almost finished. "My appointed time is near," He said shortly before His arrest (Matthew 26:18).Why did He not escape? The reason is because He knew God had sent Him into the world for one reason: To become the complete and final sacrifice for our sins. This could only be accomplished if He endured the judgment and death we all deserve for our sins— and this is exactly what happened when He went to the cross.[25]

Critical attitudes lead to harsh judgment:

> *For with the judgment you pronounce you will be judged, and with the measure you use it will be measured to you,* (Matthew 7:2, NIV.)

From the moment God made a covenant with Abraham, his off-spring became God's Chosen People:

> *For you are a people holy to the Lord your God. The Lord your God has chosen you out of all the peoples on the face of the earth to be his people, his treasured possession. The Lord did not set his affection on you and choose you because you were more numerous than other peoples, for you were the fewest of all peoples. But it was because the Lord loved you and kept the oath he swore to your ancestors that he brought you out with a mighty*

hand and redeemed you from the land of slavery, from
the power of Pharaoh king of Egypt. Know therefore that
the Lord your God is God; he is the faithful God, keeping
his covenant of love to a thousand generations of those
who love him and keep his commandments, (Deuteronomy 7:6-9, NIV.)

God did not choose a people with mighty armies feared by all
surrounding nations. When He made the promise to Abraham,
his tribe numbered only seventy. When the compact was sealed,
Abraham had no children at all—not Ishmael and not Isaac. Yet God
continued to make promises to His friend:

He promised that he would have as many descendants as there is dust on the earth (Genesis 13:16), as
there are stars in the sky (Genesis 15:15), and as there is
sand upon the seashore (Genesis 22:17; Genesis 26:4.)

These descendants would occupy much territory:
"And thy seed shall be as the dust of the earth, and thou
shalt spread abroad to the west, and to the east, and to
the north, and to the south: and in thee and in thy seed
shall all the families of the earth be blessed," (Genesis
28:14, KJV.)

They would become a great and mighty nation
(Genesis 18:18). And not only one nation, but many
nations (Genesis 17:5.)

This nation would be a ruling nation; among his
descendants would be kings. God promised to make
him exceedingly fruitful and to *"make nations of thee,*
and kings shall come out of thee" (Genesis 17:6, KJV.)

"Let people serve thee, and nations bow down to thee: be lord over thy brethren, and let thy mother's sons bow down to thee: cursed be every one that curseth thee, and blessed be he that blesseth thee" (Genesis 27:29, KJV.)[26]

God has not failed to keep a single promise.

Since the establishment of the Church, theologians seem to have adopted the mistaken philosophy that God has forsaken His Chosen People. Nothing could be further from the truth; God will never forsake either the land or His people:

> *But Israel will be saved by the LORD with everlasting salvation; you won't be put to shame or disgraced ever again,* (Isaiah 45:17, ISV.)
> *And so all Israel shall be saved: as it is written, There shall come out of Sion the Deliverer, and shall turn away ungodliness from Jacob:* (Romans 11:26, NIV.)

When speaking to the Samaritan woman about eternal life, Jesus pointed out that His heavenly Father's free gift of eternal salvation has been brought to the world via the Jews:

> *"You worship that which you do not know; we know what we worship, for **salvation is of the Jews"*** (Emphasis mine, John 4:22, ASV.)

Truthfully, Jews are sometimes, but not always, hated because they are deemed to be wealthy; Jews of every social stratum were forced into ghettos and concentration camps. Jews are not hated solely because they "crucified Christ"; that argument has never been valid. Simply, they are hated because they are Jewish. Distinguished theologian Edward H. Flannery wrote:

> It was Judaism that brought the concept of a God-given universal moral law into the world...the Jew carries the burden of God in history and for this he has never been forgiven.[27]

If the most precious gift that Christians will ever possess came by means of the Jewish prophets, leaders, teachers, and in particular, Jesus the Messiah, how can we have any attitude other than one of deep gratitude toward Jacob's offspring? We who are Gentiles should be extremely thankful that God, in His shining wisdom and gracious mercy, has allowed us *"wild olive branches"* to be grafted into the rich Tree of Israel, as revealed in Romans 11:17.

Why do so many embrace false religions? Satan encourages such beliefs. The Bible says:

> *And for this cause God shall send them strong delusion, that they should believe a lie: That they all might be damned who believed not the truth, but had pleasure in unrighteousness,* (II Thessalonians 2:11-12.)

The Enemy of our soul knows that Jesus Christ is the only Way to the Father:

> *Jesus said to him, "I am the way, the truth, and the life. No one comes to the Father except through Me,* (John 14:6, NKJV.)

Satan has no problem with people following after any of the myriad of other man-conceived religions available in the world today. He knows they all lead to a downward path of destruction.

In his New Testament letter to the Romans, the Jewish Apostle Paul went on to point out that the *"grafted in"* Gentile Church does not somehow tower over the Jewish people, as many have maintained over the centuries and still do today. Rather, it is the original covenant people that remain the bedrock "root" that supports every Christian's spiritual life:

> *...do not boast against the branches. But if you do boast, remember that you do not support the root, but the root supports you,* (Romans 11:18, ISV.)

There are more churches in America than in any nation in the world. There are more Christian bookstores, more Christian radio and television stations, and more Bible schools. The world views America as a "Christian nation." Yet, America is the number one Western nation per capita for murder, rape, drugs, alcohol, pornography, and homosexuality. If this doctrine of judgment is to be meted out, then America is finished as a nation.

Peter Wehner of *Commentary Magazine* wrote:

> Israel is far from perfect—but it is, in the totality of its acts, among the most estimable and impressive nations in human history. Its achievements and moral accomplishments are staggering—which is why, in my judgment, evangelical Christians should keep faith with the Jewish state...Israel warrants support based on the here and now; on what it stands for and

what it stands against and what its enemies stand for and against; and for reasons of simple justice. What is required to counteract the anti-Israel narrative and propaganda campaign is a large-scale effort at education... in a manner that tells a remarkable and moving story...

The suffering the Palestinian people (including Palestinian Christians) are enduring is real and ought to move one's heart. Many Palestinians suffer from circumstances they didn't create...But these circumstances they suffer under are fundamentally a creation not of Israel but of failed Palestinian leadership, which has so often been characterized by corruption and malevolence. Checkpoints and walls exist for a reason, as a response to Palestinian aggressions. Nor has anyone yet emerged among the Palestinian leadership who is either willing or able to alter a civic culture that foments an abhorrence of Jews and longs for the eradication of Israel. To my coreligionists I would simply point out an unpleasant truth: hatred for Israel is a burning fire throughout the world. Those of the Christian faith ought to be working to douse the flames rather than to intensify them.[28]

The truth is, God is much more merciful than Man. Lamentations 3:22, KJV states: *"Through the Lord's mercies we are not consumed, Because His compassions fail not."* Nowhere in His Word does God make eternal promises to America; yet He continues to show mercy. Even wicked Sodom was to be the beneficiary of God's mercy. Why? Because Abraham appealed to God to spare the cities of Sodom and

Gomorrah if only ten righteous men could be found there; regrettably, none could be found to answer the call to stand in the gap.

Perhaps the reason judgment has yet to fall on the United States is that God still has a remnant—Abraham's "ten righteous" if you will—who intercede in prayer and continue to carry the torch of righteousness in a dark and dying world.

CHAPTER SEVEN

GOD ABHORS ANTI-SEMITISM

"For he who touches you touches the
apple [pupil] of his Eye,"

(ZECHARIAH 2:8, NASB.)

A nti-Semitism is hatred against all Jews. At its very root is actually hatred of God, His Son, and His Word. You cannot love Jesus whom you have not seen (who was born a Jew) if you don't love the Jewish people whom you have seen. If you refuse to bless the House of Israel when it is in your power to do so, what evidence of true Christian love do you have to present to a Holy God?

Martin Luther King said:

> You declare, my friends, that you do not hate the Jews, you are merely anti-Zionist. And I say, let the truth ring forth from the highest mountaintops. Let it echo through the valleys of God's green earth. When people criticize Zionism, they mean Jews. Zionism is

nothing less than the dream and ideal of the Jewish people returning to live in their own land.[29]

You cannot go to church and talk about how much you love dead Jews, such as the ones in the Bible, and not accept the Jewish family across the street. That reeks of anti-Semitism, and God's judgment will come on anyone who even unknowingly touches the seed of Abraham.

Christians are Zionists if they believe the Bible. Martin Niemoller, the anti-Nazi theologian and Lutheran pastor wrote in his poem, *First they came:*

> In Germany, they first came for the communists, and I didn't speak up because I wasn't a communist. Then they came for the Jews, and I didn't speak up because I wasn't a Jew. Then they came for the trade unionists, and I didn't speak up because I wasn't a trade unionist. Then they came for the Catholics, and I didn't speak up because I wasn't a Catholic. Then they came for me... and by that time there was nobody left to speak up."

Hitler employed the anti-Semitic hoax, *The Protocols of the Learned Elders of Zion,* to murder six million Jews during World War II.

Historian Norman Cohn suggested that Hitler used the *Protocols* as his primary justification for initiating the Holocaust—his "warrant for genocide."[30]

The trend continues today among Arab countries:

> ...in the Middle East, where a large number of Arab and Muslim regimes and leaders have endorsed them

as authentic...The 1988 charter of Hamas, a Palestinian Islamist group, states that *The Protocols of the Elders of Zion* embodies the plan of the Zionists.[31] Recent endorsements in the 21st century have been made by the Grand Mufti of Jerusalem, Sheikh Ekrima Sa'id Sabri, the education ministry of Saudi Arabia, member of the Greek Parliament Ilias Kasidiaris, and young earth creationist and tax protester Kent Hovind.[32]

The former Grand Mufti was simply following the World War II lead of Haj Amin al-Husseini, who said:

> Germany is the only country in the world that has not merely fought the Jews at home but has declared war on the entirety of world Jewry; in this war against world Jewry the Arabs feel profoundly connected to Germany.[33]

The appalling historical record reveals that Jews have been the targets of fierce discrimination and persecution even in so-called Christian lands over the centuries. Vatican-inspired Crusaders deliberately murdered Jewish people during the Middle Ages. The Roman Catholic Inquisitions were directed against the Jews in Spain and elsewhere, leaving many dead or in prison. The pogroms of Russia and Eastern Europe forced Jews from their homes, and left untold numbers slaughtered.

As evil as these anti-Semitic assaults were, they all pale in comparison to the Holocaust of World War II. A full one-third of the entire Jewish race was annihilated by Hitler's Nazi forces. The utter horror of the hideous Holocaust as revealed by the testimonies of death-camp survivors cannot be overstressed. Something to which we tend to give little credence is the definition of the term "Nazi." It is often used so wantonly in this day that we forget it has an absolute meaning. It was a term coined for the National Socialist Movement, an organization devoted solely to the most malicious and deadly form of anti-Semitism.

Too late, many Germans recognized the blessings that the Jewish people brought to their society before Hitler's tragic rise to power. Jewish composers, scientists, doctors, teachers, writers, and others contributed their significant talents and intelligence to the land of Luther, and were repaid in Hitler's death chambers.

In the twenty-first century, anti-Semitism continues to raise its ugly head in the unlikeliest of places:

> Belgian Justice Minister Stefaan De Clerck shocked the country's Jewish community by voicing support for an initiative to provide amnesty to Nazi collabora-tors during WWII, and for his suggestion that it may behoove the government to "forget" its Nazi past. Dur-ing a television debate, De Clerck said that the coun-try should not focus on the crimes it committed as it was already in the past. In fairness there are plenty of crimes being committed now against Belgium's Jews. The country's anti-Semitism is partly why the safety of European Jews is at its lowest since the Sec-ond World War, with anti-Jewish attacks at postwar highs. So maybe De Clerck was saying that Belgians should focus on their present anti-Semitism rather than on their past anti-Semitism.[34]

During a trip to Israel nearly three decades ago, I spent an afternoon with brilliant Jewish scholar Benzion Netanyahu, father of Israel's prime minister. At that time, he was researching and writing a book, *The Origins of the Inquisition in Fifteenth-Century Spain* based on the Spanish Inquisition. For hours we discussed his findings. He told me what he believed to be the purpose of the Inquisition:

> The royal decree [from King Ferdinand and Queen Isabella] explicitly stated that the Inquisition was instituted to search out and punish converts from Judaism who transgressed against Christianity by secretly adhering to Jewish beliefs and performing rites and ceremonies of the Jews. No other group was mentioned, no other purpose indicated - a fact that in itself suggests a close relationship between the creation of the Inquisition and Jewish life in Spain. Other facts, too, attest to that relationship.[35]

On August 2, 1492, Ferdinand and Isabella issued an expulsion order aimed at the Jewish *conversos*—those who had converted to Christianity under duress. It read, in part:

> Whereas, having been informed that in these kingdoms, there were some bad Christians who Judaized and apostatized from our holy Catholic faith, the chief cause of which was the communication of Jews with Christians...we ordered the said Jews in all cities, towns, and places in our kingdoms and dominions to separate into Jewries [ghettos] and place apart...hoping by their separation alone to remedy this evil....But

we are informed that neither that, nor the execution of some of the said Jews...has been sufficient for a complete remedy....Therefore we...resolve to order all the said Jews and Jewesses to quit our kingdoms and never return...by the end of the month of July next, of the present year 1492...if they do not perform and execute the same, and are found to reside in out kingdoms...they incur the penalty of death.[36]

The following day, August 3, 1492, Christopher Columbus, who is thought to have been of Jewish descent, set sail on a voyage of discovery. Contrary to popular belief, his voyage was not funded by the sale of royal jewels, but by two Jewish *conversos*, both businessmen and members of the royal court. The major financiers were two court envoys, Louis de Santangel, chancellor of the royal household, and Gabriel Sanchez, treasurer of Aragon.

Can you not see God's hand at work in this enterprise? Just as the Jews of Spain were being expunged from the country, God planted a seed in the heart of an explorer who yearned to find new lands. The voyage eventually led to the shores of the North American continent and the place that would become a refuge for millions of Jews over the centuries—the United States of America. God was preparing a sanctuary for His Chosen People.

Not only did God plant the seed, the tools so necessary for exploration of later voyagers were invented by Jews:

The key tools of navigators—the quadrant and the astral lobe used during this period—were of Jewish manufacture. In fact, the type of quadrant then in use was called "Jacob's Staff"; it had been invented by

Rabbi Levi ben Gershon, also known as Gershonides. The famous atlas that Columbus and the other explorers used was known as the Catalon Atlas. It was the creation of the Cresca Family, Jews from Majorca, Spain. Not only was the Catalon Atlas considered the greatest and most significant collection of maps at the time, it had no competition to speak of. Jews had a virtual monopoly at map making then, culling information from Jewish merchants from all over the known world.[37]

Within a century of having expelled the Jews from Spain, the country was bankrupt.

The early American statesmen who crafted the Constitution based its content on Judeo-Christian values. In a letter to Reverend F. A. van der Kemp, John Adams wrote of the influence of the Jews on western nations:

> I will insist that the Hebrew have done more to civilize men than any other nation. If I were an atheist, and believed in blind eternal fate, I should still believe that fate had ordained the Jews to be the most essential instrument for civilizing the nations. If I were an atheist of the other sect, who believe, or pretend to believe that all is ordered by chance, I should believe that chance had ordered the Jews to preserve and propagate to all mankind the doctrine of a supreme, intelligent, wise, almighty sovereign of the universe, which I believe to be the great essential principle of all morality, and consequently of all civilization.[38]

President Woodrow Wilson felt strongly that the ancient Hebrews set the standard for the developing United States of America:

> Recalling the previous experiences of the colonists in applying the Mosaic Code to the order of their internal lives, it is not to be wondered that the various passages in the Bible... [were] held up before the pioneer Americans the Hebrew Commonwealth as a model government.... In the spirit and essence of our constitution, the influence of the Hebrew Commonwealth was paramount in that it was not only the highest authority for the principle, 'that rebellion to Tyrants is obedience to God,' but also because it was in itself a divine precedent for a pure democracy.[39]

President Calvin Coolidge praised the contributions of the Jews to the American Revolution:

> The Jewish faith is predominantly the faith of liberty. [He listed] some among the merchants who unhesitatingly signed the nonimportation resolution of 1765: Isaac Moses, Benjamin Levy, Samson Levy, David Franks, Joseph Jacobs, Hayman Levy Jr., Matthias Bush, Michael Gratz, Bernard Gratz, Isaac Franks, Moses Mordecai, Benjamin Jacobs, Samuel Lyon, and Manuel Mordecai Noah.[40]

Coolidge also recounted the story of Haym Salomon, Polish Jew financier of the Revolution:

Born in Poland, he was made prisoner by the British forces in New York, and when he escaped set up in business in Philadelphia. He negotiated for Robert Morris [the superintendent for finance in the Thirteen Colonies] all the loans raised in France and Holland, pledged his personal faith and fortune for enormous amounts, and personally advanced large sums to such men as James Madison, Thomas Jefferson, Baron Steuben, General St. Clair and many other patriot leaders, who testified that without his aid they could not have carried on in the cause.[41]

Near the beginning of the Revolution, when colonial soldiers were poorly armed, starving to death, and on the verge of defeat, Salomon went to the Jews in America and Europe and gathered a gift of one million dollars (an incredible amount at that time). He sent the funds to General George Washington, who used them to buy clothes and arms to outfit American troops, an act that ultimately helped the Colonies win the war. Salomon pledged his personal fortune. It is said that altogether, Salomon gifted the Continental Army with $25 million dollars and later died a pauper. Neither he nor his heirs ever collected a dime of what was due from the Government. He never even received a medal for his services...an example of the utter lack of appreciation of what the Jewish race has meant to this and other countries.[42]

In addition to his gifts, Salomon loaned the US government at least another $800,000. It has been calculated that were his loan to be repaid today at 7 percent interest, the amount owed the Salomon family would equal at least $2.5 trillion.

To show his appreciation, Washington instructed the engravers of the US one-dollar bill to include a memorial to the Jewish people over the head of the American eagle. It is still there today. If you look closely at the reverse side of a one-dollar bill, you will see thirteen stars over the eagle's head that form the six-pointed Star of David. Surrounding that is a cloudburst representing the glory in the tabernacle in Jerusalem. President Washington specified that this was to be a lasting memorial to the Jewish people for their help in winning the war for independence.

America has been blessed because she opened her doors to the Jewish people and has blessed the nation of Israel (Genesis 12:1-3). But America is in danger of moving away from the place of blessing to the place of cursing. The land-for-peace deals of recent years have placed Israel and the Jewish people in grave danger. To weaken Israel is to risk the peace of the world, for the road to world peace runs through Israel. Israel is the firewall between America and the anti-Semitic Islamic nations. America's ability to win the war on terrorism will be directly related to America's willingness to support Israel in winning the war against terrorism. Israel is the only power that restrains Islamic terrorism from the West. Jews are dying so that Christians can live. Terrorists consider the United States a Christian nation. They do not hate the US because of Israel; they hate Israel because of the US. They refer to America as the Great Satan, and Israel as the Little Satan.

Some may say, "I don't need to reach out to the suffering House of Israel. Why, the Bible says there will be wars and rumors of wars over there, until the Messiah comes. It's all part of prophecy." This Scripture is taken from Matthew 24:6. It refers to the entire world. As a matter of fact, there have only been approximately 268 years of peace on this planet in the last 6,000 years despite the signing of some 8,000 peace treaties. However, there have also been some amazing revivals during that time!

To simply say that there is no need to pray and support the Jewish people, my friend, is anti-Semitic nonsense. It is to say to Nehemiah, Esther and even our Lord that they were wrong to pray and reach out in love to the House of Israel. There are hundreds of examples of prophets, priests and kings who chose to light a candle rather than curse the darkness. Jesus is our perfect example. He fed the hungry. He gave water to the thirsty. He healed the sick. And yet, He was not afraid to deliver the truth to the skeptics of His day. He also prophesied that the Temple would be torn down, and Jerusalem left in shambles.

The Bible says the same thing about the entire world in 2 Timothy 3:1, KJV:

> *But know this, that in the last days perilous times will come.*

And in Matthew 24:6-8, KJV:

> *And you will hear of wars and rumors of wars. See that you are not troubled; for all these things must come to pass, but the end is not yet. For nation will rise against nation, and kingdom against kingdom. And there will be famines, pestilences, and earthquakes in various places. All these are the beginning of sorrows.*

If we are to do nothing for the Jewish people because they do not embrace Jesus Christ, then why do we do everything in our power to help hurting unbelievers in our own country?

The Apostle Paul warned Christians not to behave arrogantly toward the physical descendants of Jacob. However, arrogance would have been welcomed in comparison to the ugly hatred and deadly violence that has frequently been aimed at the Jewish people in the name of Christ. This alone should be reason enough for contemporary Christians to humbly uphold the Jewish people in their difficult struggle to rebuild their ancient homeland in the hostile Middle East.

CHAPTER EIGHT

COMFORT ISRAEL

*"Comfort ye, comfort ye my people saith your God.
Speak ye comfortably to Jerusalem..."*

(ISAIAH 40:1-2, KJV.)

The setting of Isaiah 40 follows the dispersion of the Jewish people to Babylon. The Children of Israel had been captives, distraught by the circumstances in which they found themselves. Those left behind in Jerusalem, ruled too by the Babylonians, were equally distressed. As a release for their grief and agitation, the book of Lamentations was written. In Lamentations 1:17, NLT, the writer records:

Jerusalem reaches out for help, but no one comforts her.

Now in Isaiah 40, change has come. The Hebrew people have paid the price for their sin and the time for comfort has come. As the author of one Bible commentary wrote, "God is now comforting you who have been punished." It is time for comfort for a people who have long been held captive. God cries out:

Comfort, oh comfort my people...Speak kindly to Jerusalem, (Isaiah 40:1-2, NASB.)

The price has been paid and comfort has come as a result of Israel's repentance, of their sighing and lamenting over the cause of their captivity. Jehovah, merciful and gracious, has now sent His spokesman to offer comfort and consolation. He has sent a servant to offer tenderness, the balm of Gilead to bind up their wounded spirits and broken hearts. God's response to their repentance is "I am with you. I have neither forgotten nor forsaken you." That theme is repeated again and again through the remainder of the Book of Isaiah.

The children of Israel had suffered through a terrible calamity. They were in need of comfort, of being assured that their time of catastrophe was coming to an end. It was time for encouragement, for knowing that God had not forsaken them. Darkness had covered the land, but Israel had not been cast aside by Yahweh. The time for restoration was at hand; the time for comfort had come. The God of all comfort had declared it is time for consolation.

In his commentary on Isaiah, Walter Brueggemann writes:

> Enough! Enough sentence, enough penalty, enough payment, enough exile, enough displacement! This is an assertion of forgiveness, but it is not cheap or soft or easy forgiveness. There is, in any case, a limit to the sentence. It can be satisfied and served out. And now it is ended![43]

The prophetic word given by Isaiah was not just for that time, it is a God-given mandate to Christians to offer comfort, encouragement, and emotional and financial support to the suffering House of Israel. If this Scripture is not for Christians then for whom is it? Nation after nation has turned its back on the Jewish people. God will not forget those who abandon Israel, just as He will not forget those who reach out in love and assistance. This assignment is echoed in Paul's second letter to the Corinthians:

> *Praise be to the God and Father of our Lord Jesus Christ, the Father of compassion and the God of all comfort, who comforts us in all our troubles, so that we can comfort those in any trouble with the comfort we ourselves receive from God,* (II Corinthians 1:3-4, NIV.)

If you and I are to be godly, if our major focus is to become more like Christ, we must offer comfort and consolation to God's chosen people. In Isaiah 6:8, NKJV, God called out, *"Whom shall I send, and who will go for us?"* Isaiah cried, *"Here am I; send me."* The Lord is saying that praying Christians can win the war being fought right now in the land of the Bible. Wake up, mighty men; wake up, mighty women! Wake up, Esthers and Nehemiahs! As Daniel so confidently stated:

> *But the people that do know their God shall be strong, and do exploits,* (Daniel 11:32, KJV).

As Christians we are called to show God's love to the suffering House of Israel as did Corrie ten Boom and her family. Almost three decades ago, in September of 1986, I traveled to Haarlem, Holland with the idea to purchase and restore the ten Boom clock shop. On April 15, 1986, I met with the owner Mr. Cor Van Der Noll and asked him if he would sell the clock shop so we could restore it to its original condition, as it was when Corrie was alive. As I prayed and waited for his answer, the clocks in the shop began to chime the noon hour. Mr. Van Der Noll looked at me and said, "Yes, I will sell. Do you know why? Today is April 15, Corrie's birthday."

On January 1, 1987, the 150th anniversary of the clock shop, the project was completed. The ten Boom clock shop has been open at no charge to the public since that time as a witness of the love Christians have for the Jewish people.

The lives and deaths of the ten Boom family—Corrie's father Casper and her sister Betsie—their love for the Jewish people, and the sacrifices they made in order to save some eight hundred Jews during the Holocaust was the inspiration for the Jerusalem Prayer Team. Their story, one of courage, faith, and determination, began on May 10, 1940, when the people of Holland came face-to-face with the reality of war. Germany was poised to invade their country, which had hoped to remain neutral. Earlier in the evening, the ten Boom family had gathered around Casper's prized radio to hear the Dutch prime minister address the country. He assured the people that there was nothing to fear. Casper was incensed by his comments. "It is wrong to give people hope when there is no hope. It is wrong to base faith upon wishes. There will be war. The Germans will attack, and we will fall."[44]

Corrie was in bed asleep when the jarring sound of explosions rent the night. She bolted upright and grabbed her robe. Slipping her arms into the sleeves, she raced downstairs, paused outside her father's room, and hearing only the sounds of his whiffling snores, moved on to her older sister Betsie's room. Corrie felt her way across the bedroom to find Betsie, who was sitting upright in the darkness. The two sisters embraced and said in unison, "War."

They curled up in Betsie's bed and drifted back to sleep. That was when Corrie dreamed that she, Betsie, their father, brother Willem, and nephew Peter, were being driven through the square in Haarlem in the back of a wagon. To her horror, they were unable to climb down from the dray that was carrying them farther and farther from their home. She jerked awake and told Betsie about the dream. Betsie reassured Corrie, "If God has shown us bad times ahead, it's enough for me that He knows about them. That's why He sometimes shows us things, you know—to tell us that this too is in His hands."[45]

Five days later the news came that Holland had surrendered and Queen Wilhelmina had fled to England. Over the next months, the Dutch people gradually became aware of the horrors of anti-Semitism. At first, it was negligible—a rock through a window or slurs painted like ugly slashes across synagogue walls and on the front doors of Jewish homes. Jews were denied service in restaurants, libraries, theaters, and other gathering places. Finally, six-pointed yellow cloth stars were handed out that had to be worn prominently on clothing, each bearing the word *Jood* (Jew). Then Jews began to silently disappear, as if they had never existed.

On one of their walks, Corrie and her father saw Jews in the public square being loaded like so many cattle into the back of a truck—men, women, and children—all bearing the ignominious yellow star. Corrie wept for the people; Casper pitied the Germans, for, he said, they were "touching the apple of God's eye."

It was Corrie's nephew Kik, Willem's son, who was responsible for helping the Weils, the ten Booms' neighbors across the street, escape the Nazi threat, and who first planted the thought in her mind of working with the Underground. Once the seed was planted, God began to water it and cultivate it until, on May 10, 1942, the seedling burst forth into the light, and the lives of the ten Boom family were forever changed. (Kik died in Bergen-Belsen. He was incarcerated for aiding a downed American pilot.)

The edict had been handed down from Nazi headquarters that the singing of the Dutch national anthem "Wilhelmus" was *verboten* (forbidden). Corrie, Betsie, and Casper were on their way to Sunday services at the Dutch Reformed Church in Velsen, a small town nearby. The German occupation had been responsible for one good thing in Holland: Churches were filled to overflowing with worshippers. Peter, another nephew, had been selected as church organist in a competition of forty entrants. He was in the organ loft, hidden from the crowd below. As the service concluded, the crowd emitted a unified gasp; Peter had pulled out all the stops on the huge organ and was playing the "Wilhelmus" at full volume.

Peter was clearly a hero to the burdened Dutch people, but Corrie worried that he might be arrested for his victorious organ recital. For several days his safety seemed secure, but then his little sister, Cocky, burst into the clock shop to inform everyone that Peter had been arrested and taken away to the federal prison in Amsterdam. For two months he would languish in a cold, dark, concrete cell at the prison before being released.

Two weeks later, the ten Boom family home became a way station on the Underground Railroad, which aided Jews in escaping the Nazis. Just before evening curfew a knock summoned Corrie to the alley door. There stood a heavily veiled woman. When the door opened, she stepped inside and identified herself as a Jew seeking asylum. Casper ten Boom welcomed her and explained that all of God's children were welcome in his home. Two nights later, another furtive knock sounded at the side door. An elderly couple stood there, also seeking asylum.

The following day, Corrie traveled to seek Willem's advice. As he talked with Corrie on how to procure ration cards, she thought of a friend who worked in the Food Office. With the help of Fred Koornstra, Corrie was able to secure enough ration cards to feed the Jewish refugees who passed through the ten Boom home.

The secret room or "The Hiding Place," as it would become known was the brainchild of one of Europe's most respected architects, whom they knew only as Mr. Smit. (Many of the underground workers were labeled "Smit." This made it difficult for other workers to identify these brave volunteers.) This elderly wisp of a man freely gave his time and energy to design and direct the workmen, who built a room so secure that the Gestapo failed to ever find it. A signal was devised to show that it was safe to enter the ten Boom home. This was an Alpina Watches sign that was hung in the dining room window.

Once the room was completed, "guests" rehearsed getting into the hiding place quickly until they could vacate the lower floors and be safely inside the compartment in less than two minutes. Corrie practiced stalling techniques to delay anyone who might come in search of the hidden Jews. One of their guests, Leendert, a schoolteacher, even installed an alarm system that would sound an early warning if unwanted visitors threatened.

Since the ten Boom home was in the center of Haarlem, Corrie worked diligently to secure other hiding places for the people who came for help. She enlisted farmers, owners of large homes, and others who wanted to give aid to the tormented Jewish population. She amassed a group of about eighty people, some of whom were teenagers, willing to risk their lives to carry coded messages between Corrie and her contacts. One coded message read:

> We have a man's watch here that's giving us trouble.
> We can't find anyone to repair it. For one thing, the face
> is very old-fashioned.[46]

That was translated as, "an elderly Jew whose facial features would give him away." This was a most difficult individual to place in a safe house. The ten Boom family took him in and provided a haven for him.

Rolf, a local policeman who provided aid to the ten Boom family, stopped at the clock shop one afternoon. He had information that the Gestapo was going to raid a local safe house that night. Corrie summoned Jop, a seventeen-year-old volunteer, and asked him to deliver a message about the planned raid. Unfortunately for Jop, the Gestapo had already swooped down on the home and was lying in wait for the unsuspecting young man. He was quickly arrested and transported to the prison in Amsterdam. When Rolf returned with the news of Jop's arrest, members of the ten Boom family were convinced they should stop their underground activities, but they refused to abandon their Jewish friends. The work had to continue.

Corrie had been in bed for two days with influenza when, on February 28, 1944, a man claiming to need help to rescue his wife from prison came to the clock shop and demanded to speak only to her. Corrie painfully rose from her bed, dressed, and went downstairs. The visitor pleaded for 600 guilders in order to bribe a policeman and secure his wife's release. She arranged for the money, sent the man on his way, and slowly climbed back up the stairs to her sickbed. Sometime later she heard the incessant buzzing of the alarm system.

Corrie supposed a drill was in progress—but that was soon followed by the realization that it was no drill. She heard the sound of boots tromping through the downstairs and heavy footfalls on the stairs below her room. She secured the trapdoor to the hiding place, set her "prison bag" in front of the panel, and dove back into her bed, feigning sleep.

The door to her room burst open and a tall, heavyset man entered demanding her name. "Cornelia ten Boom," she replied sleepily. The Gestapo leader, Kapteyn, commanded her to arise and dress. He casually asked, "So, where are you hiding the Jews?" Corrie denied any knowledge of Jews or an underground ring. He watched as Corrie pulled her clothes on over her pajamas, and with a regretful glance at her bag, which she had stuffed with necessities in case of capture, turned and walked out of the bedroom. She was prodded down the stairs into the kitchen, only to see that a uniformed soldier stood there. In the front room, Corrie was pleased to see the Alpina Watches sign lying smashed on the floor. Anyone walking past the shop would know it was not safe to enter.

Another of the Gestapo led Corrie into a separate room to be interrogated. Again and again she was asked to reveal the secret room. Each time she refused, she was hit repeatedly, but she still refused to answer, although she could taste the metallic tang of blood in her mouth. She cried, "Lord Jesus, help me." Her captor threatened to kill her if she spoke that name again, but he did stop the beating and eventually led her back to the room where other family members were being held.

Corrie was shoved inside, and Betsie was led from the room. Corrie dropped into a chair and heard sounds of wood splintering as cupboard doors were smashed in search of the suspected hiding place. One German was sifting through the treasures that had been secreted in a corner cupboard on a lower floor. As the architect of the hidden room had predicted, it was the first place the Gestapo looked in their search for Jews. The destruction continued for another half hour, yet no one was found. When Betsie returned to the room, she was bleeding and bruised but had kept silent during the interrogation.

As they were escorted from their home, their sanctuary, Corrie realized her earlier vision was about to become reality: She and her family were being arrested, and they would eventually be transported to an undetermined place from which they could not escape. They were taken first to the local police station and placed in the care of their friend Rolf. For the remainder of the day, they were forced to sit on the cold, hard floor of a large room with thirty-five members of the underground family.

Rolf entered the room, spoke briefly to Willem, and then bellowed that there were toilets available that could be used under escort. After he left the room, Willem whispered to Corrie that this would be an opportunity for those inside to dispose of any papers they did not want to fall into the hands of the Gestapo.

Later, as evening fell and darkness settled over Haarlem, Casper gathered the group around him and began to recite Psalm 119:114, KJV: *"Thou art my hiding place and my shield: I hope in thy word."* As he quoted his beloved scriptures from memory, the group was comforted by their elder, who would shepherd them through many dark days. His unwavering faith gave them renewed strength.

The following morning the prisoners were loaded onto buses and taken to Scheveningen Prison in The Hague, about twenty-four miles south of Haarlem. When they disembarked, one of the guards pointed at Corrie's father and yelled, "Did you have to arrest that old man?" Willem led his father up to the check-in desk. The head of the prison peered into Casper's eyes and said, "I'd like to send you home. I'll take your word that you won't cause any more trouble."

Those standing nearby clearly heard his reply, "If I go home today, tomorrow I will open my door again to any man in need who knocks." As the group was led to their individual cells, none knew it would be the last time they would see Casper ten Boom. He died ten days later.

Casper's dedication and determination to assist God's Chosen People came as the result of his father, Willem, having taken up the banner passed to him by his great-grandfather, a Christian Zionist, who had begun a weekly meeting to pray for the peace of Jerusalem (Psalm 122:6) in 1844. Casper continued the meetings, where the family and others gathered specifically in prayer for the Jewish people. The meetings ended on February 28, 1944, when Nazi soldiers came to the house to take the family away.

Corrie's first prison assignment was a narrow cell, which she shared with four other women. When the matron determined that she was quite ill, Corrie was transported to the hospital. The doctor diagnosed her with pre-tuberculosis, hoping that she would be allowed to stay in the hospital. It was not to be; Corrie was taken from the hospital and returned to the prison, but not before one of the nurses had slipped her a small packet containing soap, safety pins, and four individual booklets containing the Gospels.

Corrie gradually recovered from the influenza and began to wonder what had happened to the other people from Haarlem who had been transported to the prison. On Hitler's birthday, she had the opportunity to gather information. While the wardens celebrated, the prisoners were able to shout back and forth to each other and gather yearned-for knowledge of loved ones. She learned that her sister Betsie was still at Scheveningen, that her brother Willem had been released, and that her sister, Nollie, had been discharged almost a month before. It would be much later that Corrie learned of her father's death.

Shortly after the celebration, the door to Corrie's cell cracked open and a package landed with a thump on the floor. She was overjoyed to discover that it was from Nollie. Inside, she found a light blue embroidered sweater. It was like being enfolded in the comfort of Nollie's distant arms. The package also contained cookies, vitamins, a needle and thread, and a bright red towel.

As Corrie wrapped the items back up in the brown parcel paper, she noticed a discrepancy in the return address. Carefully removing the stamp she found a joyous message: "All the watches in your closet are safe." Corrie rejoiced; all six of the Jews they had been hiding had safely escaped the secret room. This, no doubt, helped her through the following four long months in solitary confinement, in which her only contact was an ant that had found its way into her cell. She was grateful to God for friendship with even one of His smallest creatures. She shared crumbs from her daily ration of bread with the tiny insect.

Corrie knew that eventually she would face a hearing at the hands of a Gestapo interrogator. Finally, on a cool May morning, she was summoned from her tiny room. She was led through a labyrinth of halls and a courtyard sparkling with the drizzle of rain before entering one of the huts where the hearings were held. As she awaited her fate, she prayed, "Lord Jesus, You were called to a hearing too. Show me what to do."

The inquisitor, Lieutenant Rahms, noticed that Corrie was shivering from the cold and built a fire in the stove. He drew a chair forward, motioned for Corrie to sit, and very gently began to question his prisoner. For the next hour he probed, feinted, and parried in the dance to gain Corrie's trust and glean information from his affection-starved detainee. He began, "I would like to help you, Miss ten Boom, but you must tell me everything."

Corrie was glad that among the drills practiced in her home in Haarlem was one of answering questions if captured by the Gestapo. Her training stood her in good stead. The officer questioned her about the ration cards and how they were obtained. She was relieved that she had no knowledge of how they had been stolen. When asked about her other activities Corrie launched into a description of her work with the girls' clubs and with the mentally disabled. The lieutenant had no idea why she found that so rewarding.

Rahms chided her for her waste of time with the disabled. Corrie responded, "God loves everyone, even the weak and feeble. The Bible says that God looks at things very differently from us." The officer abruptly ended the session and sent Corrie back to her cell. From that time forward, as long as Corrie was in Scheveningen, the lieutenant helped her as much as possible. He arranged for her to be allowed to see her family, using the pretext of the reading of Casper ten Boom's will. While they were all together, Willem slipped Corrie a small, compact Bible secreted in a pouch that she could wear around her neck.

Although the lieutenant could supply aid, he unfortunately did not have the authority to allow her and Betsie to return home. Nevertheless, Corrie spent time reading the precious Gospels that had been smuggled to her. She rejoiced that Jesus' death, though meant for evil, brought forgiveness to all who accepted His gift. She prayed that God would use her troubles to bring good to someone.

CHAPTER NINE

CORRIE TEN BOOM

*He who dwells in the secret place of the Most High
Shall abide under the shadow of the Almighty,*

(PSALM 91:1, NKJV.)

I n June 1944, the prisoners languishing in their cells at Schevenin-gen were told to pack what few belongings they had, then were lined up and marched to a train awaiting them at the station. As she stood in line to board, Corrie saw Betsie down the platform. Suffering from pernicious anemia from childhood, Betsie had been denied medication. Corrie saw at once how very ill she had become, and she wriggled her way through the throng to reach her sister. They embraced with the joy of knowing that they were, at least for the moment, together.

The train chugged down the line toward a labor camp in the south of Holland. The prisoners were assigned to barracks and forced to work long, hard hours. Corrie was dispatched to the building in which Phillips radios were made for German aircraft. She did her work in the Phillips factory with great diligence. Day after day she made as many mistakes as she dared while assembling the radios.

Life in the camp was exceedingly hard, and execution of the male prisoners was the order of the day. Yet Corrie and Betsie survived. Betsie taught Bible classes to those who gathered around each night. Eventually, a faint hope blossomed as word seeped through the camp that the Allies had invaded Europe. Rumors that Allied forces were nearing Holland swirled through the prison like leaves flying in the autumn wind. The sounds of explosions filled the air, but they were later confirmed to be the work of Germans destroying bridges and railroad lines.

Late one evening, the loudspeaker in the men's camp blared out name after name, and then just as quickly fell silent—as if the life had been squeezed from it. A sense of foreboding settled over the women's camp, when suddenly the twilight was filled with the sound of volley after volley of gunfire. When the guns were finally silenced, more than seven hundred captives lay silent on the killing field.

The next morning the women were once again commanded to gather their belongings and report for roll call in a field outside the camp. As noon approached, the women were ordered to line up and were marched from there to a railroad siding. Betsie clung to Corrie's arm, wheezing and gasping for each breath. Corrie slipped an arm around her and half carried her precious sister the final quarter mile to their destination. As the two sisters glanced around, they could see perhaps a thousand weary, hungry, thirsty, bedraggled women standing in single file along the railroad track.

Corrie looked around for the train that was to take them to their next destination but saw only what she described as "small, high-wheeled European boxcars" stretching out of sight in both directions. Soldiers marched down the line of women, stopping at each car to throw open the sliding door. Horrified, Corrie realized that they were to be herded into the small boxcars like so many cattle. Each car, which normally would have held only thirty or forty, was soon packed with eighty or more women. Those in the car with Corrie and Betsie developed a plan that would allow them, at least, to sit on the floor. With little food or water and no toilet facilities, the car soon reeked of human waste.

For three days and nights the train slowly made its way across the border from Holland into Germany. At last the lurching locomotive screeched to a halt and the doors were opened. The women scrambled out into the sunlight and were at last able to drink their fill of water. They were lined up again and then marched through the countryside to the crest of a hill, from where they could see their destination: Ravensbruck! Its reputation had reached Holland long before Corrie and Betsie were incarcerated. It was infamous as an extermination camp for female prisoners.

For the first two days in the compound, surrounded by grey concrete walls intersected by gun towers, the women were forced to stay in the open. Rain poured down on them, turning the ground into a quagmire of mud. When it wasn't raining, the sun beat down mercilessly with nothing to shade the desperate women. Finally they were processed, forced to disrobe, prodded through showers, and issued thin dresses and worn shoes.

Corrie wondered how she would be able to secure Betsie's much-needed sweater and prevent the confiscation of her beloved Bible. Then she saw an opportunity to hide them behind a bench in the latrine area. She prayed that her subterfuge would not be discovered, as she and Betsie later made their way through two searches. At last they exited the building with Betsie's sweater tied around Corrie's waist and the Bible dangling between her shoulder blades beneath her dress. As soon as she safely could, Corrie gave the sweater to Betsie, who put it on under her dress so that it could not be seen by the guards.

The two sisters were then crammed into a barracks designed to hold 400 people. Now it was home to over 1,400 women forced to sleep on rickety platform beds swarming with fleas. Yet, in this desperate room, Betsie and Corrie retrieved their beloved Bible from its hiding place and proceeded to teach the Gospel of Jesus Christ to these starving women. Betsie would read in Dutch, translate into German, and the words would flow back through the crowd in French, Polish, Russian, or Czech, coming full circle back to Dutch.

The indignity of the regular Friday searches revealed a dynamic truth about Christ's sacrifice that neither Corrie nor Betsie had ever conceived. As they stood naked and shivering before the leering eyes of the German guards, a passage from the Bible literally came alive for Corrie. She realized that Jesus, too, had been stripped of His clothing. Corrie later wrote:

> I had not known—I had not thought...The paintings, the carved crucifixes showed at least a scrap of cloth. But this, I suddenly knew, was the respect and reverence of the artist. But, oh, at the time itself, on that other Friday morning—there had been no reverence. No more than I saw in the faces around us now. I leaned toward Betsie, ahead of me in line. Her shoulder blades stood out sharp and thin beneath her blue-mottled skin. "Betsie, they took His clothes, too."[47]

A Catholic theologian, Monsignor John M. Oesterreicher wrote of the forced nakedness of the Nazi prisoners in terms of self-worth:

> The forced nakedness of the prisoners was an attempt to divest them of their dignity as persons.

Clothes not only protect and adorn the body, they also bespeak the spirit of man, his sense of beauty, his style, his respect for himself, his reverence for others. In short, clothes mark a man as a civilized being. When the victims were compelled to undress, they were robbed, therefore, of their part in civilization. They were thrown into a mass of like men, all drained of initiative, and the last flicker of resistance was snuffed out.[48]

Each morning, Corrie, Betsie, and the other women were rousted out of bed for roll call at 4:30 by the sound of riding whips striking the side of the building. Conditions inside were so deplorable, so filled with the sharp odor of unwashed bodies, strangling dust, crawling lice, and swarms of fleas, that the guards refused to go inside. Everyone had to be outside and ready for work. If even one person was missing, all the women were forced to stand stick straight for hours until all were counted again and again.

Corrie and Betsie were assigned to work in the nearby Siemens factory, pushing a cart laden with heavy metal plates to a railroad siding and then unloading it. Their eleven-hour days were broken only by a meager lunch of thin soup and a boiled potato. Corrie and Betsie felt blessed, for those who did lighter work received no lunch at all.

As the desperate days mounted, Corrie found that she was more often forced to share her hoard of liquid vitamins she had managed to hide for Betsie. The bottle had been given to her before she left Scheveningen. Corrie was stunned when she realized that though she often shared the precious drops with as many as twenty-five women in a day, the contents never ran dry. She was reminded of the woman in the Old Testament, the widow of Zarephath, whose cruise of oil held a perpetual supply as long as there was need of it—all because she willingly shared all that she had with the prophet Elijah.

One day one of the nurses from the infirmary, a young Dutch woman, smuggled a bottle of vitamins to Corrie. She rejoiced to be able to refill her small bottle. God's provision was truly confirmed that night as she held her bottle upside down to drain the last drop. No matter how long she held it or how many times she tapped the bottom, the bottle refused to give up another single drop. As God provided the new, the old ran dry.

When prisoners became ill with a fever of more than 104 degrees Fahrenheit, they were taken to the camp hospital. No treatment was given them even at the hospital, so when it grew too full to receive more patients, the weakest and sickest were placed in carts and taken to the ovens that dominated the center of the camp. The ten Boom sisters had truly reached Hell on Earth, and yet they continued to praise God for His care. No matter where Betsie found herself, she talked about Jesus to those nearby—standing in line at the dispensary, performing the backbreaking work assigned to her, waiting for her daily ration of bread—she spoke of her Lord and His desire to come into their lives.

Corrie recalled how, as the women labored in the prison yard one day, Betsie was maliciously lashed by one of the guards. She refused to allow Corrie to give in to hatred, rather praying for her captors as much as she prayed for the captives surrounding her. As the ruthlessness increased, Betsie's faith seemed to grow exponentially. She seemed to move even closer to God, her suffering but a small thing in light of His sacrifice.

When she returned to the barracks, Betsie told Corrie of her longing to have a place where people wounded in body and spirit could come to be healed after the war. One night as the sisters lay side by side in the barracks, Betsie told Corrie more of her dream:

> It's such a beautiful house, Corrie! The floors are all inlaid wood, with statues set in the walls and a broad staircase sweeping down. And gardens! Gardens all around it where they can plant flowers. It will do them such good, Corrie, to care for flowers.[49]

Betsie's desire was to tell people of the goodness of God—of what a good and wonderful Father He is. She wanted to teach people that hatred and bitterness must be left behind. Like the apostle Paul, she yearned to forget "those things which are behind," and to reach "forward to those things which are ahead," and to "press toward the goal for the prize of the upward call of God in Christ Jesus," (Philippians 3:13–14, NKJV.)

Later, Betsie revealed another vision to Corrie, one of a concentration camp. It had been cheerfully painted, flowers ringed its periphery, barbed wire was gone, and guards no longer paraded on its walls. It would house the people who had been vilely treated by Hitler's minions, or whose lives had been infiltrated by his evil. They would once again be taught to be loving and kind to those around them.

As the fall days shortened into winter's icy blast, Betsie became more and more ill. Before long her body began to fail and she coughed up blood. She was not a candidate for hospitalization, as her temperature lingered at 102 degrees. Then one fateful night, it finally topped the 104 mark, and she was placed in the hospital. Corrie accompanied her as, with the unexpected help of one of the more brutal matrons, Betsie was taken from the barracks on a stretcher to the hospital. The night was heavy with sleet as Corrie walked beside her sister and tried to shield her from the cold onslaught. When Corrie returned to the dormitory, her dorm mates assaulted her with inquiries about her beloved sister.

Daily Corrie sneaked over to the hospital to stand outside the window where she could see her sister. One day she peered through the dirty glass and saw only an empty bed. She slumped as she trudged away from her place of vigil. Suddenly she heard, "Corrie!" She turned to see the young Dutch nurse, Mien, who had provided so much assistance to those prisoners in the barracks. She grabbed Corrie by the arm and dragged her back to the hospital. "You have to see this," she pleaded. As the two neared the place where Betsie's body lay, Corrie looked at her face and there was Betsie of Haarlem. Gone were the lines of grief and hunger and disease. Betsie's face was one of repose, of peace, of radiance. At last she was home with her earthly father and her heavenly Father. Corrie took time over the next days to share Betsie's miraculous transformation with her dorm mates.

One morning at roll call Corrie heard, "Prisoner ten Boom report after roll call." She thought surely her time must be up. Would she be punished for sharing the Gospel with others, or would she be shot? When she arrived, she learned that she was to be released, but her hopes were dashed when she was ordered to report to the hospital for swelling in her feet. Corrie spent weeks hospitalized before she was declared well enough to leave. Finally her medical release was stamped.

In a shed near the front gate, she was given new clothes: under-garments, a wool skirt and silky blouse, sturdy shoes, a hat, and a coat. When she was handed a document that stated she had never been ill while in Ravensbruck, she gladly signed the form. She was overjoyed when her watch— a gift from her father—was returned, along with her mother's ring and a few Dutch guilders.

At last the heavy gates swung open and a group of about a dozen inmates were marched through them. Corrie thought there must have been some mistake. Surely she was being taken to the Siemens plant to work or to a local munitions factory. But instead of turning right toward the work places, the group was directed left toward the train station. After a grueling trip with many delays, Corrie reached Berlin on New Year's Day 1945. She and Betsie had both been liberated—Corrie to life anew and Betsie to life everlasting.

After Corrie crossed the border into Holland, she spent almost two weeks in a local hospital, recovering her strength from the cruel ordeal she had suffered. One night she was smuggled to Willem's home onboard a truck ferrying food and supplies. Sometime later, Corrie learned that she had been released from Ravensbruck by a clerical error, and a week after her departure, all women her age in the camp were brutally slaughtered.

As soon as she was fit enough, Corrie began to share her story with others. When the war ended, she shared Betsie's vision of a place of asylum with a lady, Mrs. Bierens de Haan, whose son had been miraculously returned from a German prison camp. She was so grateful for his return that she gave Corrie her home for Betsie's legacy. It was a place of peace and comfort where the wounded and scarred—physically and emotionally—could receive succor.

The story of Corrie's wartime experiences began to reach other countries. She was invited to speak in America, England, and many other nations. The most difficult place for her to go was to Germany, a land scarred by bombs and hatred. Its cities were heaps of rubble, and the citizens' minds and hearts were covered with the ashes of despair. Corrie knew that the Lord would "give them beauty for ashes, the oil of joy for mourning, [and] the garment of praise for the spirit of heaviness," (Isaiah 61:3, NKJV) if only the German citizens would surrender their lives to the living Lord.

In Corrie's own words, she described an encounter with one of the guards from Ravensbruck:

> At a church service in Munich I saw the former SS man who had stood guard outside the shower room... He came up to me and said, "How grateful I am for your message, Fraulein. To think that He has washed my sins away!" He thrust his hand out to shake mine... I who had so often preached the need to forgive kept my hand at my side... I breathed a silent prayer: Jesus, I cannot forgive him. Give me Your forgiveness. As I took his hand the most incredible thing happened... a current seemed to pass from me to him, while into my heart sprang a love for this stranger that almost over-whelmed me.[50]

A Christian organization in Germany providing relief to the German people asked Corrie to help run a camp for those whose lives had been wrecked under Hitler's malevolent rule. When she arrived, she was stunned to see living proof of Betsie's vision spread out before her. It was the abandoned concentration camp of which she had dreamed. Its dull, dreary barracks were surrounded by bales of corroded barbed wire. Upon its paths of coal ash had trodden the feet of prisoners destined for death. Inside the empty barracks stood row upon row of cots. If they could talk, oh, what tales of bravery, courage, despair, faith, or hopelessness they would be able to relate!

Corrie began to share Betsie's plan with her companions. They would need brightly painted window boxes filled with flowers, paint the color of sunshine for the inside walls, and the color of trees on the outside. And, of course, the horrid barbed wire must go before anyone would be allowed onto the grounds. That place must be a place of refuge, peace, and renewal.

Corrie was further able to spread the Good News of God's faithfulness and love to those around her. For over thirty years, she traveled from country to country calling herself "a tramp for the Lord." She shared Betsie's story and her own experiences at the hands of their captors while spreading the Gospel. She traveled to communist countries that others avoided as being too risky, and she wrote numerous books. Perhaps the most well-known was *The Hiding Place*, which later became a movie produced by Dr. Billy Graham. As her fame spread, so did her ministry.

Cornelia ten Boom suffered a debilitating stroke in 1978 that robbed her of the ability to communicate. She died on her birthday, April 15, 1983, at the age of ninety-one. Certainly, no Jew who was saved because of the sacrifice of her family, all the Jewish women with whom she and Betsie shared the Gospel and ministered to in the prison and concentration camp, and even the Germans who received the Lord due to their testimony will ever forget her, Betsie, or her family.

Corrie's favorite Psalm was the ninety-first:

> *"He that dwelleth in the secret place of the most High shall abide under the shadow of the Almighty. I will say of the Lord, He is my refuge and my fortress: my God; in him will I trust."*

Indeed, she did abide under His shadow and trust Him!

If Christians who are able to bless the house of Israel with-hold that blessing, especially by not reaching out toward those who are suffering from terrorist attacks such as the ones that happened during the Holocaust, how will Jews ever know that real Christians are different than those who claim His name but kill Jews? To comfort the house of Israel is our duty, and our privilege:

> *But when He saw the multitudes (the Jews), He was moved with compassion for them, because they were weary and scattered, like sheep having no shepherd,* (Matthew 9:36, NKJV.)
>
> *But thou, O LORD, shalt endure forever; and thy remembrance unto all generations. Thou shalt arise, and have mercy upon Zion: for the time to favour her, yea, the set time, is come,* (Psalm 102:12-13, KJV.)

CHAPTER TEN

GOD'S GIFTS AND CALL TO ISRAEL HAVE NOT BEEN REVOKED

"Can a woman forget her sucking child, that she
should not have compassion on the son of her womb?
Yea, they may forget, yet will I not forget thee,"

(ISAIAH 49:15, KJV.)

he House of Israel seems to have fallen among robbers who
have not only stolen their land but their lives. Many people
watch with little, if any, concern as Jews again become scapegoats
for the world's inequities. The economy tanks—must be the fault
of Jewish bankers. Disease runs rampant—must have been caused
by the Jews. Floods, fires, hurricanes, tornadoes, famine—the Jews
have to be somehow responsible. Right? That has certainly been
the mindset of Arab leaders for decades.

According to a recent article in the *Jerusalem Post*, there are as
many reasons Arabic-speaking people believe these lies as there are
Arabs in the region:

...A Swiss reporter interviewed a high-ranking official in the oil-rich United Arab Emirates and asked

why the school system wasn't better. Ah, explained the man, this was all due to Israel.

While the following are generalizations, they are generally true:

Arabic-speaking people live in terrible, [closed] societies marked by massive injustice and poor prospects for improvement. Their lives are increasingly governed by restrictions based on religious interpretation, large-scale segregation by gender, a contrast of which they are well aware between the repression and stagnation of their own countries and the relative freedom and progress in other parts of the world...

There is deep resentment of the West for past imperialism, its relative power and wealth and cultural and religious differences.

All of these factors are systematically fed to the masses on a daily basis by mosques, schools, leaders, opposition politicians, media and just about every other institution.

And yet we are to believe that this problem is entirely or almost entirely caused by Israel's existence, the Arab- Israeli conflict and the situation of the Palestinians. That's it? Why do people say this? One reason is ignorance. The conflict is all they know about the Middle East, and this answer is what they are constantly told by most experts and some media. Another reason is politics, as it is a talking point by those who for various reasons want to wipe Israel off the map or weaken it.[51]

Teachings from the Koran and from Sharia law deny the Jews any right to live on an earth that Muslims believe belongs to Allah, period. Christians, Buddhists, Taoists, and others have far fewer rights, if any, than Muslims. Fanatical organizations such as al Qaeda, Hamas, Hezbollah, Fatah, the PLO and the jihadists, mullahs, ayatollahs and imams who support them believe it is the sacred duty of every Muslim to attempt to convert the infidels. If rejected, then all non-Muslims must be eradicated to purify planet Earth.

Unfortunately, few heed the words Jesus spoke concerning the House of Israel:

*"For I was an hungered, and ye gave me no meat: I was thirsty, and ye gave me no drink: I was a stranger, and ye took me not in: naked, and ye clothed me not: sick, and in prison, and ye visited me not. Then shall they also answer him, saying, Lord, when saw we thee an hungered, or athirst, or a stranger, or naked, or sick, or in prison, and did not minister unto thee? Then shall he answer them, saying, Verily I say unto you, **Inasmuch as ye did it not to one of the least of these, ye did it not to me,**"* (Emphasis mine, Matthew 25:42-45, KJV.)

In the above verses, our Lord was referring to the Jews, His earthly seed. This Scripture means just what it says, and the United States finds itself at a critical crossroads: Will we believe the God of the Bible and stand with Israel? Will we turn our backs on the Jewish people and embrace the Liberal Left views of those who commiserate with Israel's enemies? Many Americans embrace the thought of religion, but have turned their backs on its reality—an adherence to the Word of God.

Since 9/11 the US has been embroiled in a war against radical Islamic groups. Our homeland has been made more vulnerable by the refusal to call a terrorist a terrorist. Those who desire to see the demise of the United States are often referred to erroneously as "freedom fighters." Presidents over past decades have pressed Israel not to retaliate against those fanatics who only want to see the Jewish people annihilated. Israel has further been compelled to give up land for peace—a futile exercise. In the entire chapter of Joel 3:1-17, God calls the nations to account for their treatment of His people:

> In those days and at that time, when I restore the fortunes of Judah and Jerusalem, I will gather all nations and bring them down to the Valley of Jehoshaphat.[b] There I will put them on trial for what they did to my inheritance, my people Israel, because they scattered my people among the nations and **divided up my land,** (Emphasis mine, Joel 3:1-3, NIV.)

The truth is that the Jews were totally rejected during the Holocaust, and this was the response by the average Christian to their cries. May it not be our retort today.

Americans are not the only ones who feel the Jews are responsible; that same feeling is palpable among young Israeli pundits. Many of them feel that "Israel is a deeply flawed democracy twisted by special laws favoring Conservative religious Jews and Judaism, by racism and segregation, by the Law of Return, by a labyrinthine separatist wall, by an ethnocentric national anthem and a Davidic flag, and by other grievous offenses to Palestinian Arabs."[52]

Conversely Christian Zionists acknowledge an enormous debt of gratitude is owed to the Jewish people. They also understand what so many fail to recognize: The Jewish people are not the reason fanatical Muslims hate the United States. Rather, the Jews are allies in the continuing fight against world domination by Islam. Until September 11, 2001, the Israelis stood their ground alone against this threat, and still today are the first line of attack by terrorists. Even though the Israeli Defense Forces do not fight shoulder to shoulder with American troops, the two military forces guard, preserve, and protect identical values.

Truthfully, all the world's nations may turn their collective backs on the Jews, but God will never forsake His people:

> For Israel hath not been forsaken, nor Judah of his God,
> of the LORD of hosts, though their land was filled with sin
> against the Holy One of Israel, (Jeremiah 51:5, KJV.)

Some say the promises of God to the Jews have been revoked; they now belong solely to the Church. If this were true, why didn't the Apostle Paul know it? If all the promises were revoked, why didn't John the Revelator know it? And why didn't our Lord and Savior who gave this revelation to John know it? You cannot read the book of Revelation and not be aware of Israel from chapters seven through twenty-one. Israel is, and will always be, God's Miracle Nation.

Some use defiance as an occasion to deny their responsibility, saying the Jews are blind. But the Word contradicts that claim:

> For I tell you, you [Believers] will not see me again
> until you say, "Blessed is he who comes in the name of the
> Lord," (Matthew 23:39, NIV.)

You cannot say you have been a blessing until you have actually been a blessing. While many professing Christians stood mute while six million Jews were murdered in our lifetime, how can we who have turned our backs on their pain expect the Jewish people to listen to anything we might have to say?

Intimidated Christians in Europe maintained their silence while Hitler's death camps spewed smoke and ashes across the landscape. If you were Jewish, how would you feel when Christians sing in their churches about Jews in the Bible (Moses, David, Jesus), yet do nothing to reach out in love to living Jews? What about when Christians remained silent as America forced Israel to give the world's most infamous terrorist organization, the PLO and its leaders, part of the Holy Land from which 10,000 terrorist attacks would be committed against innocent Jews?

Once the horrors of German concentration camps became a reality, Christian attitudes were transformed. People began to understand that the Jews had suffered horribly at the hands of the Nazis, and that their living conditions following the end of the war were equally as deplorable. A place of sanctuary was needed for those who had been so horribly abused; change was an absolute necessity. Perhaps a stimulus for any change was the understanding that if Palestine, the ancient homeland of the Jews, was not opened to Jewish immigration, those survivors would be cast on the mercy of other Western nations.

Once that decision was made, it was not long before groups such as the National Council of Churches (NCC), now a member of the World Council of Churches (WCC) founded in 1948, in conjunction with other organizations, began to denigrate the plan for a Jewish homeland in Israel. For decades, the organization has pointedly castigated the Jews. For instance, in 2002 the WCC held a conference in Volos, Greece. While not a single criticism was uttered regarding

Muslims who harass and oppress Arab Christians, there was much said against the Jews:

> The conference declared the Jewish State "a sin" and "occupying power," accused Israelis of "dehumanizing" the Palestinians, theologically dismantled the "chosen-ness" of the Jewish people and called for "resistance" as a Christian duty. The conference denied 3,000 years of Jewish life in the land stretching between the Mediterranean and the Jordan River, took sides against the very presence of Israel, likened the defensive barrier that has blocked terrorism to "apartheid," attacked Jewish homes in Judea and Samaria invoking the name of God and conceptually dismissed the Jewish state, imagining it to be a mixture—Islamic, Christian and perhaps a bit Jewish. It even legitimized terrorism when it talked about the "thousands of prisoners who languish in Israeli jails," proclaiming that "resistance to the evil of occupation is a Christian's right and duty."[53]

Paul C. Merkley, Professor Emeritus of History at Carleton University, Ottawa, Canada, wrote of the WCC:

> During the weeks previous to the Six-Day War of June 1967, when Nasser, the dictator of Egypt, was rallying the Arab world for a war of liquidation against Israel, the WCC remained silent. But immediately after Israel's victory, the WCC... announced that it "cannot condone by silence territorial expansion by armed force."[54]

From that day forward, the WCC and its constituent denominational organizations have generally portrayed Israel's behavior to be in lockstep with Arab rhetoric. They believe and declare that all subsequent wars have been fomented by Israel for the purposes of further territorial gain and for the opportunity to incorporate innocent and abject Arab populations. (Ironically, those Arab men, women, and children would benefit far more greatly by being under Israeli administration.) The WCC pressed constantly through the 1970s and 1980s for America's official contact with the PLO and denounced Israel's punitive responses to terrorism and civil disruption. It denounced the Camp David Accords of 1978 for allegedly ignoring the national ambitions of the "Palestinians." Its consistent line is that "Israel's repeated defiance of international law, its continuing occupation and the impunity it has so long enjoyed are the fundamental causes of the present violence and threaten peace and security of both peoples."[55]

In September 2001, WCC representatives attending the UN Conference on Racism, Racial Discrimination, Xenophobia, and Related Intolerance at Durban, South Africa, led the demand to officially denounce Israel for "systematic perpetration of racist crimes including war crimes, acts of genocide, and ethnic cleansing."[56]

CHAPTER ELEVEN

SILENCE IMPLIES CONSENT

For Zion's sake I will not keep silent, and for Jerusalem's
sake I will not be quiet, until her righteousness goes forth
as brightness, and her salvation as a burning torch,

(ISAIAH 62:1, NIV.)

When it became blatantly apparent in the 1960s that many in Christian churches were turning a blind eye to the plight of the Israelis, Dr. Franklin H. Littell, chairman of the Department of Religion at Temple University, felt the call to confront the Church regarding its lack of response to the Nazi-led methodical murder of six million Jews. Dr. Littell was convinced that *"Qui tacet consentit"* (silence implies consent). The good doctor was appalled when much of the Church again remained silent in the weeks leading to the Six-Day War. He felt that the lack of response indicated compliance. Dr. Littell wrote that such passivity signaled acquiescence to the Arab mandate that Israel be driven into the sea.

As Israel worked to push back its enemies, Littell worked to resurrect among Protestant churches the spirit of support for the Jewish nation that had been evident in the ACPC. Following Israel's success on the battlefield, he introduced his new organization, Christians Concerned for Israel (CCI). It was, for Dr. Littell, a testament to the effectiveness of the organizations that had come before—the PPF, CCP, and ACPC.

In 1978, the CCI became the embryo for the National Christian Leadership Conference of Israel, a much larger group whose foundation was laid during the congressional hearings to authorize the sale of AWACS (Airborne Warning and Control System) to Saudi Arabia. The sale was contested by Prime Minister Begin, as well as Senators Edward Kennedy and Bob Packwood. Despite the opposition, the sale of AWACS was finally approved by Congress in October 1981. Christians representing organizations across the United States amassed in Washington, D.C., to protest the sale. Many of the organizers were amazed at the number who responded to show their support for Israel and the determination and emotion that was exhibited.

Even though ridiculed, reviled, and rebuffed by many of the mainline churches, Christian Zionists have continued to support Israel. These dedicated men and women continue to battle anti-Semitism both through the written and spoken word. The support of Evangelicals for the descendants of Abraham, Isaac, and Jacob is genuine and should not be dismissed as irrelevant.

In light of the biblical evidence presented until now, we must conclude that Christians have a God-given mandate to honor the Jewish people, wherever they are. But how does this connect to modern Israel? Many Christians seem happy enough to salute Jewish neighbors living alongside them in largely Gentile lands, but are indifferent or even hostile to the proposition that we also have a duty to support the controversial State of Israel. Some Believers bristle at the mere suggestion that God has anything to do with Israel's amazing restoration in our era.

Centuries before the Jewish people first were forced into foreign captivity, God revealed that they would be expelled from their
covenant land due to sin. But He also promised to eventually restore
them to the Promised Land. This prophecy came via Moses—whose
parents came from the tribe of Levi—while he was in the process of
boldly leading the children of Israel from the bondage of Egypt into
Canaan:

> *That the Lord your God will bring you back from
> captivity, and have compassion on you, and gather you
> again from all the nations where the Lord your God has
> scattered you,"* (Deuteronomy 30:3, NKJV.)

This prophecy could be speaking of the return of the Jewish
people from Assyrian and Babylonian captivity hundreds of years
before the time of Christ. Yet the ancient Hebrew prophets also
foretold that Israel's loving God would restore His people to their
Promised Land in the Last Days of history, just before Messiah begins
His reign in Jerusalem. This implies that the Jews would be exiled
two times from their beloved homeland, which is exactly what has
taken place in history.

The prophets also foretold that the final Jewish ingathering
would be from all over the globe, unlike the first return from
lands directly to the east of Israel. It would be a permanent return,
meaning no additional exiles would follow. Most significantly, it
would end with the spiritual revival that King Solomon prophesied
in 2 Chronicles 7:14:

> *"If My people who are called by My name will humble
> themselves, and pray and seek My face, and turn from*

their wicked ways, then I will hear from heaven, and will forgive their sin and heal their land," (II Chronicles 7:14, NKJV.)

There are many prophetic Scriptures about this important topic in the Bible—far too many to quote them all here. But let's take a look at three of them:

I will bring back the captives of My people Israel; They shall build the waste cities and inhabit them; They shall plant vineyards and drink wine from them; They shall also make gardens and eat fruit from them. I will plant them in their land, And no longer shall they be pulled up From the land I have given them,' Says the Lord your God, (Amos 9:14-15, NKJV.)

"For behold, the days are coming," says the Lord, "'that I will bring back from captivity My people Israel and Judah," says the Lord. "And I will cause them to return to the land that I gave to their fathers, and they shall possess it, (Jeremiah 30:3, NKJV.)

Who hath heard such a thing? who hath seen such things? Shall the earth be made to bring forth in one day? or shall a nation be born at once? for as soon as Zion travailed, she brought forth her children. Shall I bring to the birth , and not cause to bring forth? saith the LORD: shall I cause to bring forth , and shut the womb? saith thy God. Rejoice ye with Jerusalem, and be glad with her, all ye that love her: rejoice for joy with her, all ye that mourn for her: That ye may suck, and be satisfied with the breasts of her consolations; that ye may milk

out, and be delighted with the abundance of her glory.
For thus saith the LORD, Behold, I will extend peace to
her like a river, and the glory of the Gentiles like a flow-
ing stream: then shall ye suck, ye shall be borne upon her
sides, and be dandled upon her knees. As one whom his
mother comforteth, so will I comfort you; and ye shall be
comforted in Jerusalem, (Isaiah 66:8-13, KJV.)

As mentioned previously, the Hebrew prophets also revealed that the full ingathering of the scattered Jewish people would only be completed when the Messiah came to earth. In other words, some Jews will still be living outside of Israel during the end of this age. However, this does not lessen or negate the fact that a large-scale return has been occurring in our day. In fact, nearly half the Jews on Earth have now returned to their biblical Promised Land. Christians worldwide should be exuberant supporters of this prophesied restoration, for it confirms that the God of Israel exists, that the prophecies of Bible are true, that He holds the future in His capable hands, that He is a covenant-keeping Lord, and that He is a merciful God who forgives the sins of His people.

Sometimes Christians ask me, "How do I know if my church is a Bible-believing church that doesn't teach replacement theology, progressive dispensationalism, or supersessionism?"

Ask yourself these questions:

> » Does my pastor encourage the church to pray for the Jewish people, for the peace of Jerusalem and Israel?

> » Does my pastor teach on Israel and its biblical significance?

» Does my pastor teach on the significance of the Church's Jewish roots?

» Does my pastor preach against replacement theology or supersessionism?

If the answer to these questions is "No," then you may be a member of a church that refuses to believe the Bible, and rejects God's eternal promises to the House of Israel. If your church seems powerless, and appears not to be blessed by God, perhaps this is the reason.

We must be part of God's dream team and support Israel and the Jewish people. Their existence and the rebirth of Israel is a miracle. As Christians, we believe in miracles; the resurrection of our Lord was the greatest of all miracles. If He can live again, it is no problem at all for Him to restore the Nation of Israel.

Israel was not born in 1948; she was born in the heart of God and revealed to Abraham many years before the birth of Isaac. God made a blood covenant with Abraham that the land of Canaan would be given to his seed through Isaac (Genesis 15:18). As part of that vision, God told Abraham that for 400 years his seed would be strangers in a land that did not belong to them (Genesis 15:13). The offspring of Isaac spent 400 years in Egypt before Moses led them out, and Israel, the nation, was born.

Unique as this religious centrality is, there is one reason above all others why committed Christians must stand with Israel: The God of the Universe, the God that we worship, has chosen to make an *everlasting* covenant with the physical descendents of Abraham, Isaac, and Jacob—the Jewish people.

The word "everlasting" has nothing temporary or conditional about it. It clearly means, "Lasting forever." Although Jews in number are found today in North and South America, Australia, Asia, Europe, many parts of Africa, and virtually every non-Muslim nation on earth, their historic spiritual and physical center has always been the Promised Land of Israel.

God's eternal covenant with the descendents of Abraham featured the promise to give them the land of Israel as an everlasting possession. This is recorded in the very first book of the Bible, Genesis, in chapter 17:

> When Abram was ninety-nine years old, the Lord appeared to Abram and said to him, "I am Almighty God; walk before Me and be blameless. And I will make My covenant between Me and you, and will multiply you exceedingly." Then Abram fell on his face, and God talked with him, saying: "As for Me, behold, My covenant is with you, and you shall be a father of many nations. No longer shall your name be called Abram, but your name shall be Abraham; for I have made you a father of many nations. I will make you exceedingly fruitful; and I will make nations of you, and kings shall come from you. And I will establish My covenant between Me and you and your descendants after you in their generations, for an everlasting covenant, to be God to you and your descendants after you. Also I give to you and your descendants after you the land in which you are a stranger, all the land of Canaan, as an everlasting possession; and I will be their God," (Genesis 17:1-8, NKJV.)

It is true God reveals in these verses that many peoples will eventually emerge from Abraham's loins, and so it has been. The Arabs, scattered in over 20 countries throughout the Middle East and North Africa, trace their ancestry to the ancient patriarch who traveled to Canaan at God's command from the town of Ur in Chaldea. Their lineage comes through Abraham's first-born son, Ishmael. However, the Scriptures go on to reveal that the special, eternal land covenant, and others, will come through the line of the son of promise, Isaac, his grandson, Jacob, and his twelve great-grandsons—the forefathers of the modern Jewish people. This is summarized in Psalm 105, verses 8 through 11, NKJV:

> *He remembers His covenant forever, The word which He commanded, for a thousand generations, The covenant which He made with Abraham, And His oath to Isaac, And confirmed it to Jacob for a statute, To Israel as an everlasting covenant, Saying, 'To you I will give the land of Canaan As the allotment of your inheritance.*

As we have seen, the belief that God has revoked His solemn land covenant with the Jewish people due to their sin and rebellion against Him is widespread in the Church today. It is certainly a fact that living peacefully in the land was conditional on obedience to God's holy law. Jacob's offspring were warned that they would be removed from the land if they disobeyed God's commands. But the Bible also foretells that a Jewish remnant would be restored to the Promised Land after worldwide exile, as is wonderfully occurring in our day.

The words "next year in Jerusalem" became a part of the Passover Seder during the Middle Ages. It was an expression of the longing of the Jewish people that Jerusalem and the Temple be rebuilt. Today Jerusalem stands; reunified under Jewish rule. It is a flourishing and modern city to which Jews of the Diaspora, forced from homes and land through the centuries, have returned. In Psalm 137, the Jews carried away to Babylon sat down and wept as they remembered their homeland and the Holy City:

There on the poplars we hung our harps, for there our captors asked us for songs, our tormentors demanded songs of joy; they said, "Sing us one of the songs of Zion!" How can we sing the songs of the Lord while in a foreign land? If I forget you, Jerusalem, may my right hand forget its skill. May my tongue cling to the roof of my mouth if I do not remember you, if I do not consider Jerusalem my highest joy, (Psalm 137:2-6, NIV.)

The captives did not dash their harps against the rocks and trees around them; their musical instruments were hung on trees that dotted the landscape, preserved for a future time—in the Holy City. It was symbolic of the hope of their return to Jerusalem when sorrow would be turned into joy, mourning into dancing, their ashes exchanged for beauty, and the spirit of heaviness replaced with the garment of praise (Isaiah 61:3.)

Additional Scripture Readings:

Boast not against the branches. But if thou boast, thou bearest not the root, but the root thee. Thou wilt say then, The branches were broken off, that I might be grafted in.

Well; because of unbelief they were broken off, and thou standest by faith. Be not highminded, but fear, (Romans 11:18-20, KJV.)

God has not cast away His people whom he foreknew, (Romans 11:2, NIV.)

I say then, Hath God cast away his people? God forbid. For I also am an Israelite, of the seed of Abraham, of the tribe of Benjamin. God hath not cast away his people which he foreknew, (Romans 11:1-2, KJV.)

Who are Israelites; to whom pertaineth the adoption, and the glory, and the covenants, and the giving of the law, and the service of God, and the promises; Whose are the fathers, and of whom as concerning the flesh Christ came, who is over all, God blessed forever. Amen, (Romans 9:4-5, KJV.)

James, a servant of God and of the Lord Jesus Christ, to the twelve tribes which are scattered abroad, greeting," (James 1:1, KJV.)

Thus says the Lord God: "When I have gathered the house of Israel from the peoples among whom they are scattered, and am hallowed in them in the sight of the Gentiles, then they will dwell in their own land which I gave to My servant Jacob. And they will dwell safely there, build houses, and plant vineyards; yes, they will dwell securely, when I execute judgments on all those around them who despise them. Then they shall know that I am the Lord their God," (Ezekiel 28:25-26, NIV.)

He will set up a banner for the nations, And will

assemble the outcasts of Israel, And gather together the dispersed of Judah From the four corners of the earth, (Isaiah 11:12, ASV.)

For I will take you from among the nations, gather you out of all countries, and bring you into your own land, (Ezekiel 36:24, NIV.)

And I will cause the captives of Judah and the captives of Israel to return, and will rebuild those places as at the first. I will cleanse them from all their iniquity by which they have sinned against Me, and I will pardon all their iniquities by which they have sinned and by which they have transgressed against Me, (Jeremiah 33:7-8, NKJV.)

CHAPTER TWELVE

GOD ALMIGHTY HAS PRESERVED ISRAEL

Behold, He who keeps Israel Shall neither slumber nor sleep. The Lord is your keeper; The Lord is your shade at your right hand. The sun shall not strike you by day, Nor the moon by night. The Lord shall preserve you from all evil; He shall preserve your soul. The Lord shall preserve your going out and your coming in From this time forth, and even forevermore,"

(PSALM 121:4-8, KJV.)

God has not permitted any power to totally exterminate the Jews, although no people has been plagued, persecuted, pursued, and pressured more throughout their history. Many attempts at annihilation have been made, but have ended in utter failure, defeat, and humiliation.

Author George Gilder wrote:

In *Dialogues and Secrets with Kings*, published after the 1967 war, the very first official ...PLO leader, Ahmad Shuqeiri [said], "I frequently called upon Arabs to liquidate the state of Israel and to throw the

Jews into the sea. I said this because I was—and still am—convinced that there is no solution other than the elimination of the state of Israel."[57]

Take a step back in time and look at Egypt and Pharaoh's edict concerning the Israelites:

> *So Pharaoh commanded all his people, saying, "Every son who is born you shall cast into the river, and every daughter you shall save alive." (Exodus 1:22, NKJV.)*

Following Pharaoh's brutal treatment of the Children of Israel, God sent Moses to deliver His people from their harsh existence under the Egyptian ruler. In order to change the heart of the Pharaoh, God sent a series of ten plagues against the captors. The first three curses affected the comfort of the Egyptian people. By turning the water to blood, He denied them what was needed for cleansing and drinking. The Nile, also worshipped as the giver of life, became instead an agent of death. Secondly, their homes were invaded with frogs. (I have never been able to understand why, as Moses asked Pharaoh when he would like to be rid of the frogs, he said, "Tomorrow." Why did he want to spend another night with slimy, green amphibians?) Thirdly, lice invaded the land, attacking the Egyptians.

When Pharaoh continued to refuse to let God's people go, a second trifecta of plagues was unleashed on the land. They targeted Egypt's false gods. The fourth plague was that of flies, perhaps to let it be known that one of their gods, Beelzebub, lord of the flies, was incapable of rescuing them from Jehovah's wrath. The fifth plague decimated their herds of cattle. Again Jehovah proved He was greater than Apis, the sacred bull worshipped by the Egyptians.

And the sixth challenged the claims of Egyptian medical shamans by causing a horrific outbreak of incurable boils. Still Pharaoh was not moved to release the people to Moses, God's chosen leader.

The last set of three plagues was designed to bring death and desolation as hail rained down on the land flattening crops and killing more cattle. That was followed by a plague of locusts that stripped any green vegetation left after the hailstorms. Then darkness descended upon the land—so comprehensive that the Bible says:

> *During all that time the people could not see each other, and no one moved. But there was light as usual where the people of Israel lived,* (Exodus 10:23, NLT.)

In Carlsbad Caverns, New Mexico, at one point during the tour, the guide asks everyone to sit. The lights are then turned off in the cavern for a few moments; the darkness is complete. You literally cannot see your hand held in front of your face. God caused just such a blackness to cover the land of Egypt for three long days. Not a chariot moved; not a shaman prognosticated; no fishermen fished, and no merchant plied his trade.

With a still obstinate Pharaoh refusing to heed the warnings of Moses, God brought forth the tenth and final plague: the death of all the firstborn in Egypt—at least among those not safe beneath the blood covering of the Passover lamb.

Theologian Arthur W. Pink wrote of the tenth plague:

> One more judgment was appointed, the heaviest of them all, and then not only would Pharaoh let the people go, but he would thrust them out. Then would be clearly shown the folly of fighting against God.

Then would be fully demonstrated the uselessness of resisting Jehovah. Then would be made manifest the impotence of the creature and the omnipotence of the Most High.[58]

Psalm 78 summarizes the battle between God and Pharaoh:

He cast upon them the fierceness of His anger, wrath, and indignation, and tribulation, by sending evil angels among them. He made a way to His anger; He spared not their soul from death, but gave their life over to the pestilence, and smote all the firstborn in Egypt, the chief of their strength in the tabernacle of Ham, (Psalm 78:49, KJV.)

The ruler who had so persecuted the children of Abraham, Isaac, and Jacob, who had ordered every Hebrew male child tossed into the Nile River lost every eldest son in the land. For some families, it might have meant the death of every male in the household—grandfather, father, eldest son, grandchild. But Jehovah God didn't stop there: while pursuing the Hebrew children into the wilderness the entire Egyptian army was drowned in the Red Sea as Pharaoh watched helplessly. God had inexorably triumphed over the enemy of His children:

Then Moses and the children of Israel sang this song to the LORD, and spoke, saying: "I will sing to the LORD, For He has triumphed gloriously! The horse and its rider He has thrown into the sea! (Exodus 15:1, NKJV.)

The Old Testament book of Esther paints a beautiful picture of God's deliverance of the Jews from the menace of anti-Semitism. Esther was a beautiful young Jewish girl who was torn from her home and taken captive to the palace where a tyrannical ruler had banished his queen from the royal throne and initiated a search for her successor. The king was captivated by Esther and chose her to be his new queen. Of course, there was also a dastardly villain, Haman, who desired to perpetrate genocide against her Jewish people.

> Then Haman said to King Ahasuerus, "There is a certain people scattered and dispersed among the people in all the provinces of your kingdom; their laws are different from all other people's, and they do not keep the king's laws. Therefore it is not fitting for the king to let them remain." (Esther 3:8, NIV.)

Esther's uncle, Mordecai, challenged Esther to approach the king (a move that could be punishable by death) and ask for the salvation of her people. In encouraging her to do so, Mordecai confronted Esther with these timeless words:

> For if you remain completely silent at this time, relief and deliverance will arise for the Jews from another place, but you and your father's house will perish. Yet who knows whether you have come to the kingdom for such a time as this? (Esther 4:14, NIV.)

Esther's response to Mordecai was magnificent in its faith:

> Go, gather all the Jews who are present in Shushan,

and fast for me; neither eat nor drink for three days, night or day. My maids and I will fast likewise. And so I will go to the king, which is against the law; and if I perish, I perish! (Esther 4:16, NIV.)

With great trepidation, Esther approached King Ahasuerus. Miraculously, he granted her an audience. The plan for the destruction of the Jews by the foul villain, Haman, was thwarted, and the king issued a decree throughout the land allowing Esther's people to defend themselves if attacked. Because of this decree, the Jews overcame every enemy and lived in peace (Esther 8-9). Yet another attempt by Satan to annihilate the Jews was foiled.

Another major example was Satan's endeavor to destroy the Jews during World War II. German leader, Adolf Hitler, declared the Jews were not the Chosen People, the Aryan race was. He determined to resolve what he called the "Jewish problem."

Hitler, born in Braunau am Inn, Austria, on April 20, 1889, was the son of Alois Schickelgruber Hitler and Klara Poelzl, both from a remote area of lower Austria. Hitler's father had been born out of wedlock to a young peasant woman, Maria Anna Schickelgruber. It was not until Alois was in his thirties that his father returned to the village, married Maria Anna, and changed the young man's last name to Hitler. Had he not come forward to claim an inheritance, Johann Hitler's grandson would have grown up as Adolf Schickelgruber. (One can't help but wonder if he would have had the same impact and garnered the same notoriety had he retained that name rather than the more familiar Adolf Hitler.)

As a child, Adolf was angry and sullen, undependable, short-tempered, and indolent. He was antagonistic toward his father, a strict disciplinarian, and intensely devoted to his industrious mother. The young Hitler "took singing lessons, sang in the church choir, and even entertained thoughts of becoming a priest."[59] He was devastated when his mother died during his teen years.

At age sixteen, Adolf made his way to Vienna with dreams of becoming an artist. He applied to the Viennese Academy of Fine Arts but was roundly rejected as lacking artistic talent by that august body. He survived in the large cosmopolitan city by doing odd jobs and selling sketches in backstreet pubs. Between drawing patrons, he would spout political rants of his ostentatious dreams for a superior Germany to anyone too drunk to walk away.

Adolf was enchanted with the manipulative methods of Vienna's mayor, Karl Leuger, and quickly adopted his affinity for anti-Semitism with its fanatical demand for "purity of blood." From the eccentric teaching of an excommunicated monk, Lanz von Liebenfels, to those of German Nationalist Georg von Schönerer, the impressionable young Hitler adopted the belief that the Jewish people were responsible for anarchy, dishonesty, and the ruin of civilization, government, and finance. According to those so-called "learned men," the purpose of the Jew was to completely weaken Germany and dilute the superior Aryan race.

Hitler enlisted in the Sixteenth Bavarian Infantry Regiment during World War I, where he served as a dispatch runner. He was awarded the Iron Cross for bravery but was caught in a gas attack shortly before the end of the war. He spent months recovering from the effects, including temporary blindness. After his recovery, he was delegated the job of joining and spying on various political factions in Munich—among them the German Workers' Party.

Hitler joined the other forty members in 1919 and the name was changed shortly thereafter to the National Socialist German Workers' Party. By 1921, he had claimed chairmanship of the organization and began to dazzle crowds with his formidable gift of oratory. Soon thereafter, the party adopted a new logo —the swastika —which Hitler believed symbolized the triumph of the Aryan man. It also adopted a new greeting, *"Heil!"* and eventually *"Heil, Hitler!"* (This can be translated as "Hail Hitler," or more ambiguously as "Salvation through Hitler.")

The mustachioed little man mesmerized his listeners with his gravelly, impassioned voice—never mind that his speeches contained little of actual value. Near the end of 1921, he had come to be known as the *der Führer*. He formed gangs to maintain control at his assemblies and to apply goon-squad tactics to disrupt those of his adversaries. These were the beginnings of the infamous storm troopers, the SS, Hitler's black-shirted and dreaded bodyguards.

Although British Prime Minister David Lloyd George was driven from office in 1922 by the opposition party and would never hold another government position, he stirred a bit of controversy even in his retirement years, when, in 1936, he traveled to Berlin to meet with Adolf Hitler. Upon his return to England he wrote an article for the *Daily Express*, in which he gushed:

> I have now seen the famous German leader and also something of the great change he has effected. Whatever one may think of his methods—and they are certainly not those of a parliamentary country, there can be no doubt that he has achieved a marvelous transformation in the spirit of the people, in their attitude towards each other, and in their social and economic outlook.... One man has accomplished this miracle. He is a born leader of men. A magnetic and

dynamic personality with a single-minded purpose, a resolute will and a dauntless heart.[60]

Of course, by the time Adolf Hitler breached the Munich Agreement, Lloyd George was no longer a proponent of appeasement or of the German leader's tactics.

CHAPTER THIRTEEN

THE UGLINESS OF
ANTI-SEMITISM

O you who love the LORD, hate evil!

(PSALM 97:10, ESV.)

I n 1922, Hitler declared the Jewish people to be Germany's No. 1 enemy, the race accountable for not some, but all the nation's internal problems. He strongly stressed what he saw as "the anti-Semitism of reason" that must lead "to the systematic combating and elimination of Jewish privileges. Its ultimate goal must implacably be the total removal of the Jews."[61] He was so convinced Germany was near collapse, that he joined forces with nationalist leader General Erich Friedrich Wilhelm Ludendorff in an attempted coup.

The ensuing riot that began in a Munich beer hall resulted in: 1) the deaths of sixteen individuals, 2) the Nazi Party being outlawed, and 3) Hitler being tried and sentenced to five years in prison. His sentence was commuted to nine months, but during his incarceration, he dictated a draft of *Mein Kampf* (*My Struggle*) to Rudolf Hess, a devoted sycophant. The tome—filled with a coarse, ill-conceived jumble of anti-Semitism, fabrication, and fantasy, evolved into the literal bible of the emerging Nazi Party. By 1939, this hodgepodge of pretense had sold five million volumes and had been translated into eleven languages.

It was also in 1922 that Hitler outlined his plan fully in a conversation with a friend, appropriately named Joseph Hell:

> If I am ever really in power, the destruction of the Jews will be my first and most important job. As soon as I have power, I shall have gallows after gallows erected, for example, in Munich on the Marienplatz— as many of them as traffic allows. Then the Jews will be hanged one after another, and they will stay hanging until they stink. They will stay hanging as long as hygienically possible. As soon as they are untied, then the next group will follow and that will continue until the last Jew in Munich is exterminated. Exactly the same procedure will be followed in other cities until Germany is cleansed of the last Jew![62]

Philosopher Houston Stewart Chamberlain wrote to encourage Hitler in a letter dated October 7, 1923. He zealously advised the Führer that he was perceived as the "opposite of a politician... for the essence of all politics is membership of a party, whereas with you all parties disappear, consumed by the heat of your love for the fatherland."[63] In a later missive to Hitler, Chamberlain asserted:

> One cannot simultaneously embrace Jesus and those who crucified him. This is the splendid thing about Hitler—his courage. In this respect he reminds one of [Martin] Luther.[64]

It is quite obvious from his writings that Chamberlain also viewed Jewish industrialists as Germany's "public enemy No. 1."

The Germans made a disastrous error in judgment in 1925: They removed the prohibition against the Nazi Party and granted permission for Hitler to address the public. Moreover, when he needed it most in order to expand the reach of the party, a worldwide economic crisis enveloped Germany. Ironically, the resulting magnitude of unemployment, panic, and anger afforded Hitler the opportunity to step forward and claim the role of redeemer and savior of the nation. On January 30, 1933, Weimar Republic of Germany President Paul von Hindenburg was persuaded to nominate Hitler as Reich Chancellor. Germany had lost its last chance to avoid a Second World War—and the Holocaust.

Hitler's determination to outfox his opponents and remove conservatives from any role in the government took little time or effort. He abolished free trade unions, removed Communists, Social Democrats, and Jews from any participation in politics, and consigned his rivals to concentration camps. He solidified his hold on Germany in March 1933 with the use of persuasive argument, indoctrination, fear, and coercion. The façade was firmly in place, and the people of Germany were soon intimidated into subjugation.

With the death of von Hindenburg in August of 1934, the Third Reich had a determined dictator who held the reins both of Führer and chancellor, as well as all the powers of state accorded to a leader. He abandoned the Treaty of Versailles, conscripted a massive army, supplied it with war materiel, and in 1938 forced the British and French into signing the Munich Agreement. Soon to follow were laws against Jews, the promotion of concentration camps, the destruction of the state of Czechoslovakia, the invasion of Poland, and a nonaggression pact with the USSR. The only obstacles standing between

Hitler and the rest of the world were President Franklin D. Roosevelt, Prime Minister Winston Churchill, and General Secretary of the Central Committee of the Communist Party of the Soviet Union Joseph Stalin, along with the armies of Western civilization.

Just one week after Franklin D. Roosevelt was sworn in for his initial term as chief executive, German laborers had completed Dachau, the original Nazi concentration camp. Within its confines some 40,000 individuals would be murdered, most of them Jews. Hitler would follow the opening of the camp by nationalizing the Gestapo and bringing it under his full control. Just three months later, he had successfully combined all commands under the aegis of the Nazi Party.

In 1935, the Nuremberg Laws were instituted and German Jews lost their citizenship with its rights and privileges. They were then totally under the cruel fist of Hitler and his rabid Jew-hatred. Like many of the Jews in the earlier days of Hitler's rule, Roosevelt, too, was deceived by the picture presented to the world at the 1936 Olympics. American historian and author Deborah Lipstadt wrote:

> The sports competition was a massive exercise in propaganda and public relations, and many American reporters were uncritical about all that they saw.... Americans, particularly non-German speaking ones who only knew Germany from the Games—departed convinced that the revolutionary upheavals, random beatings, and the murders of political opponents had been greatly exaggerated or were a thing of the past. Those bedazzled included not only the athletes and tourists, but personages such as newspaper publisher Norman Chandler and numerous American

businessmen. This period marked the beginning of Charles Lindbergh's love affair with the Reich. One reporter was convinced that as a result of the Games visitors would be...inclined to dismiss all anti-German thought and action abroad as insipid and unjust. [The visitor] sees no Jewish heads being chopped off, or even roundly cudgeled.... The people smile, are polite, and sing with gusto at the beer gardens. Visitors to Berlin described it as a warm, hospitable place and Germany as a country well on its way to solving the economic and unemployment problems which still plagued America.[65]

While Hitler was making plans to wreak havoc in Europe, the Jewish community in 1938 Jerusalem was trying to persuade the British to increase immigration quotas. The British, however, saw increased allotments only as putting a match to the Arab fuse—a short one at that. So we read the agonizing accounts of Jewish refugees struggling to escape Hitler's iron fist only to perish in the waters of the Mediterranean in unseaworthy ships that could find no safe harbor.

As events of the mid-to-late 1930s led ominously toward a Second World War, the Nazis under Hitler had already been searching for a "final solution" for what they considered the Jewish problem.

On January 20, 1942, Hitler's architects of death met at the beautiful Wannsee Villa located in a serene lakeside suburb of Berlin. Their stated objective was to find a "Final Solution to the Jewish Question."

Presiding over the conference was SS-Lieutenant General Reinhard Heydrich, chief of the Security Police and Security Service.

As the meeting began, Heydrich was determined that none should doubt his superiority or his authority, which was not limited by geographical borders. He briefed those in the room on measures that had already been taken in an attempt to eradicate the Jews from both the German culture and homeland.

In attendance were fourteen high-ranking German military and government leaders, among them Adolf Eichmann. Over a 90-minute luncheon, fifteen men changed the world forever. After years of this continuous rhetoric, it took ninety minutes—a mere ninety minutes—for Adolf Hitler's henchmen to determine the fate of six million Jews. During that period, roughly the time it would take to drive from Jerusalem to Tel Aviv during peak traffic time, the Holocaust became a heinous reality. January 20, 2012, marked the 70th anniversary of that fateful conference. We dare not let these dubious anniversaries pass without marking how little time it takes to alter the course of history.

Initially, steps had been implemented to allow German Jews to emigrate to whatever countries would accept them, but the move proved to be too slow for the Führer and the Reich. Now the men gathered to implement Hitler's new solution. Heydrich provided a list of the number of Jews in each country; a total of eleven million Jews were to be involved. In his zeal he determined:

> In large, single-sex labor columns, Jews fit to work will work their way eastward constructing roads. Doubtless, the large majority will be eliminated by natural causes. Any final remnant that survives will doubtless consist of the most resistant elements. They will have to be dealt with appropriately because otherwise, by natural selection, they would form the germ cell of a new Jewish revival.[66]

Translation: All must die.

According to the minutes of the meeting, Jews were to be purged, beginning in Germany, Bohemia, and Moravia. After that, they were to be expunged in Europe from east to west. Many questions arose as to how to identify those considered to be Jews. The issue was not resolved during the Wannsee meeting.

Of course, this was not the beginning of the extermination of the Jewish people. Many of the Nazi elite in attendance had already participated in mass murders since the summer of 1941. Even before the gathering at Wannsee, more than a half million Jews had been executed behind army lines. The question was how to attain the goal of total extermination in areas outside the battle zone. A more efficient way needed to be found to eliminate larger numbers. No, the meeting had not been called to determine how to begin the process but rather to spell out how the "final solution" would be achieved. By January, death camps equipped with gas chambers and ovens were under construction.

The ordinary citizenry of Germany did not enter the war determined to annihilate six million of their neighbors. It began with a subversive program of anti-Semitism aimed at blaming the Jewish people for all the ills that had beset Germany following its losses in World War I. Perhaps even Hitler did not begin with total extermination in mind. That seed probably began to germinate only after Jews were denied entry into other countries. It seemed to him that he had then been given a green light to do whatever he wished with the Jewish population. Ultimately, his "final solution" was the Holocaust—the deaths of six million Jewish men, women, and children murdered in the most horrific of ways.

The preservation of a remnant of Jews through all the suffering, wars and afflictions over the centuries is further evidence that Israel and the Jewish people are God's miracle. Why have the Jews been hated so? Because Satan's only adversary would come through the Jews: The Messiah. Ultimately He would destroy the powers of Satan.

Our God keeps His covenants; He remains faithful even when we are faithless (2 Timothy 2:13). It is He who has sovereignly decided to preserve the Jewish people as a separate, identifiable people before Him and then to restore them to their biblical homeland. These truths are revealed in numerous Scriptures. That they would remain on Earth until the end of time as a distinct people group is foretold in Jeremiah, Chapter 31:

> *Thus says the Lord, Who gives the sun for a light by day, The ordinances of the moon and the stars for a light by night, Who disturbs the sea, And its waves roar (The Lord of hosts is His name): "If those ordinances depart From before Me, says the Lord, Then the seed of Israel shall also cease From being a nation before Me forever,"* (Jeremiah 31:35-36, NKJV.)

The next verse makes crystal clear that the God of Abraham has no intention of ever forsaking His special covenant with Jacob's children, despite their many failures:

> *I will direct their work in truth, And will make with them an everlasting covenant. Their descendants shall be known among the Gentiles, And their offspring among the people. All who see them shall acknowledge them, That they are the posterity whom the Lord has blessed"* (Isaiah 61:8-9, NKJV.)

God calls the land of Israel, "My Land" (Ezekiel 38:16), and He gave it to Israel by a blood covenant that cannot be annulled. God has assigned the land of Israel to the children of Israel, and has never cancelled that which He assigned.

God said that Israel would be scattered among the heathen and they were. But He also said they would be re-gathered and they have been:

> *He will set up a banner for the nations, And will assemble the outcasts of Israel, And gather together the dispersed of Judah From the four corners of the earth,* (Isaiah 11:12, ASV.)

> *I will bring back the captives of My people Israel,* (Amos 9:14, NKJV.)

> *For I will take you from among the nations, gather you out of all countries, and bring you into your own land,* (Ezekiel 36:24, NKJV.)

> *I will bring them back to this place, and I will cause them to dwell safely,* (Jeremiah 32:37, NKJV.)

> *I will plant them in their land, And no longer shall they be pulled up From the land I have given them,* (Amos 9:15, NKJV.)

> *I will say to the north, "Give them up!" And to the south, "Do not keep them back!" Bring My sons from afar, And My daughters from the ends of the earth,* (Isaiah 43:6, NIV.)

Thus says the Lord God: "Behold, I will lift My hand in an oath to the nations, And set up My standard for the peoples; They shall bring your sons in their arms, And your daughters shall be carried on their shoulders," (Isaiah 49:22, NIV.)

Isaiah predicted the people of Israel would fly to their homeland hundreds of years before the invention of the airplane.

Who are these who fly like a cloud, And like doves to their roosts? (Isaiah 60:8, NIV.)

He also predicted that they would return by ships:

Surely the isles shall wait for me, and the ships of Tarshish first, to bring thy sons from far, their silver and their gold with them, unto the name of the LORD thy God, and to the Holy One of Israel, because he hath glorified thee, (Isaiah 60:9, KJV.)

The final restoration of Jews to their homeland comes with a wonderful promise:

And I will bring again the captivity of my people of Israel, and they shall build the waste cities, and inhabit them; and they shall plant vineyards, and drink the wine thereof: they shall also make gardens, and eat the fruit of them. And I will plant them upon their land, and they shall no more be pulled out of their land which I have given them, saith the LORD thy God, (Amos 9:14-15, KJV.).

CHAPTER FOURTEEN

TWENTIETH CENTURY CONFLICT

A prophecy against Damascus: "See, Damascus will no longer be a city but will become a heap of ruins,

(ISAIAH 17.1, NIV)

T he Arab–Israeli conflict grew out of the political tension and military skirmishes between both sides. As we have discussed, however, its more recent roots lie in the rise of Zionism and Arab nationalism in the latter half of the nineteenth century. The underlying reason for the conflict was based on the return of the Jewish people to their biblical homeland—a land claimed by Palestinian Arabs. The culmination came in 1948 when the modern State of Israel was recognized by the United Nations.

Open strife between the two sides began following the collapse of the Ottoman Empire after World War I, with questions of territorial rights shifting over the years from regional issues to more local Israeli–Palestinian concerns. Open hostilities generally ended with the cease-fire following the 1973 Yom Kippur War, but covert activities have relentlessly continued.

Peace agreements between Israel and Egypt were signed in 1979 and then between Israel and Jordan in 1994. The so-called Oslo Accords led to creation of the Palestinian National Authority in 1993, while precarious cease-fires currently exist between Israel and both Syria and Lebanon. Clashes between Israel and Hamas-ruled Gaza resulted in a 2009 cease-fire (although sporadic fighting continues with periodic missile launches into Israel proper.)

Various Muslim groups invoke religious arguments to support their uncompromising hatred for Israel and the Jewish people. The contemporary history of the Arab–Israeli conflict is unquestionably affected by those religious beliefs and the Arab desire to occupy all of the territory deeded to Israel from the time of Abraham, Isaac, and Jacob.

The Land of Canaan or *Eretz Yisrael* was, as outlined in both the Hebrew and Christian Bibles, promised by God to the Children of Israel. In his 1896 manifesto, *The Jewish State*, Theodor Herzl repeatedly refers to the biblical Promised Land concept.

Out of a total of 12 political parties now extant in Israel, Likud is currently the most prominent to include the biblical claim to the Land of Israel in its platform. Conversely, Muslims revere many sites in Israel, including the Cave of the Patriarchs and the Temple Mount. Over the past 14 centuries, Muslims have constructed Islamic landmarks on these ancient sites, such as the Dome of the Rock and the Al-Aqsa Mosque a scant distance from the Western Wall, the holiest site in Judaism. This close proximity has, as much as anything, brought the two groups into sometimes open conflict over rightful possession of Jerusalem.

Muslim teaching proclaims that Muhammad passed through Jerusalem on his first journey to heaven. Hamas, (the Palestinian Sunni Islamist organization) which governs the Gaza Strip, claims that all of the land of Palestine (the current Israeli and Palestinian territories) is an Islamic *waqf,* or indisputable religious legacy in Islamic law, that should only be governed by Muslims.

The Middle East, including Southern Syria (later Mandatory Palestine), had been under the control of the Ottoman Empire for nearly 400 years. Near the end of the empire, the Ottomans began to exert their Turkish ethnic identity, leading to discrimination against the Arabs. Hopes of liberation from the Ottomans led many Jews and some Arabs to support the Allied Powers during World War I.

In the late nineteenth century European and Middle Eastern Jews increasingly immigrated to Southern Syria, purchasing land from the local Ottoman landlords. At that time, the city of Jerusalem did not extend beyond its protective walled area and contained a population of only a few tens of thousands. During 1915–16, with World War I underway, the British High Commissioner in Egypt, Sir Henry McMahon, secretly communicated with Husayn ibn 'Ali, patriarch of the Hashemite family, and with the Ottoman governor of Mecca and Medina. McMahon convinced Husayn to lead an Arab revolt against the Ottoman Empire, which was then aligned with Germany against Britain and France. McMahon assured Husayn that if the Arabs supported Britain in that endeavor, the British government would establish an independent Arab state under Hashemite rule in the Arab provinces of the Ottoman Empire, which included Palestine. That revolt, led by T. E. Lawrence (mentioned earlier as Lawrence of Arabia) and Husayn's son Faysal, was successful in defeating the Ottomans, and Britain took control of much of the area.

In 1917, Southern Syria had been conquered and the British government issued the Balfour Declaration stating that Britain favorably viewed "the establishment in Palestine of a national home for the Jewish people" but that "nothing shall be done which may prejudice the civil and religious rights of existing non-Jewish communities in Palestine". The Declaration was issued as a result of the belief by Prime Minister David Lloyd George, and other key members of the British government, that Jewish support was essential to winning the war. As one might imagine, the declaration was not received at all well in the Arab world.

Following the war, the area remained under British rule and became known as the British Mandate of Palestine. It included what is today Israel, the Palestinian Authority and the Gaza Strip. Transjordan was eventually designated a separate British protectorate—the Emirate of Transjordan, which gained autonomy in 1928. A major crisis among Arab nationalists had taken place with the failed establishment of the Arab Kingdom of Syria in 1920. With the disastrous outcome of the Franco-Syrian War, the self-proclaimed Hashemite kingdom with its capital in Damascus was defeated and Sharif Hussein bin Ali, the Hashemite ruler, took refuge in Mandatory Iraq. The crisis saw the first of many confrontations between nationalist Arab and Jewish forces, the Battle of Tel Hai, which led to the establishment of the local Palestinian version of Arab nationalism, with the return of Hajj Amin al-Husseini from Damascus to Jerusalem in late 1920.

Jewish immigration to Mandatory Palestine continued, but less documented immigration was occurring in the Arab sector, bringing workers from Syria and other neighboring areas. Palestinian Arabs saw this rapid influx of Jewish immigrants as a threat to their homeland and their identity as a people. Moreover, Jewish practices of purchasing land and prohibiting the employment of Arabs in Jewish-owned industries and farms was not well received in Palestinian Arab communities. Demonstrations protesting what the Arabs felt were unfair preferences for the Jewish immigrants set forth by the

British mandate that governed Palestine proliferated. Resentment led to outbreaks of violence later that year. Winston Churchill's 1922 White Paper attempted to reassure the Arab population by stipulating that the creation of a Jewish state was not the intention of the Balfour Declaration.

Political demonstrations at the Western Wall in 1929 resulted in riots that soon expanded throughout Palestine; Arabs murdered 67 Jews in the city of Hebron, in what became known as the Hebron Massacre. During that week, at least 116 Arabs and 133 Jews were killed and 339 were wounded.

By 1931, seventeen percent of the population of Mandatory Palestine was Jewish, an increase of six percent since 1922. Immigration would soon peak after the Nazis rose to power in Germany, causing the Jewish population in British Palestine to double.

In the mid-1930s Izz ad-Din al-Qassam arrived from Syria and established the Black Hand, an anti-Zionist and anti-British militant organization. He recruited and arranged military training for peasants; by 1935 al-Qassam had enlisted several hundred men. The cells were equipped with bombs and firearms used to kill Jewish settlers in the area, as well as engaging in a campaign of vandalism aimed at Jewish settler plantations. By 1936, escalating tensions led to the 1936–1939 Arab revolt in Palestine.

In response to Arab pressure, British authorities greatly reduced the number of Jewish immigrants to Palestine. Those restrictions remained until the end of the Mandate, a period which coincided with the Nazi Holocaust and attempts by Jewish refugees to escape Hitler's Europe. As a consequence, the majority of Jewish entrants to Palestine were considered to be illegal, further increasing tension. Following several failed efforts to solve the problem diplomatically, the British petitioned the newly-formed United Nations for help. In May of 1947, the General Assembly appointed a United Nations Special Committee on Palestine (UNSCOP), composed of representatives from Australia, Canada, Czechoslovakia, Peru, Sweden, Guatemala, Yugoslavia, India, Iran, Netherlands, and Uruguay.

Christian Zionist John Stanley Grauel is credited in some circles with literally making Israel possible. You might recognize the name of the refugee ship, *SS Exodus*, made famous by *Exodus*, the Leon Uris novel released in 1958. Uris had earlier covered the fighting in Israel as a war correspondent. His novel would become an international bestseller—the biggest since Margaret Mitchell's blockbuster, *Gone with the Wind*. Director Otto Preminger turned the book into a movie in 1960 with the lead role going to Paul Newman. Perhaps one of the book's characters was based on Grauel.

Grauel was born in Worchester, Massachusetts, in 1917. In 1941, John bowed to his mother's wishes and entered the Methodist Theological Seminary in Bangor, Maine. She would hold great sway over his education regarding the Jewish people and the path John would take in later life.

During his last year at seminary, John met and married. Sadly, he lost both his wife and son in childbirth and never remarried. Shortly after graduation, John essentially became a circuit-riding preacher, as he was sent to pastor several small towns. However, his heart was soon captured by news of the war raging in Europe, and specifically by the suffering of the Jewish people under Hitler's regime. It was his friendship with Judge Joseph Goldberg in Worcester, Massachusetts, that sparked Grauel's interest in Zionism. The judge, whose background was Russian and Jewish, loaned Grauel books on the subject. It sparked his life-long interest in the return of the Jews to their homeland.

Although he could have claimed an exemption from military service as a conscientious objector due to his pastorate, Grauel could not escape his desire to do something to aid the Jews. He solicited the advice of Judge Goldberg and was sent to meet Dr. Carl Herman Voss, the head of the American Christian Palestine Committee (ACPC). Voss persuaded Grauel to take the position as executive director of the ACPC office in Philadelphia. It would totally change the direction of his life.

In 1944, at his first Zionist conference, John met David Ben-Gurion. From him he learned of the Haganah, the Jewish underground army in Palestine. After returning home, Grauel soon noticed a steady stream of young men going in and out of an adjoining office. One day his curiosity got the better of him, and he walked next door to introduce himself to the man in charge, Bucky Karmatz. Over a lunch of sandwiches at Karmatz's desk, John discovered that the office was a recruiting station for Haganah. When the two men parted company, John recorded, "I knew I had found my niche. I would join Haganah. . . to become part of that organization to rescue those who could be helped to leave Europe. I liked that affirmation of life after the war."[67]

During Haganah meetings at the Hotel Fourteen in New York City, John rubbed elbows with the men and women who would be totally invested in the future of Israel: David Ben-Gurion, Golda Meir, Teddy Kollek, Nachum Goldman, Meyer Wisgal, and others of note who attended the meetings occasionally. At one session, John was informed that an ocean liner had been secured and would be outfitted to transport Jewish immigrants from Europe to the Holy Land. The ship had been named after the owner of the Baltimore Bay Line, the uncle of Wallace Warfield Simpson, who would become the paramour and later wife of Edward VIII, once king of England.

Grauel arrived at the docks in Baltimore expecting to see the luxurious *SS President Garfield*, but was met instead by the derelict and rotting hulk of the *SS President Warfield*. He was horrified at the thought of crossing the Atlantic in the old liner but was determined to fulfill his commitment. He boarded the ship and later said:

> By the grace of God and a touch of insanity, I passed from the world of Reverend John Stanley Grauel to John Grauel, ordinary seaman.... There were thousands of leaks...it took the crew days of scrubbing, sanding, polishing, and mending just to make some order out of chaos.[68]

On March 29, 1947, after a storm delay had set them back by a month, John and the crew set sail for Marseille aboard the ship renamed *Exodus*. He was there ostensibly as an undercover correspondent for the *Churchman*, an Episcopal journal. With that designation, he secured a visa from the British Consulate in Paris, enabling him to legally enter Palestine. His assignment was to make certain the world knew of the events surrounding the ship. Previous attempts to transport Jewish refugees to Palestine had met with ships being seized and destroyed. One ship, the *Struma*, was sunk by a Russian torpedo after having been towed into the Black Sea by the Turks. It carried 769 men, women, and children.

Once he had arrived in Europe, Grauel's job was to arrange for the transfer of refugees from displaced persons camps to the *Exodus*. His tasks were many and varied—cook, distributor of supplies, administrator, and contact person between the refugees and the crew. The ship steamed toward Palestine with more than 4,550 refugees packed aboard. Just as she neared Haifa on the Mediterranean coast, the ship was rammed by the British Royal Navy cruiser *Ajax*, in a convoy with five destroyers, and was boarded by sailors. This was not an easy task, as the *SS Exodus* had been fortified with barriers and barbed wire to discourage such actions. The British reportedly bombarded the ship with tear gas grenades in order to subdue the passengers. Captain Ike Aronowicz and his crew challenged the boarding party. One crewmember, First Mate William Bernstein, a sailor from California, and two passengers were bludgeoned to death.[69]

The ship that had brought such hope to so many had been attacked by the British navy a mere seventeen miles offshore, in international waters. It was a wanton act of piracy for which the Royal Navy commanders were never charged. Grauel reported that, as the *Exodus* staggered into the port at Haifa, those still able to stand gathered on the deck of the ship and sang "Hatikvah," the hymn of hope.

Grauel, the only passenger onboard with a valid visa, was arrested but soon escaped with help from none other than the future mayor of Jerusalem Teddy Kollek and the Haganah. He was approached by a reporter, who was a member of the Jewish organization. The unnamed reporter shepherded Grauel to the men's room, from which he was whisked out a back door into a waiting car displaying American press credentials. The Jews onboard the *SS Exodus* were then forced to disembark in Haifa and were eventually and unwillingly returned to British-controlled camps in Germany. Against this setting, Rabbi Judah Magnes rose to present testimony to the United Nations. Assuming what surely must have been a sadly pious look, he postulated:

> We are here in this country [Palestine] with two peoples; so long as it is inhabited by two peoples, the Jewish people will have to do without a state, as it has done for many hundreds of years.[70]

Grauel was summoned to Kadimah House in Jerusalem to give a firsthand account of his experiences during the voyage with the refugees to the United Nations Committee on Palestine. As he stood before that group, he leveled his heartfelt accusations regarding the treatment of the Jewish passengers on the *SS Exodus*. He later said of his testimony:

> There was great gratification for me in knowing that my eyewitness report was now a matter of record. Inherent in the nature of the relationship between Christians and Jews was the fact that because I was a Christian, in this situation my testimony would be given greater credence than that of a Jewish crew member.[71]

Grauel's witness proved to be an effective means of gaining compassion and support for the Jewish cause. His eloquent speech to the UNSCOP later earned him the moniker of "the man who helped make Israel possible." Prime Minister Golda Meir believed it was Grauel's recounting of the events surrounding the *SS Exodus* that persuaded the UN to support the creation of a Jewish state.[72]

After five weeks of study in Palestine, the UNSCOP group returned to the General Assembly in September 1947 with a report containing both a majority and a minority plan. The majority proposed a Plan of Partition with Economic Union; the minority proposed an Independent State of Palestine.

With only slight modifications, the Plan of Economic Union was recommended and adopted on November 29, 1947. The Resolution carried by 33 votes to 13 with 10 abstentions. As expected, Arab states, which constituted the Arab League, voted against it. At the time, Arab and Jewish Palestinians fought openly to control strategic positions in the region. In the weeks prior to the end of the Mandate, the Haganah (the clandestine military wing of the Jewish leadership that became the basis for the Israeli Defense Force) launched a number of offensives to gain control over all the territory allocated to the Jewish state by the UN, creating a large number of refugees and capturing the towns of Tiberias, Haifa, Safad, Beisan and, in effect, Jaffa.

Early in 1948, the United Kingdom announced it would terminate the Mandate in Palestine on May 14. In response, President Harry S. Truman proposed UN trusteeship rather than partition, stating that "unfortunately, it has become clear that the partition plan cannot be carried out at this time by peaceful means."[73] Further, he commented that "...unless emergency action is taken, there will be no public authority in Palestine on that date capable of preserving law and order. Violence and bloodshed will descend upon the Holy Land. Large-scale fighting among the people of that country will be the inevitable result."[74]

On May 14, 1948, the day on which the British Mandate expired, the Jewish People's Council gathered at the Tel Aviv Museum and approved a proclamation declaring establishment of a Jewish state in *Eretz Yisrael*, to be known as the State of Israel. In an official cablegram from the Secretary-General of the League of Arab States to the UN Secretary-General on May 15, 1948, the Arabs stated publicly that various Arab Governments were "compelled to intervene for the sole purpose of restoring peace and security and establishing law and order in Palestine."[75]

That same day, the armies of Egypt, Lebanon, Syria, Jordan, and Iraq invaded what had ceased to be the British Mandate just the day before. It marked the beginning of the Arab-Israeli War. The newly-formed Israeli Defense Force repulsed the Arab League nations from part of the occupied territories, thus extending Israel's borders beyond the original UNSCOP partition.

By December 1948, Israel controlled most of that portion of the Mandate including Palestine west of the Jordan River. The remainder of the Mandate consisted of Jordan, the area that today is called the West Bank (controlled by Jordan), and the Gaza Strip, now controlled by the Palestinian Authority and the terrorist organization, Hamas. Prior to and during this conflict, 713,000 Palestinian Arabs fled their original lands to become Palestinian refugees due, in part, to a promise from Arab leaders that they would be able to return when the war had been won. The war came to an end with the signing of the 1949 Armistice Agreements between Israel and each of its Arab neighbors.

CHAPTER FIFTEEN

THE STRUGGLE CONTINUES

Joshua said to them, "Do not be afraid; do not be discouraged. Be strong and courageous,"

(JOSHUA 10:25, NIV.)

Before the adoption by the United Nations in November 1947 and the declaration of the State of Israel in May 1948, several Arab countries had begun using discriminatory measures against their local Jewish populations. The status of Jewish citizens in Arab states worsened dramatically during the 1948 Israeli-Arab war. Anti-Jewish riots had erupted throughout the Muslim world in December 1947, and Jewish communities were hit particularly hard in Syria and Aden, with hundreds of dead and injured. By mid-1948, almost all Jewish communities in Arab states had suffered attacks and their status rapidly deteriorated.

Jews under Islamic regimes were uprooted from their longtime residences and many became political hostages. With anti-Jewish violence and persecution escalating, a large number of Jews fled or were forced to emigrate from Arab countries and other Muslim countries as well.

In Libya, Jews were deprived of their citizenship, and in Iraq, their property was seized. Egypt expelled most of its Jewish community in 1956, while Algeria denied its Jews citizenship upon its independence in 1962. The majority fled due to worsening political conditions and rabid anti-Semitism, although some emigrated for ideological reasons.

As a result of Israel's victory in its 1948 War of Independence, Arabs caught on the wrong side of the ceasefire line were unable to return to their homes in what became Israel. Likewise, any Jews on the West Bank or in Gaza were exiled from their property and homes. Today's Palestinian refugees are the descendants of those who left at the strong suggestion of the Arabs in countries that surround Israel. The responsibility for their exodus continues to be a matter of dispute between the Israelis and the Palestinians. The world at large points a finger at Israel for the disparity while seemingly dismissing any Arab complicity.

In 1956, Egypt closed the Strait of Tiran to Israeli shipping, and blockaded the Gulf of Aqaba, in contravention of the Constantinople Convention of 1888. Many argued that this was also a violation of the 1949 Armistice Agreements. Further, on July 26, 1956, Egypt nationalized the Suez Canal Company, and closed the canal to Israeli shipping. Israel responded on October 29, 1956, and with British and French support invaded the Sinai Peninsula. During the Suez Canal Crisis, Israel captured the Gaza Strip and Sinai Peninsula.

The US and the UN soon pressured Israel into a ceasefire. Jewish leaders agreed to withdraw from Egyptian territory, and Egypt acceded to freedom of navigation in the region and the demilitarization of the Sinai. Also, the United Nations Emergency Force (UNEF) was created and deployed to oversee the demilitarization. It is noteworthy that the UNEF was only deployed on the Egyptian side of the border. Israel refused to allow UNEF on its own territory.

The PLO (Palestinian Liberation Organization) was established in 1964, under a charter including a commitment to "the liberation of Palestine [which] will destroy the Zionist and imperialist presence..."[76] On May 19, 1967, Egypt expelled UNEF observers, and deployed 100,000 soldiers to the Sinai Peninsula. It again closed the Strait of Tiran to Israeli shipping, returning the region to its alignment in 1956 when Israel was blockaded.

On May 30, 1967, Jordan signed a mutual defense pact with Egypt. Egypt mobilized Sinai units, crossing UN lines (after having expelled the UN border monitors) and amassed troops and equipment on Israel's southern border.

On June 5, Israel launched a surprise, pre-emptive strike on Egypt, and then on Jordan, Syrian, and Iraqi forces. The results of the war continue today to affect the geopolitics of the region.

At the end of August 1967, Arab leaders in response to the war met in Khartoum to discuss the Arab position toward Israel. They reached consensus that there should be no recognition, no peace, and no negotiations with the State of Israel, the so-called "three no's". In 1969, Egypt initiated the War of Attrition, with the goal of forcing Israel into surrendering the Sinai Peninsula. The war ended following Gamal Abdel Nasser's death in 1970.

Also in 1970, following an extended civil war, King Hussein expelled the Palestine Liberation Organization from Jordan. September 1970 is known as Black September in Arab history; sometimes referred to as the "era of regrettable events". It was the month when King Hussein of the Hashemite Kingdom of Jordan moved to quash the autonomy of Palestinian organizations and restore his monarchy's rule over the country. The violence resulted in the deaths of tens of thousands of people, the vast majority of them Palestinians.

Armed conflict lasted until July 1971 with the expulsion of the

PLO and thousands of Palestinian fighters to Lebanon and mounted raids into Israel.

On October 6, 1973, Syria and Egypt staged a surprise attack on Israel on Yom Kippur, the holiest day of the Jewish calendar. The Israeli military was caught off-guard and unprepared, and took about three days to fully mobilize. This led other Arab states to send troops to reinforce the Egyptians and Syrians. These Arab countries also agreed to enforce an oil embargo on industrial nations including the U.S, Japan and Western European Countries.

These OPEC countries increased the price of oil fourfold, and employed that as a political weapon to gain support against Israel. The Yom Kippur War brought about indirect confrontation between the US and the Soviet Union. When Israel had turned the tide of war, the USSR threatened military intervention. The United States, wary of a possible nuclear war, secured a ceasefire on October 25.

Following the Camp David Accords of the late 1970s, Israel and Egypt signed a peace treaty. Under its terms, the Sinai Peninsula would be returned to Egypt, and the Gaza Strip would remain under Israeli control, to be included in a future Palestinian state. The agreement also provided for free passage of Israeli ships through the Suez Canal and recognition of the Strait of Tiran and the Gulf of Aqaba as international waterways.

In June 1981, Israel attacked and destroyed Iraq's newly-built nuclear facilities in Operation Opera.

During the Gulf War in 1991, Iraq fired 39 Scud missiles into Israel, in the hopes of uniting the Arab world against the coalition which sought to liberate Kuwait. At the urging of the United States, Israel did not respond to these attacks in order to prevent an outbreak of all-out war.

In 1981, Syria allied with the PLO and moved missiles into

Lebanon. In response, Israel invaded Lebanon in June, 1982. Within two months the PLO agreed to withdraw.

In March 1983, Israel and Lebanon signed a ceasefire agreement. However, Syria pressured President Amin Gemayel into nullifying the truce. By 1985, Israeli forces withdrew to a 15-kilometer-wide southern strip of Lebanon, following which the conflict continued on a reduced scale, with relatively low casualties on both sides. In both 1993 and 1996, Israel launched major operations against the Shiite militia of Hezbollah, which had become a growing threat. In 2000, as part of a greater plan for a peace agreement with Syria, Israel abandoned its occupation of Southern Lebanon.

In October 1994, Israel and Jordan signed a peace agreement, which stipulated mutual cooperation, an end of hostilities, securing the Israel-Jordan border, and several other issues. The conflict had cost roughly 18.3 billion dollars. The peace agreement was also closely linked with efforts to create peace between Israel and the Palestinian Liberation Organization representing the Palestinian National Authority (PNA). It was signed on October 26, 1994 and made Jordan only the second Arab country (after Egypt) to normalize relations with Israel. Contrarily, Israel and Iraq have been inexorable foes since 1948.

In 2006, as a response to a Hezbollah cross-border raid, Israel launched air strikes on the militant group's strongholds in Southern Lebanon, initiating the Lebanon War. The conflict lasted 34 days, and resulted in the creation of a buffer zone in Southern Lebanon along with deployment of Lebanese troops south of the Litani River for the first time since the 1960s. Hezbollah withdrew its fighters from the border areas, and Israel eventually turned over its occupied areas in Lebanon to UN peacekeepers. Both sides declared victory in the conflict.

The 1970s were marked by a large number of major, international terrorist attacks, including the Lod (now Ben-Gurion) Airport Massacre and the Munich Olympics Massacre in 1972, and the Entebbe hostage taking in 1976, with over 100 Jewish captives of different nationalities kidnapped and held in Uganda.

In December 1987, the First Intifada (or shaking off) began. It was a mass uprising against Israeli rule in the Palestinian Territories. The rebellion began in the Jabalia refugee camp and quickly spread throughout Gaza, the West Bank and East Jerusalem. Palestinian actions ranged from civil disobedience to violence. In addition to general strikes, boycotts on Israeli products, graffiti and barricades, Palestinian demonstrations that included stone-throwing by youths against the Israel Defense Forces brought the Intifada international attention. Conversely, the Israeli army's heavy-handed response to the demonstrations, with live ammunition, beatings and mass arrests, brought international condemnation. The PLO, which until then had never been recognized as leaders of the Palestinian people by Israel, was invited to peace negotiations the following year, after it recognized Israel and formally renounced terrorism.

In mid-1993, Israeli and Palestinian representatives engaged in peace talks in Oslo, Norway. This resulted in both Israel and the PLO signing the Oslo Accords, known as the *Declaration of Principles* or Oslo I. In side letters, Israel recognized the PLO as the legitimate representative of the Palestinian people while the PLO recognized the right of the state of Israel to exist and renounced terrorism, violence and its desire for the destruction of Israel.

The Oslo II agreement was signed in 1995 and detailed the division of the West Bank into Areas A, B, and C. Area A was land under full Palestinian civilian control with the Palestinians being responsible for internal security. Area B outlined Palestinian civil control and joint Israeli-Palestinian security control. That area includes many Palestinian towns, villages and areas, with no Israeli settlements. Area C details full Israeli civil and security control which, by the year 2011 included 61% of the West Bank.

The pact further states: "Areas of the West Bank outside Areas A and B, which, except for the issues that will be negotiated in the permanent status negotiations, will be gradually transferred to Palestinian jurisdiction in accordance with this Agreement".[77]

The Second Intifada forced Israeli leaders to rethink the relationship and policies towards the Palestinians. Following a series of suicide bombings and attacks, the Israeli army launched Operation Defensive Shield. It was the largest military action conducted by Israel since the Six-Day War.

As violence between the Israeli army and Palestinian militants intensified, Israel expanded its security apparatus around the West Bank by re-taking many parts of land in Area A. The nation established a complicated system of roadblocks and checkpoints around major Palestinian areas to deter violence and protect Israeli settlements. However, in 2008, the IDF began to slowly transfer authority to Palestinian security forces.

Israeli Prime Minister Ariel Sharon instituted a policy of unilateral withdrawal from the Gaza Strip in 2003. This policy was fully implemented in August 2005. Sharon's announcement to disengage from Gaza came as a tremendous shock to his critics both on the left and on the right. A year previously, he had commented that the fate of the most far-flung settlements in Gaza, Netzararem and Kfar Darom, was regarded in the same light as that of Tel Aviv.

The formal announcements to evacuate seventeen Gaza settlements and another four in the West Bank in February 2004 represented the first reversal for the settler movement since 1968, and divided Sharon's party. The move was strongly supported by Trade and Industry Minister Ehud Olmert and Tzipi Livni, the Minister for Immigration and Absorption, but Foreign Minister Silvan Shalom and Finance Minister Benjamin Netanyahu strongly condemned it. It was also uncertain whether this was simply the beginning of further evacuation.

In June 2006, Hamas militants infiltrated an army post near the Israeli side of the Gaza Strip and abducted Israeli soldier Gilad Shalit. Two IDF soldiers were killed in the attack, while Shalit was wounded after his tank was hit by a rocket. Three days later Israel launched Operation Summer Rains to secure the release of Shalit. In October 18, 2011, Gilad was exchanged for 1,027 Palestinian prisoners. It speaks of the value the Israelis place on the life of just one of their own.

In July 2006, Hezbollah fighters crossed the border from Lebanon into Israel, attacking and killing eight Israeli soldiers, and abducting two others as hostages, setting off the 2006 Lebanon War which caused wide-spread destruction in Lebanon. A UN-sponsored ceasefire went into effect on August 14, 2006, officially ending the conflict. Over a thousand Lebanese and over 150 Israelis were killed, the Lebanese civil infrastructure was severely damaged, and approximately one million Lebanese and 300,000–500,000 Israelis were displaced, although most were later able to return to their homes. After the ceasefire, some parts of Southern Lebanon remained uninhabitable due to unexploded Israeli cluster bomblets.

In the aftermath of the Battle of Gaza, where Hamas seized control of the Gaza Strip in a violent civil war with rival Fatah, Israel placed restrictions on its border with Gaza and ended economic cooperation with the Palestinian leadership based there. Israel and Egypt have imposed a blockade on the Gaza Strip since 2007. Israel maintains the blockade is necessary to limit Palestinian rocket attacks from Gaza and to prevent Hamas from smuggling advanced rockets and weapons capable of hitting Israeli cities.

On September 6, 2007, in Operation Orchard, Israel bombed an eastern Syrian complex which was reportedly a nuclear reactor being built with the assistance of North Korea.

In April 2008, Syrian President Bashar Al Assad told a Qatari newspaper that Syria and Israel had been discussing a peace treaty for a year, with Turkey as a go-between. This was confirmed in May 2008 by a spokesman for Prime Minister Ehud Olmert. As well as a peace treaty, the future of the Golan Heights was being discussed. President Assad said there "would be no direct negotiations with Israel until a new US president takes office."

Speaking in Jerusalem on August 26, 2008, then-United States Secretary of State Condoleezza Rice criticized Israel's increased settlement construction in the West Bank as detrimental to the peace process. Rice's comments came amid reports that Israeli construction in the disputed territory had increased significantly over 2007 levels.

A fragile six-month truce between Hamas and Israel expired on December 19, 2008 and attempts at extending the truce have failed amid accusations of breaches from both sides. Following the expiration, Israel launched a raid on a tunnel suspected of being used to kidnap Israeli soldiers which killed several Hamas fighters. Following this, Hamas resumed rocket and mortar attacks on Israeli cities, most notably firing over 60 rockets on December 24. Three days later, Israel launched Operation Cast Lead against Hamas. Numerous human rights organizations accused Israel and Hamas of committing war crimes.

In 2009 Israel placed a 10-month settlement freeze on the West

Bank. Hillary Clinton praised the freeze as an "unprecedented" gesture that could "help revive Middle East talks."

A raid was carried out by Israeli naval forces on six ships of the *Gaza Freedom Flotilla* in May 2010. On the MV *Mavi Marmara*, activists clashed with an Israeli boarding party. During the fighting, nine activists were killed by Israeli Special Forces. Widespread international condemnation followed. Relations between Israel and Turkey were strained, and Israel subsequently eased its blockade on the Gaza Strip. Several dozen other passengers and seven Israeli soldiers were injured.

Following the latest round of peace talks between Israel and the PA, thirteen Palestinian militant movements led by Hamas initiated a terror campaign designed to derail and disrupt the negotiations. Attacks on Israelis have increased since August 2010, after 4 civilians were killed by Hamas militants. On August 2, Hamas militants launched seven Katyusha rockets at Eilat and Aqaba, killing one Jordanian civilian and wounding 4 others.

Intermittent fighting has continued since then, including 680 rocket attacks on Israel in 2011. On November 14, 2012, Israel killed Ahmed Jabari, a leader of Hamas' military wing, launching Operation Pillar of Cloud. A week later Hamas and Israel agreed to an Egyptian-mediated ceasefire.

The Palestinian Centre for Human Rights claimed that 158 Palestinians were killed during the operation, of which: 102 were civilians, 55 were militants and one was a policeman; 30 were children and 13 were women. B'Tselem (The Israeli Information Center for Human Rights in the Occupied Territories) stated that according to its initial findings, which covered only the period between 14 and 19 November, 102 Palestinians were killed in the Gaza Strip, 40 of them civilians. According to Israeli figures, 120 combatants and 57 civilians were killed. International outcry ensued, with many criticizing Israel for what much of the international community perceived as a disproportionately violent response. Protests took place on hundreds of college campuses across the US, and in front of the Israeli consulate in New York. Additional protests followed throughout the Middle East, Europe, and in parts of South America.

However, the governments of the United States, United Kingdom, Canada, Germany, France, Australia, Belgium, Bulgaria, Czech Republic and Netherlands have expressed support for Israel's right to defend itself, and/or condemned these on-going Hamas rocket attacks on Israel.

And so, the relentless conflict between two entities and two religions continues, abated only occasionally by short-lived pacts, agreements, and accords that are broken with impunity.

CHAPTER SIXTEEN

ISRAEL'S GOVERNMENT LEADERS

Now the leaders of the people lived in Jerusalem,

(NEHEMIAH 11:1, ESV.)

srael is overseen by a multi-party legislative system, roughly analogous to the democracy practiced in the United States. The role of president in Israel is chiefly ceremonial and is not a part of the three branches of government. The legislative authority is the Knesset, Israel's parliament, and includes 120 members elected by nationwide ballot for a term of four years. The prime minister heads the executive branch and is the most powerful political figure in Israel.

Following an election, a member of the Knesset is nominated by the President of Israel after having polled party leaders to determine their choice among possible candidates. The person selected must present a platform to the president and receive a vote of confidence from his peers in the Knesset in order to become prime minister. Generally, the one selected is the head of the largest party or has formed a coalition consisting of various parties. Ministers that head the government are then appointed by the prime minister from among the ranks of parties in the coalition. Currently, the top twelve parties are Likud, Yesh Atid, Labor, Jewish Home, Shas, United Torah Judaism, Hatnuah, Meretz, United Arab List, Hadash, Balad, and Kadima. In 2013, there were an additional twenty-one parties for which votes were cast.

A total of twelve people, eleven men and one woman, have served as prime minister; five have served on two non-consecutive occasions. One person, Yigal Allon, has served solely as interim prime minister. The other two who served as interim prime minister went on to become prime minister.

In 1904 eighteen-year old David Grün found himself in the streets of Warsaw, hungry and struggling to earn enough to buy food. Even with minimal education, he worked as a teacher and strove to further his education despite limitations on Jews attending Russian schools. As he became more and more aware of growing anti-Semitism in his world, he and two friends established a youth club, *Ezra,* to promote Hebrew studies and encourage Jews to emigrate to the Holy Land, which only whetted his own appetite to leave Poland behind for Palestine. While studying at the University of Warsaw, David joined *Poalei Zion,* the Social-Democratic Jewish Workers' Party.

Eighteen months later, Grün would set out upon his journey to Palestine, where he would take the name David Ben-Gurion and help bring about the birth of a dream—a homeland for the Jewish people.

When David arrived in a Palestine then under the control of the Ottoman Empire, he joined forces with agricultural workers to establish communes, which ultimately became the *kibbutzim* (collective

farms or settlements.) He also became involved in pro-independence and socialist activities. By the start of World War I, he must have been on all the lists of people most likely to be a disruptive influence. He and Yitzhak Ben-Zvi (instrumental in forming the Jewish defense group *Hashomer* and Israel's second president after its rebirth) were soon apprehended and deported by the Ottoman rulers.

Unwelcome and ousted from Palestine, Ben-Gurion traveled to New York City to plead the Zionist cause to Jews in the United States. While there, he met and married Paula Monbesz, who was also involved with the *Poalei Zion* organization. David and Ben-Zvi returned to Palestine in 1918 as members of the Jewish Legion in the British Royal Fusiliers. The two men had left Ottoman-controlled Palestine only to return to a land under the jurisdiction of the British.

Back in the Holy Land and still believing it would be Jewish labor that would provide the bedrock foundation for a new state, Ben-Gurion dove right into local politics. He established trade unions, specifically the General Federation of Labour or *Histradut*. As its representative, David attended World Zionist Organization and Jewish Agency meetings. In 1935, he was elected chair of both groups.

David crusaded unstintingly for Zionist ideas and ideals both in the United States and in Europe, as he also worked tirelessly to develop military strength in Palestine. At the onset of the Second World War, he actively encouraged Palestinian Jews to enlist in the Allied cause. At the same time, he was busy organizing an underground railroad to liberate Jews from the Nazis and help them escape to Palestine. Following the end of the war, as resistance against British rule became the focus, Ben-Gurion strongly denounced right-wing extremists who resorted to terrorism to make their case.

Ben-Gurion achieved his passion for a Jewish state and was then entrusted with its guardianship. When Israel issued its declaration of statehood in 1948, Ben-Gurion assumed the offices of prime minister and defense minister. He demanded that the various armed factions merge into one fighting force—the Israel Defense Force. He masterminded the creation of many of the new state's institutions and various internal projects to aid development (i.e., Operation Magic Carpet to airlift Jews from unfriendly Arab countries, the founding of new towns and cities, and the national waterworks along with other infrastructure projects). He continued to encourage pioneering and farming in remote areas of the land.

As Yoram Hazony, author, philosopher, and political theorist, wrote:

> From the time David Ben-Gurion came to Palestine at the age of twenty, he regarded himself as personally responsible for the fate of the Jewish people. Even the act of immigrating to Palestine came in the wake of Herzl's death, and Ben-Gurion's decision to come and build the Jewish State with his own hands expressed his effort to ameliorate his people's loss in the only way he knew.
>
> And it was this relationship of guardianship that was in evidence at every moment of Ben-Gurion's nearly fifteen years at the head of the Jewish state itself.[78]

When Ben-Gurion stepped to the podium at 4:00 pm on that warm Friday afternoon in May, he carefully read the statement that would declare Israel's sovereignty. The following day, May 15, Egypt launched its aircraft toward Tel Aviv. As Egypt had planned, it was Shabbat, and there would be no official response until the conclusion of the holy day. As the prime minister again delivered a news bulletin to his awaiting audience, Ben-Gurion announced that an Egyptian warplane had been shot down, its pilot imprisoned, and the aircraft added to the Israeli Air Force. He also reported that the United States had been the first nation to recognize Israel's independence.

During his first term as prime minister, Ben-Gurion established what were known as "nationality laws." This was likely the most important step toward fusing Israel into the cohesive state is has become. Simply stated, it meant that all immigrating Jews were immediately registered as Jewish nationals. The Star of David was chosen for Israel's flag;, the state seal exhibited the image of a *menorah*, and "Hatikvah" (the Hope) was chosen as the Jewish national anthem. All official holidays were centered on the Jewish calendar, and Shabbat was declared to begin at sundown on Friday and end at sundown on Saturday. Ben-Gurion urged the Ministry of Education to establish schools that would educate nonreligious Jews in the religious way of life, which included wearing the prayer shawl and *tefillin* (phylacteries) when in prayer and observing bar and bat mitzvahs, among other customs.

Ben-Gurion left political life in 1953 and returned to his first love, *Kibbutz Sde Boker* in the Negev, but was called back into service in 1955 as minister of defense and then again to the office of prime minister following the two-year term of Moshe Sharett.

Moshe Sharett served as Israel's prime minister between David Ben-Gurion's two terms (1953-1955). Sharett was one of the signatories of Israel's Declaration of Independence, and was first elected to the Knesset in 1949. His term of office was clouded by what came to be known as the "Lavon Affair," which affected not only Sharett but also Ben-Gurion's eventual second term as prime minister.

The Affair was so named because Sharett's Minister of Defense Pinhas Lavon was charged with overseeing a rogue intelligence operation that was designed to inflict damage to US and British interests in Egypt. The purpose of what came to be known as "Operation Susannah" was to cause disruption between the regime of Gamal Abdul Nasser and the West, or to in effect turn Israel's allies against her avowed enemies. Its overall aim was to convince the British not to withdraw from the Suez Canal Zone, which was deemed necessary to maintain a peaceful climate in the region.

One of the recruited spy cells was charged with placing homemade bombs on the shelves of libraries in Alexandria and Cairo, Egypt, and another group set off a firebomb in an Alexandria post office. A theater owned by a British company was also targeted with an explosive device. It was fortunate that the acid and nitroglycerin devices did little damage and resulted in no injuries or deaths.

The operation was calamitous for Israel, as one of the infiltrators turned informant and was later exposed as a double agent for the Egyptian government. The plan was made even more provocative with the use of Egyptian Jews as the moles. The Israelis charged that President Nasser's regime staged the trial only for show. Two of the saboteurs were condemned to death by hanging. The Egyptian court, on the other hand, spared the majority of the participating infiltrators the death penalty. After serving part of their sentences, the Jewish partisans involved were eventually deported from Egypt to Israel. Sharett never quite escaped the political disgrace caused by the Lavon Affair. He wrote that Lavon had "incessantly advocated acts of lunacy, inculcating the army command with the diabolical notion of igniting the Middle East, fomenting disputes, bloody assassinations, attacks on objectives and assets of the powers, desperate and suicidal acts."[79]

Lavon met with Prime Minister Sharett and disavowed any knowledge of "Operation Susannah." Reportedly the political ranks at the Ministry of Defense believed that Benjamin Givly, military intelligence chief and the prime minister's protégé, had formed a spy ring. Givly proclaimed the minister of defense a liar and an inquiry was set in motion. The group assigned to the case was unable to uncover irrefutable evidence that Lavon had actually sanctioned the mission. Lavon then tried to implicate Chief of Staff Moshe Dayan and sought to bring charges of insubordination and criminal negligence against Defense Ministry Secretary General Shimon Peres. When Lavon was forced to resign, Sharett convinced Ben-Gurion to return to the post of minister of defense. Soon thereafter, the prime minister resigned and Ben-Gurion once again assumed that office.

Levi Eshkol was elected to serve as the third Prime Minister of Israel in 1963. When Ben-Gurion resigned in June 1963, Eshkol was elected party chairman with a broad consensus, and was subsequently appointed prime minister. However, his relationship with Ben-Gurion soon turned acrimonious over the latter's insistence on investigating the Lavon Affair.

In 1964, US President Lyndon Johnson was approached by Israeli Ambassador Abraham Harman, who had been advised by Prime Minister Eshkol to seek a military alliance with the United States. The president replied that such a treaty was unnecessary, as America was committed to Israel's security, a pledge recognized by other world powers and Arab countries. When Egypt closed the

Straight of Tiran to ships bound for Haifa and to Israeli ships seeking passage, Prime Minister Eshkol sought Johnson's assistance. After conferring with former President Dwight Eisenhower, LBJ reiterated that the Israelis were guaranteed the "right of access to the Gulf of Aqaba" and that this "was definitely part of the 'commitment' we had made to them... the Gulf of Aqaba is an international waterway and the blockade of Israeli shipping is, therefore, illegal."[80]

Even as Johnson contemplated Nasser's move, the grandson of Winston Churchill, another Winston, was interviewing David Ben-Gurion at the King David Hotel in Jerusalem. A Kol Israel radio newsman announced the closure of the Strait. The Egyptian leader had effectively severed Israel's lifeline for oil imports. According to Winston:

> Ben-Gurion, with a gesture of the hand, ordered his assistant to switch off the radio and, shaking his great mane of white hair gravely, declared with sorrow: "This means war. I am very frightened. Not for Israel, for she will survive—we cannot afford otherwise—but for the younger generation. It is always the best of their generation who never return."[81]

Israel was ultimately forced to take action against Nasser and the countries that backed him. In six days during June of 1967, the Israelis blitzed the Arab armies. Not only were they victorious in the conflict, but Jerusalem was once again reunited and in Jewish hands. Israeli commander Motta Gur expressed the feelings of a grateful nation:

> For some two thousand years the Temple Mount was forbidden to the Jews.... The Western Wall, for which

every heart beats, is ours once again. Many Jews have taken their lives into their hands throughout our long history, in order to reach Jerusalem and live here. End-less words of longing have expressed the deep yearn-ing for Jerusalem that beats within the Jewish heart. You have been given the great privilege of completing the circle, of returning to the nation its capital and its holy center ... Jerusalem is yours forever.[82]

The first Israeli Prime Minister to die in office, Levi Eshkol suc-cumbed to a heart attack in 1969.

Yigal Allon served as interim prime minister upon the death of Eshkol. An Israeli politician, a commander of the Palmach, (acronym for *Plugot Maḥatz* or "strike forces", the elite fighting force of the Haganah, the underground army of the Jewish community during the period of the British Mandate for Palestine) and Allon was a gen-eral in the IDF. He operated as the acting head of government until March 1969 when Golda Meir was chosen leader of the Labor Party. Under Meir's government, he was appointed Minister of Education and Culture and Deputy Prime Minister, a post he held until 1974. Yigal Allon died of heart failure in 1980. His funeral was attended by tens of thousands of mourners, with condolences extended by many world leaders, including Egyptian president Anwar Sadat.

Golda Meir, elected prime minister in 1969, became something of an Israeli icon. Israel's first and the world's third woman to hold such an office, long before Britain's Margaret Thatcher was awarded the epithet, Meir was described as the "Iron Lady" of Israeli politics. Former Prime Minister David Ben-Gurion called Meir "the best man in the government". Golda was born on May 3, 1898, in Kiev, Russian Empire (present-day Ukraine). Her father left to find work in New York City in 1903. In 1905, he moved to Milwaukee, Wisconsin, in search of higher-paying work and found employment in the workshops of the local rail yard. The following year, he had saved up enough money to bring his family to the United States. In 1913 Golda had begun dating Morris Meyerson. When they married in 1917, settling in Palestine was her precondition for the marriage. She was a committed Labor Zionist and he was a dedicated socialist. Together, they left their jobs to join a kibbutz in Palestine in 1921.

Golda became an official in the Histadrut Trade Union, and served until she was asked to assume Moshe Sharett's role as head of the Jewish Agency Political Department. In 1948, Golda was appointed to Ben-Gurion's Provisional Government, and was covertly dispatched to Jordan to try to dissuade King Abdullah from joining an attack against Israel.

By 1956, Golda had been appointed foreign minister, a post in which she served until 1966. Prime Minister Levi Eshkol died suddenly in 1969, and the 71-year old Meir assumed the post of prime minister. At a press conference in 1969, the feisty Ms. Meir said to Anwar Sadat:

> When peace comes we will perhaps in time be able
> to forgive the Arabs for killing our sons, but it will be
> harder for us to forgive them for having forced us to
> kill their sons.[83]

It was during Meir's watch as prime minister that on October 6, 1973, Yom Kippur, the Day of Atonement and holiest day of the Jewish year the Arab Coalition, comprised of Egypt, Syria, and Jordan, struck Israel with a sneak attack in the hope of finally driving the Jews into the Mediterranean. Israel was tragically again caught off-guard, as most of its citizenry were in synagogues, and its national radio was off the air. Because people were enjoying a restful day of reflection and prayer, Israel had no immediate response to the coordinated attacks. Israeli intelligence had not seen the assault coming, and the military was ill-prepared for war.

At the outset of hostilities, Egypt attacked across the Suez Canal. The battle raged for three days, and then the Egyptian army established entrenchments, which resulted in an impasse. On the northern border, Syria launched an offensive at the Golan Heights. The initial assault was successful but quickly lost momentum. By the third day of fighting, Israel had lost several thousand soldiers. More Israeli soldiers fell on that first day than in the entire Six-Day War of 1967. Forty-nine planes, one-third (more than five hundred) of her tank force, and a sizeable portion of the buffer lands gained in the Six-Day War were lost. The Israelis seemed to once again be on the brink of a Holocaust.

On the fourth day of the war, Prime Minister Golda Meir reportedly opened up several nuclear silos and pointed the missiles toward Egyptian and Syrian military headquarters near Cairo and Damascus.[84] Army Chief of Staff Moshe Dayan was reported to have said, "This is the end of the Third Temple," in one of the crucial meetings. Later he told the press, "The situation is desperate. Everything is lost. We must withdraw."[85]

In Washington, President Richard Nixon lit a fire under those who were inundated by legislative lethargy. Nixon came straight to the point, announcing that Israel must not lose the war. He ordered that the deliveries of supplies, including aircraft, be sped up and that Israel be told that it could freely expend all of its consumables—ammunition, spare parts, fuel, and so forth—in the certain knowledge that these would be completely replenished by the United States without delay. Earlier in his presidency, according to one report, "Nixon made it clear he believed warfare was inevitable in the Middle East, a war that could spread and precipitate World War III, with the United States and the Soviet Union squaring off against each other."[86] He was now staring down the barrel of that war.

Nixon's insistence that armaments be airlifted to Israel to ensure her victory was because the president assigned a great sense of exigency to the task. White House aide Alexander Haig said of Nixon's focus on Israel:

As soon as the scope and pattern of Israeli battle losses emerged, Nixon ordered that all destroyed equipment be made up out of U.S. stockpiles, using the very best weapons America possessed....Whatever it takes, he told Kissinger... save Israel. The president asked Kissinger for a precise accounting of Israel's military needs, and Kissinger proceeded to read aloud from an itemized list. "Double it," Nixon ordered. "Now get the hell out of here and get the job done."[87]

In a *Jerusalem Post* editorial, Nixon insider Leonard Garment was quoted as saying: "It was Nixon who did it. I was there. As [bureaucratic bickering between the State and Defense departments] was going back and forth, Nixon said, 'This is insane....' He just ordered Kissinger, 'Get your [behind] out of here and tell those people to move.'"[88]

Secretary of Defense Arthur Schlesinger suggested that the United States dispatch three transports loaded with war materiel in what became known as "Operation Nickel Grass." When he presented the proposal to the president, Nixon, angry that nothing had been done, sent the secretary to do his bidding. When Secretary of State Henry Kissinger returned later to explain yet another delay in the president's orders being carried out, Nixon snapped that the delayed planes were to get off the runway immediately. He barked, "You get the stuff to Israel. Now. Now!"[89]

Every available American plane transported conventional arms to Israel. The resulting supply to defend Israel was larger than the Berlin airlift that had followed World War II, and it literally turned the tide of the war. Nixon's quick action saved Israel from almost certain extermination and the world from possible nuclear war. He had carried Kennedy's agreement to militarily support Israel to the next logical level—a full military alliance.

The Israel Defense Forces launched a counteroffensive within the week and drove the Syrians to within twenty-five miles of Damascus. Trying to aid the Syrians, the Egyptian army went on the offensive, all to no avail. Israeli troops crossed the Suez Canal and encompassed the Egyptian Third Army. When the Soviets realized what was happening, they scrambled to further assist Egypt and Syria. The Soviet threat was so real Nixon feared direct conflict with the USSR and elevated all military personnel worldwide to DefCon III, meaning increased readiness that war was likely. However, a ceasefire was finally worked out between the United States and the USSR, adopted by all parties involved, and the Yom Kippur War was ended.

There are those who ascertain that Nixon acted only because he had been threatened with the use of nuclear weapons by the original "Iron Lady". That is rebutted by Mordechai Gazit, who thought Israel's relationship with the United States was not solidified sufficiently for Nixon to have been so manipulated by Meir.

In 1974, after the end of the Yom Kippur War, Golda Meir resigned as prime minister. She died in 1978 of lymphoma.

CHAPTER SEVENTEEN

POLITICIANS, STATESMEN AND GENERALS

O LORD, lead me in Your righteousness because of my foes;
Make Your way straight before me,

(PSALM 5:8, NASB.)

Y itzhak Rabin, an Israeli politician, statesman and general, was the fifth prime minister of Israel, serving two terms in office, 1974–77 and 1992 until his assassination in 1995.

In 1968, Robert Kennedy followed in the footsteps of his brother, John, and ran for the presidency on the Democratic ticket. He was in California on June 5, where he won that state's primary—which just happened to be the anniversary of the outbreak of the Six-Day War. Kennedy's staff requested a photo opportunity with the visiting Ambassador Rabin. He had been Israel's chief of staff in 1967 and had been named ambassador to the United States. Bobby wanted to commemorate the victory with a photo of himself and the ambassador. However, the photo opportunity never took place. That same evening he was shot to death by a young Jerusalem-born Jordanian named Sirhan Bishara Sirhan. Or, at least, Sirhan was considered a

Jordanian before the 1967 war. After that war, Jordanians born in the West Bank territories and East Jerusalem became known as Palestinians. As Rabin wrote in his memoirs:

> The American people were so dazed by what they perceived as the senseless act of a madman that they could not begin to fathom its political significance.[90]

What was that political significance? According to a report made by a special counsel to the Los Angeles County District Attorney's office, Sirhan shot Kennedy for his support of Israel and had been planning the assassination for months. In an outburst during his trial, he confessed, "I killed Robert Kennedy willfully, premeditatedly, and with twenty years of malice aforethought."[91] It was a reference to Bobby's brief stint as a journalist in Jerusalem.

In a notebook found in Sirhan's apartment, investigators found a passage written on May 18, 1968, at 9:45 am: "Robert F. Kennedy must be assassinated before 5 June 68"—the first anniversary of the beginning of the Six-Day War. Mr. and Mrs. John Weidner, who owned the health food store where Sirhan worked, testified that he had told them, "The State of Israel had taken his home, and the Jewish people were on top and directing the events in America."[92] It also came out during the trial that it had "provoked a heavy shock in Sirhan" when Senator Kennedy pledged during a speech in late May or early June of 1968 to send fifty Phantom jets to Israel.[93]

On the night Sirhan was apprehended for the assassination, among other things in his pockets were two newspaper clippings, one inviting the public "to come and see and hear Senator Robert Kennedy on Sunday, June 2, 1968, at 8:00 pm, Coconut Grove, Ambassador Hotel, Los Angeles," and the other was a story by columnist David Lawrence, which noted part of Senator Kennedy's speech stating he "favored aid to Israel with arms if necessary."[94]

Robert F. Kennedy was more correct than he would ever know when he quoted in one of his articles a Palestinian who vowed vehemently:

> We shall bring brigades from Pakistan, we shall lead a religious crusade for all loyal followers of Mohammed, we shall crush forever the invader. Whether it takes three months, three years, or 30, we will carry on the fight. Palestine will be Arab. We shall accept no compromise.[95]

In 1994, Rabin won the Nobel Peace Prize together with Shimon Peres and Yasser Arafat. He was assassinated by a right-wing Israeli radical who was opposed to Rabin's signing of the Oslo Accords. Yitzhak Rabin was the first native-born prime minister of Israel, the only prime minister to be assassinated and the second to die in office after Levi Eshkol.

The story is told of the trip Ted Kennedy, brother of Bobby and John, made to Israel to attend the funeral of Prime Minister Yitzhak Rabin, also the victim of an assassination. According to Massachusetts Governor Deval Patrick:

> Before leaving, Kennedy collected handfuls of dirt from the graves of his slain brothers, Jack and Robert, in Arlington National Cemetery. After the funeral had ended and everyone had gone, Kennedy went back and spread the soil he'd brought on Rabin's grave. "No publicity—just a good man doing a sweet thing."[96]

Menachem Begin was an Israeli politician and founder of the Likud party. Before Israel's independence, he was the leader of the Zionist militant group Irgun, the Revisionist breakaway from the larger Jewish paramilitary organization Haganah.

Both Jimmy Carter and his successor, Ronald Reagan, greatly underestimated Israeli Prime Minister Begin. Though small in stature, he had the heart of a giant when it came to his beloved homeland, and Reagan came to recognize that fiercely protective stance. Begin worked closely with Carter to try to bring peace to his people—at least with the country of Egypt. When he and Anwar Sadat were awarded the Nobel Peace Prize in 1978 for their efforts, Begin said: "… if through your efforts and sacrifices you win liberty and with it the prospect of peace, then work for peace because there is no mission in life more sacred."[97]

The future Israeli leader was born August 16, 1913, to Ze'ev Dov and Hassia Begin in Brest-Litovsk, Russia (a town well-known for its Talmudic intellectuals). Menachem had a strong line of ancestors. His mother's family included a list of noted rabbis, while his father was a merchant and leader in the community. Ze'ev Dov was also an ardent Zionist and a devotee of Theodor Herzl. Menachem's birth was overseen by none other than future Israeli Prime Minister Sharon's grandmother. It seems as though he was destined to take his place in the hierarchy of Israeli politics.

At an early age, Menachem followed his father's example and became an enthusiastic Zionist. He joined Ze'ev Jabotinsky's youth movement, *Betar,* and quickly rose in the ranks of management. By the time he was twenty-three, he had been given control of Betar in Czechoslovakia, and two years later, the organization in Poland. He oversaw the armaments training of its members, who were to help shield Polish Jews. He was also involved in underground attempts to transport what were then considered illegal immigrants to Palestine, as well as preparing refugees for work in the fields of agriculture and communication. While on a Betar-related trip to Poland, Menachem met Aliza Arnold. One month later the two were married.

His efforts to assist the Polish Jews won Begin a place in one of Josef Stalin's Siberian labor camps in 1940. When the Nazis overran the USSR in 1941, surprisingly, Begin was freed because he was a Polish citizen. When he returned to Poland, he was able to find his sister—the only living member of his family. He and others who had escaped Nazi and Soviet capture joined the Free Polish Army. Those soldiers joined with Western allies in fighting the battles of France and Britain, and they eventually morphed into the fourth largest army in World War II.

In 1943, Begin found himself in Palestine, and by 1944 had begun to make contact with members of Irgun, the then-inactive Jewish underground. Begin worked tirelessly to resurrect the dormant organization. He ordered the Acre prison breakout (a failed attempt to rescue 41 of the 163 Jews held in the facility). He also ordered the attack on the British military command and the British Criminal Investigation Division administrative offices at the King David Hotel in 1945.

Begin was widely criticized for his role in the attack. What few acknowledge, however, is that he had strongly emphasized his desire to prevent civilian losses at all costs. Three calls were made: one to the hotel, one to the French Consulate, and another to the *Palestine Post*. All were warned that explosives had been placed in the King David Hotel. The call to the hotel was intercepted by a British official, who cavalierly said, "We don't take orders from the Jews."[98] As a result of his insouciance, the dead and injured toll was high: 91 killed and 45 injured.

According to an editorial by Benjamin Netanyahu, for decades the British refuted that any warning had been received, but in 1979, a British Member of Parliament provided proof that a warning had been given by members of the Irgun. One British officer overheard others in the hotel bar joking about a supposed threat of explosives having been planted in their headquarters. The officer left the hotel immediately and survived the bombing.[99]

Under Begin's guidance, the Irgun launched an attempt to import a load of weapons on the French ship *Atalena* in order to arm its members. Believing that Begin and his fighting force were about to stage a coup, Ben-Gurion ordered the ship to be sunk. Reluctantly, Begin disbanded the Irgun and assumed the role of opposition leader in the Knesset. He later became a passionate speaker *for* Zionism and *against* Germany's offer of restitution for the heinous crimes committed during the Holocaust.

In 1948, Begin founded the Herut Party, which in 1965 joined with the Gahal Party to set the stage for the emerging Likud Party. He became the party's first prime minister in 1973, followed by Yitzhak Shamir, Benjamin Netanyahu, Ariel Sharon, and then Benjamin Netanyahu for a second term. From the time of Israel's rebirth until 1977, the country was administered by coalition governments (i.e., several parties joined together to form a ruling body). A national unity government led by Golda Meir and consisting of all its political parties (except for two divisions of the Communist Party of Israel) governed during the Six-Day War in 1967. The day following the start of the war, Begin became a minister without portfolio in the Knesset. He served until 1970, when he resigned because of disagreements over the content of the Suez Canal cease-fire. Begin wanted one of the conditions of the peace treaty to be that Egyptian President Nasser would recognize Israel.

Begin was again elected prime minister in 1977. He represented his country during the Camp David Accords and managed to hammer out a peace agreement with Egypt's Anwar Sadat. That was followed two years later by an Israel–Egypt peace treaty.

Before his election to office, politics in the Jewish state had been controlled by the more secular Labor Party. Begin's Likud Party was led by strong military figures, such as Ariel Sharon, and undergirded by a progressively influential settler movement and small Orthodox religious groups. Likud voters used the biblical names of "Judea" and "Samaria" for the West Bank area and utilized the argument that the land of Israel had been given by God solely to the Jews. They contended this afforded them the privilege to make a home anywhere in the Land. This interpretation was widely welcomed by US Evangelicals, who agreed heartily with the prime minister's explanation.

When Begin and the Likud Party assumed leadership in Israel, the prime minister was the first to cultivate pro-Israel Evangelicals. It was apparently his belief that the sheer numbers in the Christian Right would provide strong support for Israel and should be courted by his party. Begin openly welcomed the most influential Evangelical leaders—Jerry Falwell, Pat Robertson, and Hal Lindsey, among others. His resolve to maintain a hold on the Land, which God had bestowed upon the Jewish people, and his employment of biblical precedents in defending his beliefs won him wide acceptance. He was determined not to give up one inch of the Holy Land to those demanding that Palestine be returned to its Arab neighbors.

When I interviewed Prime Minister Begin in 1980 for the book *Israel: America's Key to Survival,* he began our conversation by sharing his first meeting with President Carter. The two men were in the cabinet room when Mr. Carter asked a very negative question regarding the West Bank settlements, which he considered to be illegal. Rather than answer his question, the prime minister asked one of his own: Would the governor of Pennsylvania proclaim that anyone could live in Bethlehem, Shiloh, Hebron, or Bethel Park, Pennsylvania, except for Jews?

The president replied that it would be foolish; the governor would be accused of racism. Mr. Begin pointed out that he was in essence the governor of the state in which lay the original cities he had named. Then he asked, "Do you expect me to say that everyone could live in those cities except Jews? Of course not!"[100]

Mr. Begin continued:

> This land we occupy is *Eretz Israel*, the land of Israel, since the days of the prophet Samuel, three thousand years ago…even the Romans called us Judea until after the Bar-Kokhba revolt in the second century. Then, because the Jewish resistance had been so fierce and heroic, and because the Emperor Hadrian had suffered such severe casualties, he decided to try to remove all memory of the connection between that people and that land. The Romans had done it with Carthage, why not here? So he renamed the area *Syria et Palestina*, the name of our ancient enemies, the Philistines. So the word Palestine came into all languages. Thus the preamble to the British Mandate after World War I used these words: "recognition having been given to the historical connection between the Jewish people and Palestine." So, in spite

of Hadrian, nobody could forget that it was our land. Every intelligent person understands that Palestine is a misnomer for the land of Israel. So we have a right to live in Judea and Samaria, and we will live there. But that does not mean we will evict even one Arab from his village or town. We never wanted to do that. And for us living there today there is an even more press-ing need for these settlements. That is our national security. Without Jewish settlements in those hills, [our enemies] could easily hide in them and descend into the plain to kill our people whenever they liked.[101]

When asked about the seeming determination of the Arabs in the region to force the Jewish people from their homeland, Begin explained why this was unacceptable:

You know, there are twenty-one sovereign Arab states from the Persian Gulf to the shores of the Atlantic Ocean. I would like every man with a mole-cule of feeling of justice to ask himself: Should the Arab people have twenty-two states and the Jews none? If the Arabs occupied twenty-two sovereign states, we would be trapped on a narrow plain between the hills and the Mediterranean. They would get up there in those hills. . . and they would make a hostage of every child in Israel. They haven't abandoned their plan to "liquidate the Zionist entity," as they like to call us. No nation in the world would agree to that.

A Palestinian state is a mortal danger to Israel and a great peril to the Free World. And we never agreed to a Palestinian state at Camp David. What we agreed to was autonomy as a way to solve the problem of the Palestinian Arabs. With autonomy they could elect their own ministers of council to deal with daily affairs and we shall not interfere at all. This would be a great historic change for them. Under Turkish, British, and Jordanian occupation they lived under the whip. The only thing we want to do is retain the matter of security.[102]

In 1981—despite US objections, and perhaps providentially for much of the Western world—Mr. Begin proceeded with a plan to bomb Iraq's *Osirak* nuclear reactor. The efficacy of this move was perhaps never more apparent than during the 1991 Persian Gulf War. Upon being told of the bombing by his National Security Advisor Richard V. Allen, President Reagan responded with a wink and commented, "Boys will be boys." With the exception of the war in Lebanon in 1982, which exposed some philosophical differences between the two countries, Reagan's government favored Israel and emphasized her importance as an ally. Organizations favoring Israel labeled the president as having the "most pro-Israel ever" administration.

When Israel, in an attempt to secure its border with Lebanon, was drawn into a war in 1982, the outcome was devastating for Prime Minister Begin. He learned that Israeli troops had stood by while Lebanese Christian militiamen massacred hundreds of Palestinian refugees at the Sabra and Shatila camps. An investigation was ordered to determine culpability, and the conclusion was that, indeed, the soldiers had done nothing to stop the attack. The Begin government survived, but the prime minister, assaulted by screams of "murderer" even during the Knesset debates, was shaken both politically and personally.

On June 6, 1982, Beirut witnessed one of the most traumatic days in its history with air, sea, and land bombardments from all sides, as Israel sought to oust the infamous terrorist organization, the PLO, and put an end to attacks against Israeli cities in northern Israel. Within minutes of the attack, pink leaflets warning residents to flee were dropped from Israeli jets and littered the streets. Israel swept north to Beirut, driving the PLO northward. There was little bloodshed in the first three days. Most of the terrorists chose to run rather than fight. The Shi'ites and Christians in southern Lebanon were celebrating. Israel was at the point of entering Beirut and rooting out the PLO once and for all, but the Arab-favoring US State Department lobbied President Reagan to stop Israel.

The Lebanese Red Crescent (the equivalent of the American Red Cross) sent a picture to the president of a child with limbs blown off. He was told that the Israelis had done that, and that a holocaust was taking place in Lebanon. Reagan was deeply moved and disturbed. It was later discovered that the picture had been fabricated. The injuries to the child were not at all the result of the Lebanese invasion, but of a birth defect.

Under tremendous pressure, Prime Minister Begin hesitated for three weeks, during which time the PLO became entrenched in Beirut. I met with Begin in Jerusalem, and he asked me to host a Christian delegation at the Waldorf Astoria in New York City. It was the only Christian delegation with whom he would meet before his appointment with President Reagan on June 21, 1982. We joined in prayer for the prime minister and for his meeting with the president.

Before he flew back to Israel, Reuven Hecht, Mr. Begin's advisor, called from the White House to tell me that something "magical" had happened in the relationship between Menachem Begin and Ronald Reagan. President Reagan's attitude toward Begin completely changed, and some very significant but classified things had transpired in the meeting.

By that time, the prime minister had experienced three heart attacks and was suffering related medical issues. His burden became almost overwhelming when his wife, Aliza, to whom he had been married for forty-three years, died of heart failure. At the time, Begin was in the United States to deliver an address commemorating the 50th anniversary of the General Assembly of the Council of Jewish Federations. He flew home immediately. Following Aliza's death, the prime minister became increasingly lethargic, attending Parliament sessions but participating little. He submitted his resignation on August 28, 1983, and moved into his daughter Leah's apartment in Jerusalem. After his departure from politics, he was rarely seen outside the home. A very small group of friends maintained contact, as did Yehiel Kadashai, Begin's dear friend and former adviser, who paid daily visits to the ailing former leader to help him with correspondence.

Begin's most significant achievement as prime minister was the signing of a peace treaty with Egypt in 1979, for which he and Anwar Sadat shared the Nobel Prize for Peace. In the wake of the Camp David Accords, the Israel Defense Forces withdrew from the Sinai Peninsula, which was captured from Egypt in the Six-Day War. Later, Begin's government promoted the construction of Israeli settlements in the West Bank and the Gaza Strip. It was Begin who authorized the bombing of the *Osirak* nuclear plant in Iraq and the invasion of Lebanon in 1982 to fight PLO strongholds there, igniting the 1982 Lebanon War.

Menachem Begin, the man who had become the modern-day

advocate for Christian Zionism, died on March 9, 1992, at the age of seventy-eight. He had requested a simple burial—no state pomp and ceremony—and was buried on the Mount of Olives outside Jerusalem. Despite his wishes, a convoy of fifty buses and some 75,000 mourners walked the two-and-a-half-mile route from the funeral home to the burial site.

CHAPTER EIGHTEEN

INTO THE TWENTY-FIRST CENTURY

Do not forsake your own friend or your father's friend...

(PROVERBS 27:10, NKJV.)

Yitzhak Shamir served two terms as prime minister (1983–84 and 1986–1992). Before establishment of the State of Israel, he was a leader of the militant Zionist group Lehi. After its establishment he served in the Mossad (the national intelligence agency of Israel) between 1955 and 1965, was a Knesset Member, a Knesset Speaker and Foreign Affairs Minister. He was the country's third longest-serving prime minister after David Ben-Gurion and Benjamin Netanyahu.

As I left one of the meetings during the October 1991 Madrid Peace Conference, the Syrian foreign minister stopped me, pulled a picture of Yitzhak Shamir from his pocket and told me he intended to accuse the prime minister of being a terrorist. Shamir had been a member of the *Irgun* (an early Israeli paramilitary organization). I borrowed a cell phone and called Benjamin Netanyahu to relate what I had been told. The next morning before the beginning of Shabbat and in the presence of President George H.W. Bush, President Gorbachev, and other world leaders, Mr. Shamir stood and said, "I have to leave now. I am an Orthodox Jew, and I leave these proceedings to my able delegation." Thirty minutes after he departed, the Syrian foreign minister stood to speak but faced only an empty chair where Shamir had sat.

In 2004, Shamir's health declined with the progression of Alzheimer's disease, and he was moved to a nursing home. Yitzhak Shamir died on June 30, 2012.

Shimon Peres, who served twice as prime minister and as president, has been a member of 12 cabinets in a political career spanning over 66 years. Peres succeeded Rabin as party leader prior to the 1977 elections when Rabin stepped down. He held several diplomatic and military positions during and directly after Israel's War of Independence. At the age of 90, Peres is currently the world's oldest living head of state as well as the fourth oldest head of state ever under a republican constitution.

In an interview with President Peres, I asked if David Ben-Gurion fully understood the significance of his role in creating the modern-day State of Israel. He responded in the affirmative:

> No other nation has had so many prophets as we did and they really directed all of them. So now we are strong in prophesy and poor in administration. When Moses started to administrate he was mistaken for an expert. He told them how to organize the nation to a point the commanders were managers of ten and

managers of a 100. But we later found we don't have enough statesmen. We are better on prophets than on statesmen. He [Ben-Gurion] saw in the Bible the mandate of our existence, the source of our existence, and he brought the people back to the Bible, and the Bible back to the people with a little bit of statesmanship. Ben-Gurion was a genius.[103]

I also asked the president how he saw Israel's survival through several wars that could have been disastrous for the Jewish people. His response was heartening:

It was against all norms. What is a miracle? It is the abolishment of all norms. We were outgunned, outmanned. We have had a war before we have had a state, before we had an army. But the readiness of the men that sacrificed their lives was higher. So here, it was quality against quantities. Everybody fought like a lion.[104]

Peres was elected by the Knesset in June 2007 to a seven-year term as Israel's ninth president. It was a historical move by the governing body as it was the first time a former prime minister had been tapped to serve as the nation's president. In June 2012, US President Barack Obama presented the Israeli leader with the Presidential Medal of Freedom, the United States' highest civilian tribute, for his "meritorious contributions to world peace."

Benjamin Netanyahu is, at this writing, serving a second time as Prime Minister of Israel. He is also currently a member of the Knesset, the Chairman of the Likud party and Minister of Public Diplomacy and Diaspora Affairs. Born in Tel Aviv to secular Jewish parents, Netanyahu is the first Israeli prime minister born in Israel after the establishment of the state. Between 1956 and 1958, and again from 1963 to 1967, his family lived in the United States in a suburb of Philadelphia, where he attended and graduated from the Cheltenham High School and was active in a debate club. To this day, he speaks American English with a Philadelphia accent.

After graduating from high school in 1967, at the age of eighteen, Netanyahu returned to Israel to enlist in the IDF during the Six-Day War. One of the most daring raids in which he participated was a raid on Sabena Airlines flight 571:

> On May 8, 1972 a Boeing 707 passenger aircraft operating that service captained by English pilot Reginald Levy...was hijacked by four terrorists from the Black September organization and landed at Lod Airport (later Ben-Gurion International Airport.) The attack was planned by Ali Hassan Salameh and carried out by a group of two men and two women, armed with pistols, led by Ali Taha.
>
> Twenty minutes out of Vienna, the hijackers rushed the cockpit....Soon after the hijacking, the hijackers separated Jewish hostages from non-Jews and sent them to the back of the aircraft.... On May 9, 1972 at 4:00 p.m. the rescue operation began: a team of 16 Sayeret Matkal commandos [a special counter-terror-ism and hostage rescue force], led by Ehud Barak and

including Benjamin Netanyahu, both future Israeli Prime Ministers, approached the airplane. The commandos were disguised as airplane technicians in white overalls, and were able to convince the terrorists that the aircraft needed repair. The commandos stormed the aircraft and took control of the plane in ten minutes, killing both male hijackers and capturing the two women. All the passengers were rescued. Three of the passengers were injured, one of whom eventually died from her wounds.

Netanyahu was wounded during this operation. He was discharged from the IDF after six years of service having attained the rank of captain following the Yom Kippur War. Following his discharge, Netanyahu studied at MIT in Boston and received a B.S. in architecture and an M.S. in Management Studies. He also studied political science at MIT and Harvard University.[105]

Benjamin was devastated by the death of his eldest brother, Jonathan, the lone fatality during the famous 1976 raid on Entebbe to free passengers of an Air France plane hijacked by terrorists and flown to Uganda.[106]

My first meeting with my dear friend Benjamin took place when I visited the home of his father, Benzion, to offer my condolences on the anniversary of the death of his son. The elder Mr. Netanyahu was a considerate host. He greeted me graciously and invited me into his home. Soon thereafter a young man walked into the room. About thirty years old, he was dressed in a suit and carried himself with

resolve. He glanced at me and shyly smiled when his father introduced us.

I told him the purpose of my visit, and as I looked in Benjamin's
eyes, the pain at the loss of his brother was palpable. I stood slowly, put
my hand on his shoulder, and said, "You loved your brother Jonathan
as the Jonathan of old loved his friend David. From the ashes of your
despair will come strength from God. Yet unlike Jonathan, who died
in battle defending his country, you will accede to the seat of power.
One day you will become the prime minister of Israel, not once but
twice. The second time will be the most crucial in Israel's history."

Then I asked if I could pray with him. Benjamin acquiesced, and
I reached in my pocket for a small vial of oil I had purchased earlier
that day. I anointed his head with oil and prayed for the favor of God
upon his life. Since that time, Bibi, as he is widely known, has been a
more than capable leader of Israel, and has been compared by some
to British statesman Winston Churchill.

Beginning in 1982, Netanyahu served as Deputy Chief of Mission
under Ambassador Moshe Arens. That appointment was followed
by a stint as ambassador to the United Nations—a position he held
for four years. Soon after his return to Jerusalem in 1988, he ran for
office as a member of the Likud party and was elected to the Knesset.
He was appointed Deputy Minister of Foreign Affairs during which
time Israel endured the first Gulf War followed by the Madrid Peace
Conference.

In 1993, he was Likud's candidate for prime minister. He lost
that bid for election, but won the seat of prime minister in 1996 by
defeating Shimon Peres. When Netanyahu ran for prime minister
that year, US President Bill Clinton did not find him to be as malleable
as Prime Minister Yitzhak Rabin had been. In fact, Netanyahu posed
such a barrier to the president fulfilling his dreams for history, that

he did something unprecedented: Clinton sent his own democratic campaign advisors to try to help Shimon Peres win the election.

A few weeks before the elections, Rahm Emanuel, Clinton's senior advisor on internal affairs, arrived in Israel. Emanuel had gone to assess what could be expected in the elections and to coordinate the possibility of helping Peres's staff with the campaign. The American Embassy in Tel Aviv invited a number of Israeli political experts, such as Yitzhak Herzog, Yaron Ha'ezrahi, Rafi Smith, and others for a meeting with Emanuel. All the machinations were to no avail; Netanyahu held the day and won the election.

Right at the start of the 1999 election campaign in Israel, Clinton sent a very clear message as to what he wanted: he again dispatched the team that had run both of his successful election campaigns to lead Ehud Barak's campaign. Composed of James Carville, Stanley Greenberg and Bob Shrum, this team was said to be worth more than a million dollars, and regarding the activities for which the three were responsible, much more than that.

Stanley Greenberg had already been involved in the process of figuring ways to win against Netanyahu back in 1998. He kept in close contact with Barak. As the most prominent figure among the three, Greenberg did public opinion surveys and analyzed focus group data. While the general opinion in the US and Israeli press during 1998 was that Netanyahu would be in power for at least four more years, Greenberg found, and told Barak, that there was a way to beat Netanyahu. The method was to cross the security image threshold, and stick to the economy and social affairs—the same strategy Clinton had used to win his second term in office with the sleight-of-hand slogan "It's the economy, stupid!" It kept Americans focused on their wallets, and he did as he pleased while they weren't looking. That was the main input of the Americans, said Tal Silberstein, one of Barak's top advisors for the campaign. "They structured the research, they came with the insights, and we adapted it to Israel."[107]

Some of the top donors to Clinton and the Democratic Party were mobilized for Barak's campaign as though this were another election the Democrats must win.

Overall, the Labor Party spent between $50 and $80 million on its anti-Netanyahu contest, roughly ten times what Netanyahu's own Likud Party spent. In early 2000, the state comptroller of Israel produced a report that in doing so, the Labor Party had grossly violated strict Israeli campaign finance laws. The government fined the campaign an unprecedented $3.2 million.[108]

Clinton personally contributed to Ehud Barak by continuing his warm meetings with Arafat in the White House, while freezing out Prime Minister Netanyahu and receiving Barak and Yitzhak Mordechai, the two candidates running against Netanyahu in the election. "Clinton helped Barak more than he had to", says one of Barak's men.[109]

After his defeat by Ehud Barak, Netanyahu held several posts in the Knesset—Minister of Foreign Affairs and Minister of Finance—until 2009 when he formed a coalition government and became prime minister for the second time. Unfortunately, his second term coincided with that of President Barack Obama. Shortly after taking office, Obama did his best to alienate American Jews and their Israeli counterparts. He made every effort to visit Muslim countries, including two trips to Indonesia and Afghanistan, and one each to Turkey, Iraq, Saudi Arabia (where he was caught on camera bowing to King Abdullah), and Egypt. In an article for *Front Page Magazine*, Joseph Kline criticized Obama's treatment of Prime Minister Benjamin Netanyahu:

Obama's latest blast at Netanyahu recalls his snub of Netanyahu during the prime minister's first visit to the Obama White House in March 2010. Obama presented Netanyahu with a list of demands, including a halt to all settlement construction in East Jerusalem. When Netanyahu resisted Obama's charms, Obama picked up his marbles. He stormed out of the meeting and declared, "I'm going to the residential wing to have dinner with Michelle and the girls." Obama also refused the normal protocol of a joint photograph with the Israeli leader.[110]

In 2011 during a global summit, French leader Nicolas Sarkozy was captured by an open microphone intoning: "I cannot bear Netanyahu; he's a liar."[111] Obama's response, "I have to deal with him more often than you,"[112] was not designed to build a lasting relationship with the Israeli leader.

Rapport between Netanyahu and Obama reached a new low during the late 2013 breakthrough in negotiations with Iran, which the Israeli leader labeled—rightfully so, I believe—"a historic mistake." This is not a simple disagreement between two heads of state; it is a life-and-death debate that could cost Israel dearly.

In March 2013 Netanyahu was able to form another coalition that allowed him to retain a hold on the reins of government in Israel.

✦ ✦ ✦

Ehud Barak served as prime minister from 1999 to 2001. He held the posts of Minister of Defense and Deputy Prime Minister in Benjamin Netanyahu's second government from 2009 to 2013. He is a graduate in physics, mathematics, and economics from the Hebrew University of Jerusalem and Stanford University. Barak served as an officer in the Israel Defense Forces. Following a highly decorated career, he was appointed Chief of General Staff in 1991, serving until 1995. He announced that he would retire from politics after January 2013 election.

In 2010, Secretary of State Hillary Clinton was tapped to head a second round of peace talks between Israel and the Palestinians in Sharm-el-Sheikh–an Egyptian resort town on the Red Sea. There Netanyahu and Palestinian Authority President Mahmoud Abbas were expected to work out the framework for the implementation of an interim agreement. The demand was that all core issues were to be resolved within the one-year timeline laid out by President Obama.

Israeli Defense Minister Ehud Barak jumped into the fray. He had first set tongues wagging in March of 2008, when he told *Al-Jazeera* that some Jerusalem neighborhoods might become part of a Palestinian capital. "We can find a formula under which certain neighborhoods, heavily populated Arab neighborhoods, could become, in a peace agreement, part of the Palestinian capital that, of course, will include also the neighboring villages around Jerusalem," Barak said.[113]

Born in 1942 in Kibbutz Mishmar Hasharon, Barak joined the IDF at the age of seventeen. Having served as a Tank Brigade Commander, head of the IDF Intelligence Branch and as a soldier during both the 1967 and 1973 wars, Barak was ultimately awarded the Distinguished Service Medal and additional honors for bravery and operational merit.

Although not elected to the Knesset until 1996, Barak held the offices of Minister of the Interior and Minister of Foreign Affairs under Shimon Peres and Yitzhak Shamir. After his election to the Israel government in 1996, Barak served as a member of the Knesset Foreign Affairs and Defense Committee. That same year, he was tapped as Chairman of the Labor Party. Barak was elected prime minister in 1999.

As prime minister he pulled the Israel Defense Forces out of Lebanon, proposed giving the Golan Heights back to Syria, and even offered the late and unlamented Yasser Arafat the Temple Mount. Barak's "solution" for Jerusalem:

> West Jerusalem and 12 Jewish neighborhoods that are home to 200,000 residents will be ours. The Arab neighborhoods in which close to a quarter million Palestinians live will be theirs. There will be a special regime in place along with agreed upon arrangements in the Old City, the Mount of Olives, and the City of David.[114]

According to Barak, a special regime would be put in place along with agreed-upon arrangements in the Old City, the Mount of Olives and the City of David. In the negotiations between Netanyahu and Abbas (or Abu Mazen as he was known when he helped orchestrate the 1972 Munich Massacre), the Palestinian leader will be paid handsomely for his participation, and in turn will furtively fill the pockets of his Palestinian cabinet and legislators with U.S. tax-payer dollars.

This is the same Ehud Barak, who as prime minister publicly declared on Jerusalem Day, in June 2000—marking the city's reunification in the Six-Day War—that Israel's sovereign capital would never again be divided. He assured his audience:

Jerusalem shall forever remain ours, because it is in our souls. Never again will Jerusalem be under foreign sovereignty. Only someone who has no sense of reality, who does not understand anything about Israel's yearning and longing and the Jewish people's historical connection to Jerusalem for over 3,000 years would even consider making any concessions over the city.[115]

Having experienced Arab rule in part of Jerusalem prior to 1967, why would Ehud Barak again want to subject the Jewish people and Christians worldwide to such indignity? Israeli prime ministers have allowed themselves to be dragged from one bargaining table to another and have been forced again and again to give up land for a peace that has never materialized. The only thing the Jewish people have received from the Palestinians has been two *intifadas*, terrorist attacks too numerous to recount, civilians maimed and slaughtered, and the disdain of the world at large.

In December of 2000, Barak announced his resignation from the post of prime minister:

I will officially advise the president of my resignation (and) in 60 days...go to special elections for prime minister... Due to the emergency situation the country is in...And the need to continue reducing the violence and moving forward the chances of peace negotiations, I have decided to ask again for the mandate of the people of Israel.[116]

Barak's stunning pronouncement was seen as a cunning political maneuver. Only then-Knesset members could stand for reelection in specially-called balloting. He thought to deter the man he thought of as his primary opponent, Benjamin Netanyahu, who was not then a member of the Knesset. Barak erroneously supposed he could easily win over Likud Party leader, Ariel Sharon. A mere sixty days later, Sharon was in, but Barak remained in office as prime minister until his term had been completed in early 2001.

In 2007 Prime Minister Ehud Olmert selected Barak for the role of Deputy Prime Minister and Minister of Defense, two offices he continued to hold after Netanyahu was reelected prime minister in 2009. Ehud Barak declared in 2012 that he would retire from politics following the elections in January 2013.

Ariel Sharon, an Israeli statesman and retired general, served as Israel's eleventh prime minister. Sharon was born in 1928 at Kfar Malal. In 1942 at the age of fourteen, he enlisted in the Haganah. As a paratrooper and then an officer, he participated prominently in the 1948 War of Independence. While serving in the IDF, Sharon attended law school at Tel Aviv University.

Sharon commanded an armored division during the Six-Day War in 1967. He resigned from the military in 1972, but was reactivated during the Yom Kippur War in 1973. It was Sharon who led the troops crossing the Suez Canal, a move which ultimately led to victory for Israel and an eventual peace accord with Egypt.

Elected to the Knesset in 1973, Sharon withdrew in 1974 to serve as Security Advisor to Prime Minister Rabin. He was appointed Defense Minister in 1981 under Prime Minister Begin, a post he held during the Lebanon War. Remaining in the Knesset, he held the post of Minister without Portfolio and then Ministry of Industry and Trade from 1984-1990. This was followed by a stint as a member of the Foreign Affairs and Defense Committee.

Perhaps one of the most chaotic occurrences of Sharon's political career took place on September 28, 2000. He and a small group of people scheduled a visit to the Temple Mount, one of the holiest sites in all Judaism. The Palestinian Liberation Organization spread the word that Sharon had come to the area with a multitude of IDF soldiers. The truth is that Internal Security Minister Shlomo Ben-Ami allowed Sharon to go to the Temple Mount only with the approval of Jabril Rajoub, Palestinian Authority security chief. He assured Ben-Ami that if Sharon avoided the mosques there would be no problems. During Sharon's 34-minute stay, he was careful to meet the stated criteria. The following day, approximately 1,500 Palestinian youth rioted, throwing rocks at Israeli police who returned fire with rubber-coated bullets. Four people were killed and 200 wounded, including fourteen Israeli policemen.

Fatah leader, Marwan Barghouti, initiator of the riot told *Al-Hayat,* a daily Arabic language newspaper:

> The night prior to Sharon's visit, I participated in a panel on a local television station and I seized the opportunity to call on the public to go to the Aksa Mosque in the morning, for it was not possible that Sharon would reach al-Haram al- Sharif [the Temple Mount area] just so, and walk away peacefully.[117]

Although Palestinians claimed that the Sharon visit was the cause of the violence, US Senator George Mitchell and the committee appointed to investigate the occurrence concluded:

In this view, Palestinian violence was planned by the PA leadership, and was aimed at "provoking and incurring Palestinian casualties as a means of regaining the diplomatic initiative."[118]

In 2001, Sharon was elected prime minister by special election. President George Bush first met Sharon when he was governor of Texas. When they next met it would be over tea in the Oval Office in March 2001 just months after Mr. Bush's inauguration. The president indicated to Mr. Sharon that he would strongly support Israel. An anonymous source in attendance reported that Bush indicated he would use force if necessary.[119]

In December 2005 Sharon suffered a minor stroke that doctors assured him would cause no permanent damage. Sadly, that was not to be. On January 4, 2006, Ariel Sharon suffered a massive brain hemorrhage which left him in a permanent vegetative state. His duties as prime minister were assumed by Deputy Prime Minister Ehud Olmert. After eight years in a coma, Ariel Sharon died on January 11, 2014 at the age of 85.

Ehud Olmert, former mayor of Jerusalem, held the office of prime minister from 2006 to 2009. He had previously held the post of cabinet minister for two terms. Interspersed with those duties, he served as mayor of Jerusalem for ten years—from 1993 to 2003. In 2003 Olmert was re-elected to the Knesset where he had earlier served eight terms. He became a cabinet minister and acting prime minister in the government of Ariel Sharon.

Facing a challenge for leadership of the Kadima political party in

2008, Olmert announced that he would not seek re-election as party head and would resign from his position as prime minister immediately after a new Kadima leader was named. Attempts at forming a new government were unsuccessful, and instead an election was scheduled for February 2009. Israeli President Peres then chose Benjamin Netanyahu to become the new prime minister and asked him to form a Coalition Government, after there was no clear victory in the elections. Netanyahu succeeded Olmert in March 2009. In August of that same year an indictment against Olmert was served at the Jerusalem District Court. The indictment included the following five criminal counts: obtaining by fraud under aggravating circumstances, fraud, breach of trust, falsifying corporate documents, and tax evasion. Olmert was convicted on one count of breach of trust over the investment center case and given a one year suspended sentence. He was exonerated over two others. According to a *Los Angeles Times* article:

> The lighter sentence clears the way for Olmert to return to politics if he wishes, though he is still fighting an indictment in a separate bribery case involving a real estate deal during his tenure as Jerusalem mayor...Olmert has shrugged off questions about his political future, though he called the court's ruling and its sentence a vindication. He had long characterized the corruption case against him as a political witch hunt.[120]

CHAPTER NINETEEN

BLESSINGS ABUNDANTLY

*Happy are you, O Israel! Who is like you, a people
saved by the LORD, The shield of your help And the
sword of your majesty! Your enemies shall submit to
you, And you shall tread down their high places."*

(DEUTERONOMY 33:29, NKJV)

J ust as God blesses those who stand with Israel, so He has
blessed His Chosen People. Media focus on this tiny Middle
Eastern country is normally consumed with conflicts between the
Jews and their neighbors who decry the very existence of God's
Chosen People. Rather than be cowed by all the negative attention
derived from international criticism, Israelis have chosen to take
the high road and continue to work on inventions and discoveries,
and boast a society that benefits the world population in general.

The culture of Israel combines some of the best of Eastern ethnic
and religious traditions, along with those of Western civilization.
The cities of Tel Aviv and Jerusalem are considered by most to be the
artistic centers of the country.

Ethnicity is represented by immigrants from five continents and
more than one hundred countries. Significant subcultures are added

by the Arabs, Russian Jews, Ethiopian Jews and the Ultra-Orthodox. All the while, it is a family-oriented society with a strong sense of community.

In the nineteenth and twentieth centuries, the then-existing culture was infused with both the mores and traditions of those who had lived outside Palestine or modern Israel. David Ben-Gurion led the trend of blending the many immigrants who, in the first years of the state, arrived from Europe, North Africa, and Asia, into one melting pot that would unify newer immigrants with veteran Israelis.

Gradually, Israeli society has become more interconnected. Critics consider it to have been a necessity in the first years of the state, but now aver that there is no longer a need for it. Others, mainly Mizrahi Jews (descended from local communities of the Middle East, as opposed to those from Europe), along with Holocaust survivors, have criticized the earlier move to unify the country. According to them, they were forced to conceal their diaspora heritage and philosophies brought from other countries, and adopt a new Sabra culture.

Since the Jewish infusion from other countries classical music in Israel has been especially vibrant as hundreds of music teachers and students, composers, instrumentalists and singers, as well as thousands of music lovers, streamed into the country, driven first by the threat of Nazism in Europe. Israel is home to several world-class classical music ensembles, such as the Israel Philharmonic and the New Israeli Opera. The founding of The Palestine Philharmonic Orchestra (today's Israel Philharmonic Orchestra) in 1936 marked the beginning of Israel's classical music scene. In the early 1980s, the New Israeli Opera began staging productions, reviving public enthusiasm for operatic works. Russian immigration in the 1990s boosted the classical music genre with new talents and music lovers.

The Israel Philharmonic Orchestra plays at venues throughout the country and abroad, and almost every city has its own orchestra, many of the musicians having emigrated from the former Soviet Union. Israeli filmmakers and thespians have won acclimation at international film festivals. In recent years, Jewish literature has been widely translated, and several Israeli writers have gained international recognition.

While Hebrew and Arabic are the official languages of the State, an incredible 83 tongues are spoken in the country. As new immigrants arrived, learning Hebrew became a national goal. Special schools for the teaching of Hebrew were set up all over the country.

The initial works of Hebrew literature in Israel were written by authors rooted in the world and traditions of European Jewry. Native-born writers who published their works in the 1940s and 1950s, often called the "War of Independence generation," have brought a 'Sabra' mentality and culture to their writing. The word 'Sabra' originally described the new Jew that had emerged in Palestine, particularly when contrasted with the old Jew from overseas.

From the beginning of the twentieth century, visual arts in Israel have shown a creative orientation, influenced both by the West and East, as well as by the land itself. Their developments, the character of the cities, and stylistic trends have been imported from art centers abroad. In painting, sculpture, photography, and other art forms, the country's varied landscape is prominent: the hill terraces and ridges produce special dynamics of line and shape; the foothills of the Negev, the prevailing grayish-green vegetation, and the clear luminous light result in distinctive color effects; and the sea and sand affect surfaces. Local landscapes, concerns, and politics ensure the uniqueness of Israeli art.

Traditional folk dances of Israel include the Hora and Yemenite dances. Modern dance in Israel has won international acclaim. Israeli

choreographers are considered among the most versatile and original international creators working today. Notable dance companies
include the Batsheva Dance Company and the Kibbutz Contemporary
Dance Company. People come from all over Israel and many other
nations for the annual dance festival in Karmiel staged each July. It is
the largest celebration of dance in Israel, featuring three or four days
and nights of dancing, with 5,000 or more dancers and a quarter of
a million spectators in the capital of Galilee. Begun as an Israeli folk
dance event, festivities now include performances, workshops, and
open dance sessions for a variety of dance forms and nationalities.
Famous companies and choreographers from all over the world have
come to Israel to perform and give master classes.

Israel has the highest number of museums per capita in the world,
with over 200 bringing millions of visitors annually. Jerusalem's Israel
Museum has a special pavilion showcasing the Dead Sea scrolls and a
large collection of Jewish religious art, Israeli art, sculptures and Old
Masters paintings. Newspapers appear in dozens of languages, and
every city and town boasts a local newsletter.

The emergence of Hebrew theatre predated the state by nearly
fifty years. The first amateur Hebrew theatre group was active in
Palestine from 1904 to 1914. The first professional Hebrew theatre,
Habimah, (The Stage) was founded in Moscow in 1917, and moved to
Palestine in 1931, where it became the country's national theater. The
Ohel Theatre was founded in 1925 as a workers' theatre that explored
socialist and biblical themes.

Filmmaking in Israel has undergone major development since
its inception in the 1950s. Initial features produced and directed by
Israelis often tended, like Israeli literature of the period, to be cast in
the heroic mold. Even some recent films remain deeply rooted in the

Israeli experience, dealing with such subjects as Holocaust survivors and their children. Others examine issues of modern-day Israeli life.

The Israeli film industry continues to gain worldwide recognition through international awards nominations. For three years consecutively, Israeli films were nominated for Academy Awards. The Spielberg Film Archive at the Hebrew University of Jerusalem is the world's largest repository of film material on Jewish themes as well as on Jewish and Israeli life.

Israel's diverse culture is also manifested in its cuisine, a combination of local ingredients and dishes and diasporic dishes from around the world. An Israeli 'fusion' cuisine has developed, with the adoption and continued adaptation of elements of various Jewish styles of cuisine and many foods traditionally eaten in the Middle East. Israeli cuisine is understandably influenced by geography, featuring foods common in the Mediterranean region such as olives, chickpeas, dairy products, fish, and fresh fruits and vegetables.

The main meal is usually lunch rather than dinner. Jewish holidays influence the cuisine, with many traditional foods served. Shabbat (the Jewish day of rest and seventh day of the week) dinner, eaten on Friday night, is a significant meal in many Israeli homes. While not all Jews in Israel keep kosher, the observance of *kashrut* influences the menu in homes, public institutions and many restaurants. Kashrut is the set of Jewish dietary laws. Food that may be consumed according to Jewish law is termed "kosher" in English, or fit for consumption. Most of the basic laws of kashrut are derived from the Torah's Books of Leviticus and Deuteronomy. While the Torah does not state the rationale for most kashrut laws, many reasons have been suggested, including philosophical, practical and hygienic.

Physical fitness is important in Jewish culture, and this approach received a boost in the 19th century from the physical culture campaign of Max Nordau. The Maccabiah Games, an Olympic-style event for Jewish athletes, was inaugurated in the 1930s, and has been held in Israel every four years since then.

To date, Israel has won seven Olympic medals since its initial victory in 1992, including a gold medal in windsurfing at the 2004 Summer Olympics. Unquestionably the most memorable Olympics took place in 1972 in Munich, Germany, when members of Black September, a militant extremist group with ties to Arafat's Fatah organization, took eleven members of Israel's Olympic team hostage. After hours of negotiations between the leaders of the terrorist group and the German police, the eleven Israelis, five terrorists, and one German police officer would die during a bloody gun battle at the NATO airbase in Firstenfeldbruck.

PLO leader Yasser Arafat blithely swore he was not responsible for the actions of the renegade arm of Fatah. However, Abu Daoud, the man who helped the terrorists scale the walls of the Olympic village on September 5, 1972, refutes that assertion both in his memoirs and in an interview with *Sports Illustrated*.

Daoud's book, *Palestine: From Jerusalem to Munich*, confirms "what many terrorism experts and Israeli officials long suspected...that the Black September organization, which Yasser Arafat and the Palestine Liberation Organization always claimed was a renegade outfit, was in fact tightly controlled by Arafat. Even more shocking, however, was the allegation that [a top Arafat deputy, Mahmoud] Abbas... provided the financing for the massacre."[121][122]

Jealousy could likely be the reason fundamental Islam fanatically targets not only the Jews in Israel but the United States' citizens, according to noted Jewish lecturer, Irwin N. Graulich:

> In addition, during that same period [1948–current], Israel totally embarrassed the entire Arab/Muslim

world by defeating them economically, technologically, intellectually, culturally, religiously, medically, socially and morally. Since America's accomplishments are that much greater, it is no wonder that the Arab/Muslim nations feel totally frustrated. They subscribe to a religious belief that promises world greatness, strength and domination, while reality shows them trailing very far behind.[123]

Not only are there numerous inventive and creative people in Israel, there is a sense of generosity and compassion few of its neighbors deign to recognize and/or accept. For example, a World News article on NBC.com revealed a heartwarming story of unheralded assistance to a family in Syria:

> The young girl was dying when she arrived in the land of her country's enemy. A heart condition had left the 4-year-old Syrian struggling to walk or even talk. But in Israel—a country still in a state of cease-fire with Syria after the Yom Kippur War four decades ago—she found her saviors. Admitted in early 2013 to the Wolfson Medical Center, south of Tel Aviv, she underwent life-saving surgery. The girl is now recuperating on a ward along with children from the West Bank and Gaza Strip, Sudan, Romania, China and Israel. "She would have definitely died if she wouldn't have arrived here," Ilan Cohen, one of the doctors who treated her, said. "A lot of patients arrive here from enemy countries and view Israelis as demons. They are surprised that we are human without horns on our heads," he added. "This is

the first time they see Israelis without a uniform and I think it's a good surprise." Her treatment was the work of "Save a Child's Heart," an Israeli nonprofit organization started by the late Ami Cohen, who moved to Israel from the United States in 1992. He joined the staff of the Wolfson with a vision to mending children's hearts from around the world. The organization he began has since helped treat 3,200 children from 45 countries.[124]

The story told of the mother's fear of reprisal upon their return home. It seems incredible that hatred could be so strong as to fault a family for trying to save a beloved child; and yet it is. The other side of that story is the men and women who provided the techniques and services that saved the life of the young girl.

In the sixty-five-plus years since Israel was recognized as a state in the mid-1940s, amazing strides have been made in science, technology, medicine, farming, and communication thanks to the diligence of the people who live in the Holy Land.

There have been some mind-boggling discoveries in the field of medicine:

In 1954, Ephraim Frei discovered the effects of magnetism on the human body. His exploration led to the advancement of the T-scan system, a breakthrough in the advancement for detecting breast cancer.

In 1956, Professor Leo Sachs developed amniocentesis to uncover the benefits of examining amniotic fluid in the diagnosis of prenatal anomalies. It has become a major obstetrics tool in aiding pregnant women and their unborn babies. In 1963, Sachs became the first to grow lab-bred blood cells, a tool used to help chemotherapy patients.

Ada Yonath, awarded the Nobel Prize in Chemistry in 2009, laid the groundwork for the advent of drugs that are used to treat some strains of leukemia, glaucoma and HIV, as well as antipsychotic and antidepressant medicines.

The time it takes to heal a broken bone may soon be cut in half thanks to an intelligent "wrapping paper" from Israeli company Regenecure. The "wrapping paper," technically called a membrane implant, enables bones to heal faster and more evenly by attracting healing stem cells and fluids while keeping soft tissues from growing around the broken bone. The membrane looks and feels like plastic wrap, it can be cut with a pair of scissors to fit any bone in the body and is naturally absorbed into the body after 10 months. The material has already been used in dental procedures to replace bone grafts and has been used on animal bones, where it cut the healing time in half when used along with a traditional bone graft.[125]

Added to these inspired and ingenious men and women are Meir Wilcheck, the discoverer of blood detoxification; Elli Canaani, inventing a drug to treat chronic myelogenous leukemia; Avram Hershko and Aaron Ciechanover, improving cellular research to better determine the cause of ailments such as cervical cancer and cystic fibrosis; and, the creation of Copaxone, the only non-interferon treatment for multiple sclerosis. These are only a few of the many advancements in detection and management of a myriad of diseases and serious health conditions. Amazing and innovative techniques have originated in the field of spinal surgery, treatment of Parkinson's disease, tumor and small bowel (Pillcam) imaging, in first-aid in the form of innovative field dressings that are now the global standard, the Lubocollar used to treat trauma patients worldwide, helping paraplegics walk, treating diabetes, artificial limb improvements, and more.

Israel has silently and steadily blossomed into an enthusiastic and impressive proving ground for entrepreneurs and inventors. In the field of technology, just a few examples are:

> The Uzi machine gun developed by Major Uzi Gaf; millions are in use globally.
>
> The WEIZAC computer introduced by the Weizmann Institute in 1955 was one of the first, "large-scale stored program computers in the world."[126]
>
> A solar energy system that today is used to power the majority of hot water heaters worldwide.

We must also include color holograms, desalination processes, drone aircraft, computer processors, digital information sharing, terrorist detectors, and thousands of other technology-based products.[127]

Farmers worldwide have enjoyed the benefits of advances such as the super cucumber and disease resistant potatoes, improved food storage systems, drip irrigation, extracting water from the air, bee preservation, advanced fish farming, water purification, and more ecologically-friendly food packaging.

Add to this list baby monitors, instant messaging, office

equipment, the Babylon computer dictionary, flash drives, micro-computers, miniature video cameras, computer chips, advances in airport safety, and missile defense systems. It is an incredible list; a testament to the ingenuity and inventiveness of the Jewish people.

Many of these inventions capture Nobel prizes for those responsible, but the awards are not confined to science and technology. Now, they are shared by authors, poets, mathematicians, peacemakers and economists.

It is amazing to discover that 22 percent of all individual Nobel Prize winners worldwide between the organization's inception in 1901 and 2012 have been of Jewish descent. That alone is an incredible number to contemplate.

Two Jewish laureates were honored after having endured incarceration in concentration camps during the Holocaust: Imre Kertész and Elie Wiesel. At the age of 14, Kertész was rounded up with other Hungarian Jews and sent first to Auschwitz, and then to Buchenwald. He was a prolific writer whose best-known novel, *Sorstalanság*, (Fatelessness) unveiled the experiences of a teenage boy who was sent to the camps at Auchwitz, Buchenwald, and Zeitz. He was awarded the Prize in 2002 "for writing that upholds the fragile experience of the individual against the barbaric arbitrariness of history."[128]

Elie Wiesel, who was also sent to Auschwitz, Buna, and Buchenwald during World War II, received the Nobel Prize in 1986. The committee characterized him as a "messenger to mankind," stating that through his struggle to come to terms with "his own personal experience of total humiliation and of the utter contempt for humanity shown in Hitler's death camps", as well as his "practical work in the cause of peace", Wiesel delivered a powerful message "of peace, atonement and human dignity" to humanity.[129]

In 2009, I was invited to speak at a communications and law conference held at Ariel University in Israel. It was my distinct privilege to meet Nobel Laureate, Professor Robert Aumann of Hebrew University, and founder of the Game Theory Society. I had been asked to attend the conference by my good friend, the late Ron Nachman, mayor of the city of Ariel, and was able to see firsthand the genius of the professor.

Born in Germany, Aumann and his family escaped just fourteen days before the ravages of *Kristallnacht,* a series of coordinated attacks against Jews in Nazi Germany and parts of Austria. In a 2005 Jerusalem Post article, journalist Hilary Leila Krieger wrote:

> The year was 1938 and the Aumanns desperately wanted to leave their native Germany. Salvation dangled in the form of US visas, available for passport holders who swore they wouldn't be a burden on their new country and passed a test of basic American terms and concepts. Robert "Yisrael" Aumann saw his parents studying hard and thought he should do likewise. After his parents passed the exam, his mother confided in the consular official that her son had also prepared very diligently and would like to be presented with a test question. The consul leaned over to the eight-year-old and asked him to name the president of the United States - at the time Franklin D. Roosevelt. Aumann answered enthusiastically: "Rosenfeld!" The consul burst out laughing. He also granted the boy a visa. The qualities Aumann displayed at a ripe age - a propensity for hard work, a fierce intellect and a commitment to Jewish values - and has continued to

exhibit throughout adulthood, earned him [the 2013] Nobel prize in economics.[130]

When presented with the Nobel Prize in 2005, the Professor titled his acceptance speech "War and Peace." He said to the assembled audience:

> Simplistic peacemaking can cause war, while arms race, credible war threats and mutually assured destruction can reliably prevent war.[131]

Ernest Hemingway wrote: "The world breaks everyone, and afterward, some are strong at the broken places."[132] Adversity has forged a people of great strength, resiliency, insight, and intelligence. As the psalmist wrote in Psalm 115:12, ESV: "The LORD has remembered us; he will bless us; he will bless the house of Israel..."

The list of brilliant men and women who have sprung from Abraham, Isaac, and Jacob is long and impressive: Nelly Sachs, Shmuel Yosef Agnon, Saul Bellow, Ada Yonath, Isaac Bashevis Singer, Dan Shechtman, Menachem Begin, Yitzhak Rabin, and Shimon Peres.

Brilliance, tenacity, and determination are not confined to Nobel Prize winners. It is found in all men and women who are determined to work hard, teach their children, bless their neighbors, feed the hungry, extend a helping hand to those in need, and build on the foundations of the past to reap the blessings of Jehovah, He who blesses the House of Israel.

Twenty-first century Jewish scientists and inventors can again be found at the forefront of invention and technological genius. Just as in past decades, Israelis are not simply marginal participants in new and innovative discoveries; they are at the very epicenter of modern ingenuity.

The Word of God is very explicit in Genesis 12:3 which records, "I [God] will bless them that bless thee"; and in the New Testament book of Luke:

> Give, and it will be given to you. A good measure, pressed down, shaken together and running over, will be poured into your lap. For with the measure you use, it will be measured to you, (Luke 6:38.)

CHAPTER TWENTY

THE VALUE OF INTERCESSORS

I have set watchmen upon thy walls, O Jerusalem,
which shall never hold their peace day nor night:
ye that make mention of the LORD, keep not
silence, And give him no rest, till he establish, and
till he make Jerusalem a praise in the earth,

(ISAIAH 62:6-7, KJV.)

God has a purpose and a plan for our lives. The lives of those in the United States and the nation of Israel are dependent on prayer. His will and His blessings are bound up in prayer. The fuel that moves the engine of humanity is prayer. Almighty God created the nation of Israel. His purposes and plans are more important than anything Man can do. Conversely, to engage in prayer is one of the most important things we can do. God invited His people:

Call unto me, and I will answer thee, and shew thee
great and mighty things, which thou knowest not, (Jeremiah 33:3, KJV.)

As Jeremiah prophesied to the Jewish people during their captivity in Babylon, he was given this promise. The Jews were ultimately delivered from captivity, and revival came to Israel.

Prayer is a vital part of our relationship with our heavenly Father. If you were to ask any John Doe on the street to loan you $200, it is highly likely he would simply laugh. If, however, you were to approach someone of longstanding friendship—someone who knew that you were honest, honorable, and trustworthy, the odds of a loan being granted would increase exponentially. God wants His people to build a relationship with Him, to communicate with Him frequently, to trust Him and to recognize His sovereignty in our lives as did men such as Daniel, Abraham, and David.

Daniel in Babylon (Iraq) refused to obey the decree of the king. The king had ordered that no one ask any petition of any God or man for 30 days. Daniel who had faced Jerusalem and prayed three times each a day (Daniel 6:1-23) continued to pray just as he had done before this command. The God Daniel worshipped honored him and shut the mouths of the lions in their den. Daniel's prayers prevailed in the midst of Israel's captivity in Babylon and beyond:

> For thus saith the LORD, That after seventy years be accomplished at Babylon I will visit you, and perform my good word toward you, in causing you to return to this place. For I know the thoughts that I think toward you, saith the LORD, thoughts of peace, and not of evil, to give you an expected end. Then shall ye call upon me, **and ye shall go and pray unto me, and I will hearken unto you**. And ye shall seek me, and find me, when ye shall search for me with all your heart. And I will be found of you, saith the LORD: and I will turn

*away your captivity, **and I will gather you from all the nations**, and from all the places whither I have driven you, saith the LORD; and I will bring you again into the place whence I caused you to be carried away captive"* (Emphasis mine, Jeremiah 29:10-14, KJV.)

Abraham is a striking example of the power of prayer. For Lots' sake, he interceded for Sodom and God delayed judgment. He would have even spared Sodom for ten righteous souls (Genesis 18:20-33). Abraham thought surely Lot, his wife, his daughters, his sons and sons-in-law would be righteous and total more than ten; he was wrong. Even Lot's wife turned to look longingly at the worldly treasures and pleasures she was leaving behind.

Whenever Abraham, a praying man, pitched his tent and camped for a season with his household, he erected an altar of sacrifice and of prayer. In another example, God said to Abimelech, Abraham *"is a prophet, and he shall pray for thee, and thou shalt live"* (Genesis 20:7, KJV). God heard Abraham's prayers, and He hears ours. Moses interceded forty days for Israel. The result was a mighty deliverance for the nation. God's movement to bring Israel from bondage had its inception in prayer (Exodus 2:23-25; 3:9.)

September 11, 2001 was an assault from hell, planned by demonic spirits, and carried out by their representatives on earth. The terrorist attacks in Israel are also a result of the same evil powers, ones that cannot be defeated without prayer. Praying saints are God's agents to carry out His will on earth. America is helpless without prayer, as is Israel. If Daniel and Abraham found it necessary to pray regularly, and if Jesus said that He could do nothing without prayer, then we surely cannot hope to accomplish anything of eternal significance and value without prayer.

A Christian who refuses to pray is like a swimmer refusing to get in the water. All the talking in the world of how much we know about swimming will only bring those we are trying to influence to laughter. For a Christian, to refuse to make prayer the number one priority is like saying to al Qaeda, "We refuse to fight; you win!" Our weapons of war and our Commander in Chief are waiting to win the battle; we only need to speak the Word:

> *Then one of the seraphim flew to me, having in his hand a live coal which he had taken with the tongs from the altar. And he touched my mouth with it, and said: "Behold, this has touched your lips; Your iniquity is taken away, And your sin purged,"* (Isaiah 6:6-7, ASV.)

Darkness flees when we pray! Demons tremble when we pray. Heaven moves when we pray, and angels receive assignments when we pray. Prayer affects three realms: The Divine, the Angelic, and the Human. Without it, demons rule uncontested (Ephesians 6.)

Hannah's petition for a son (1 Samuel 1:11) began a great prayer movement in Israel. Her prayers brought about the birth of Samuel the Prophet who would anoint a shepherd boy to become the king of Israel and rule over the City of David. Samuel was a man of prayer. He stood before the people on one occasion and said, *"Far be it from me that I should sin against the Lord in ceasing to pray for you"* (1 Samuel 12:23.)

We cannot make contact with God without prayer. If we don't make contact with Him, no matter how sincere our intentions, we will see no change in the circumstances of our life.

When King Solomon prayed at the dedication of the Temple, God exhibited His great power and revealed His plan to Solomon (2

Chronicles 7:12-15). He called unto God in prayer and Jehovah was there:

> *Then you shall call, and the Lord will answer; You shall cry, and He will say, "Here I am," (Isaiah 58:9.)*

King Solomon prophesied that a mighty national revival was coming to Israel. It has not happened yet; and it can only come through the power of prayer. You and I can help usher in that revival through prayer.

Hezekiah was another example of God's response to prayer and repentance. During a dark hour of Israel's history, the Assyrians demanded heavy tribute from the king.

> *And Hezekiah prayed to the Lord: "Lord, the God of Israel, enthroned between the cherubim, you alone are God over all the kingdoms of the earth. You have made heaven and earth. Give ear, Lord, and hear; open your eyes, Lord, and see; listen to the words Sennacherib has sent to ridicule the living God. "It is true, Lord, that the Assyrian kings have laid waste these nations and their lands. They have thrown their gods into the fire and destroyed them, for they were not gods but only wood and stone, fashioned by human hands. Now, Lord our God, deliver us from his hand, so that all the kingdoms of the earth may know that you alone, Lord, are God,"* (II Kings 19:14-19, NIV.)

In response, Hezekiah stripped the Temple of its gold and silver in order to meet the demand. Still that was not enough. The Assyrians mounted an attack against the city. Hezekiah bowed before God, and prayed. God responded with an amazing victory! He sent a plague that killed 185,000 Assyrian soldiers.

In great gratitude for God's mercy, Hezekiah cleansed, repaired, and reopened the Temple of God. Worship of Jehovah was restored; daily sacrifices were resumed. The Passover Feast was celebrated by the nation.

The world has been trying to find an answer to the ongoing crisis in the Bible land. That answer is in your hands and mine—through intercessory prayer:

> *You do not have because you do not ask,* (James 4:2, NIV.)

> *So I say to you, ask, and it will be given to you; seek, and you will find; knock, and it will be opened to you. For everyone who asks receives, and he who seeks finds, and to him who knocks it will be opened,* (Luke 11:9-10, NIV.)

You may be like the prophet Jonah who did everything but pray. He knew what God wanted him to do, but kept resisting. Jonah fled, and ended up in the belly of a big fish. There he cried out to God against whom he had sinned. God intervened and caused the fish to vomit Jonah out onto dry land. Even the fish of the sea are subject to the power of prayer! When those in Nineveh saw this stinking, praying prophet, they repented quickly and God sent revival.

CHAPTER TWENTY-ONE

STAND WITH ISRAEL

Their descendants will be recognized and honored among the nations. Everyone will realize that they are a people the Lord has blessed,

(ISAIAH 61:9, NLT.)

I f the revealed will of God and the record of history mean anything to followers of the Jewish Messiah—as they must—we can only conclude that Christians have a God-ordained duty to love and support the Jewish people in every possible way. More than a duty, it should be considered a great privilege to bless the people of the Book who have blessed us; especially by being the channels through which our sacred Bible and our precious salvation have come to us.

Jesus Himself said that the Son of Man will pass judgment on the nations when He comes to rule on His glorious throne as King of Kings:

> *When the Son of Man comes in his glory, and all the angels with him, then he will sit on his glorious throne,*
> (Matthew 25:31, ESV.)

He went on to reveal that the main criteria for judgment would be how Gentiles treated His brethren in the House of Israel:

> *And the King will answer them, "Truly, I say to you,*
> *as you did it to one of the least of these my brothers, you*
> *did it to me,"* (Matthew 25:40, ESV.)

Of course, we who are faithful followers of the Great Shepherd are the Lord's spiritual brethren. Jesus' Jewish kin, however, will always be His basic family stock, and thus His particular brethren. There is good reason to believe that these are the ones to whom the Lord referred in Matthew 25.

Paul confirms that Christians are to especially bless the Jewish people. Indeed, these Scriptures reveal that Jewish Believers in Jesus—who are once again greatly multiplying in our day—should be the direct recipients of financial blessings from Gentile Believers:

> *For it pleased those from Macedonia and Achaia to*
> *make a certain contribution for the poor among the saints*
> *who are in Jerusalem. It pleased them indeed, and they*
> *are their debtors. For if the Gentiles have been partakers*
> *of their spiritual things, their duty is also to minister to*
> *them in material things,* (Romans 15:26-27, NIV.)

Christians have been blessed beyond words by being grafted into the rich olive tree of Israel. Therefore, we must minister to the Jewish Believers in the Promised Land in many ways, but especially by actively upholding their right to live there. This is doubly important since widespread anti-Semitism has again reared its ugly head in recent years.

We Christians have a date with destiny! The Church cannot fulfill its eternal purpose if it is not salt and light to Israel (Acts 1:8.) When we support Israel, we are standing with the only nation created by an act of God: The royal land grant (See Appendix C) that was given to Abraham and his seed through Isaac and Jacob, with an everlasting and unconditional covenant.

> *My mercy will I keep for him for evermore, and my covenant shall stand fast with him. His seed also will I make to endure forever, and his throne as the days of heaven. If his children forsake my law, and walk not in my judgments; If they break my statutes, and keep not my commandments; then will I visit their transgression with the rod, and their iniquity with stripes. Nevertheless my loving kindness will I not utterly take from him, nor suffer my faithfulness to fail. My covenant will I not break, nor alter the thing that is gone out of my lips. Once have I sworn by my holiness that I will not lie unto David. His seed shall endure forever, and his throne as the sun before me. It shall be established forever as the moon, and as a faithful witness in heaven. Selah, (Psalm 89:28-37.)*

On December 12, 1988, the United Nations invited Yasser Arafat to speak in Geneva. The goal was to unify the world behind his plan for a PLO state in Israel. He was asked to simply say the words, "I denounce terrorism." He did...not only then, but thousands of times before his death, mostly after another round of terrorist murdered Jews under his orders and with his financing.

In December 1988, I flew to Geneva, Switzerland, and checked into the Hilton Hotel. I believed God would open doors with leaders of nations, and to my amazement, I was allowed into the facility where the General Assembly meetings were being held. It looked as if I would only be permitted to sit upstairs in the nosebleed section. After PLO Chairman Yasser Arafat had delivered his speech, it was concluded that he had not clearly stated that he would denounce terrorism as had been expected. He was forced to hold a press conference, which was predominantly peopled by the PLO executive council and organization members. The location had not been divulged to the general public.

The moment I heard of the meeting, I walked the halls of the building and prayed. The Spirit of God directed me to go to room 401. Once inside, He sent me to the second row of seats next to a long table. There I was impressed to put my locked briefcase on the center chair and then leave the room.

Hours later, as Arafat's minions filled the room strict security was in place to keep out those who were unwanted. When the room was completely filled, I approached one of the terrorists acting as a security guard and requested that I be allowed to find my seat.

"What seat? You have no seat here. You cannot enter," he snapped.

My reply was: "Go to the front row of chairs. You will see my briefcase on the second row, middle seat. Open it; the combination is 0001. Inside you will see my passport and several other things."

He reluctantly turned and stalked up the aisle. Shortly he came back and escorted me to the chair that held my briefcase. Minutes later, Arafat entered. I was directly in front of him in the middle row. The camera crews had been assigned row three—just behind me. Not even the PLO executive council had been permitted to sit in rows one and two. The cameramen were incensed because my head was in the way.

Before me was a table where Arafat and the few men who would accompany him were to sit. They entered the room, and the PLO chairman delivered his speech. Afterwards, he said, "I shall allow three of you to speak. You may choose among yourselves."

Knowing I would not be chosen, I clutched my Bible, stood to my feet, and held aloft a copy of the PLO charter. "Mr. Arafat, if you denounce terrorism, then denounce this covenant that calls for the destruction of Israel." Raising my Bible in the other hand, I began to recount the biblical position of the Jewish people.

Arafat screamed: "Shut up, shut up! What must I do to make you shut up?" When he paused in his rant, I turned and was met by eyes filled with murderous hatred because of what I had said. Suddenly, it was as if a carpet had been rolled out. I saw a path of escape. I walked quickly through the midst of the gathering into the dark hallway, found an exit, climbed into a taxi and was taken back to the hotel.

When I arrived in my room at the Hilton Hotel in Geneva the phone was ringing. It was my friend Reuven Hecht from the prime minister's office.

"Mike, we are hearing you in Israel. Do you know where you are? How many bodyguards do you have? Arafat and his people are terrorists," Reuven advised me of what I already knew.

The following day, I was asked to speak in defense of Israel. At the podium, I lifted my Bible heavenward and declared, "This is the final Word; it is non-negotiable. The land belongs to God Almighty, and He has decided its destiny."

In 1994, my dear friend, Prime Minister Yitzhak Rabin was asked by President Clinton to take a "brave gamble" for peace during another round of meetings between the Israeli leader and Yasser Arafat. I appealed to Rabin in person and by letter (Appendix D) not to believe that lie. My appeal was not heard by this beloved man who later died at the hand of an assassin.

Again at Camp David in July 2002, President Clinton almost

succeeded in dividing Jerusalem. He placed the pen in the hands of Arafat to sign the agreement that would have accomplished that. Arafat refused to sign; the president was shocked. If Arafat had complied, Jerusalem would have been divided. All Christian sites would now be under Islamic rule of law! This includes Mount Calvary and the Garden Tomb, and even the Christians who live there. The Bible says Jerusalem will be in the hands of the Jewish people when Messiah returns. America was challenging God Almighty and His prophetic plan. Not a wise thing to do.

Why did Arafat not sign the agreement? He wanted ALL of the Temple Site! Why did he not succeed in his efforts to exert control over this site? The sons of Esau live in the desert, and run their oppressive governments by the bullet, not the ballot. Those who take a stand against Israel will be fighting God himself. Arafat could not win in a battle against God Almighty. Why? For thousands of years, their fathers have spoken curses over Jacob's seed. When the wars of the Middle East have finally ended, Jacob's sons will rule. Who will win the conflict in the Middle East? Those who bless Israel will be triumphant. Who will lose the battle in the Middle East? Those who fight the State of Israel will go down in defeat. God created Israel; God defends Israel.

Consider the nation of Egypt. Joseph birthed a generation of wealth. After his death, there arose a Pharaoh who persecuted the Jewish people, and enslaved them. He not only starved them, but also drowned their children in the Nile River. Why? He was trying to control that nation. As a result of Pharaoh's enslavement of His people, God sent plagues. The first-born child in every Egyptian home was slain by the Death Angel. In some Egyptian homes, that meant every family member died.

For every Hebrew baby that died in the Nile River, an Egyptian child died. For every Hebrew father who died at the oppressive hands of the Egyptian overseers, an Egyptian father died. For every Hebrew mother who died of starvation, or of a broken heart, an Egyptian mother died. What you do to another, God will cause to come to you.

An angry, bitter Pharaoh gathered his terrified, demoralized troops, and pursued the Hebrew children as they departed Egypt. He led his army directly into the path of God's wrath, and all drowned in the Red Sea. Overnight, Egypt became a land of poverty and disease. It remains that way 4,000 years later...because it chose to curse the Jewish people, rather than bless them.

In the twenty-first century Israel faces a much more dire threat than the PLO; it faces the possibility of annihilation by a country that plans to soon be armed with nuclear weapons—Iran.

Most nations of the world agree that a freeze on Iran's nuclear program is absolutely necessary for a peaceful Middle East. The halt of production of both highly-enriched uranium and a means to deliver an atomic bomb is essential. Yet, Iran has continued to ignore the warnings of world leaders as well as the International Atomic Energy Agency and the United Nations. As a result, strict sanctions have been instituted as a means to end Iranian nuclear pursuits.

The country most vocal about the danger Iran presents to the world is the smallest of nations in the crosshairs—Israel. It is a predicament no twenty-first century nation should have to face—annihilation. Only one member-nation in the United Nations has another member calling for it to be "wiped off the map"—Israel. There is little reason to believe it is merely a threat as it is so often repeated by Iran's leaders.

An article posted on Alef website, one with ties to the Iranian supreme leader, calls for the destruction of Jews everywhere:

...the opportunity must not be lost to remove "this corrupting material. It is a "'jurisprudential justification" to kill all the Jews and annihilate Israel, and in that, the Islamic government of Iran must take the helm... Khamenei announced that Iran will support any nation or group that attacks the "cancerous tumor" of Israel. Though his statement was seen by some in the West as fluff, there is substance behind it...The article then quotes the Quran (Albaghara 2:191-193): "And slay them wherever ye find them, and drive them out of the places whence they drove you out, for persecution [of Muslims] is worse than slaughter [of non-believers]... and fight them until persecution is no more, and religion is for Allah."[133]

Repeated calls for the destruction of Israel issued from Tehran were at their loudest and most vociferous under the leadership of former President Mahmoud Ahmadinejad. With the advent of a new president in August 2013, the rhetoric has been dialed back a bit, but few think Iran's intentions towards the Jewish state have been rescinded. With all the calls for détente with Iran, only one scripture comes to mind:

> When people are saying, "Everything is peaceful and secure," then disaster will fall on them as suddenly as a pregnant woman's labor pains begin. And there will be no escape, (I Thessalonians 5:3, NLT.)

There is little doubt that the desire to destroy Israel is foremost in the minds of Supreme Leader Ali Khamenei and his henchmen as has been proven by the continual supply of arms from Iran to her proxies Syria, Hezbollah in Lebanon and Hamas in Gaza. Rocket attacks launched from both Lebanon and Gaza have plagued Israeli towns in the past; it would be unthinkable for Israel to be faced with the ramifications of a nuclear-armed Iran.

The United States has been very vocal about what is and is not acceptable from Iran but it has been all talk and little, if any, substance. The saber-rattling has been mere noise. The conclusion might very well be that the US is totally intimidated by Iranian oratory. Why would anyone make that assumption? Iran's nuclear program has grown from one centrifuge to as many as 3,000 working to more quickly enrich uranium. This has been accomplished while most world leaders have stood by wringing their collective hands. Should both the US and Israel fail to make a stand against the threats issued by the supreme ayatollah in charge in Tehran, more than face would be lost.

Even scarier is the thought of how the landscape in the Middle East would be changed when dominated by a nuclear-armed Iran. That notwithstanding, it is one thing to aver that a nuclear-armed Iran is unacceptable and enact sanctions, but quite another to take the steps necessary to stop the achievement of that goal. Thus far, all the grandiloquence has done nothing but cause sniggers behind closed doors in Tehran.

Perhaps the question of greatest import is this: Would the US stand with Israel if it were overtly targeted by Iran? Maybe; maybe not. The difference may be measured by how direct the threat would be to the United States, the country the Ayatollah Khomeini labeled the "Great Satan." The time to close the barn door is not after the horses have galloped down the road. The time to stop Iran's nuclear threats is before the first atomic weapon rolls off the assembly line. No one seems to know exactly when that will be.

Of greater concern to Israel may be attempts by Iran's current President Hassan Rouhani to persuade the West to lessen sanctions against his country. Talks in Geneva in November 2013 were aimed at doing just that if concrete changes were made to Iran's nuclear program. Unfortunately, with so much done clandestinely how could anyone be certain of compliance by Iran's rulers?

French leaders were the first to express doubts regarding Iran's long-sought lessening of sanctions in return for a more transparent nuclear program. According to French Foreign Minister Laurent Fabius, Paris could not agree to a "sucker's deal". As evidence, he pointed to the reservations that the Iranians would continue their stealthy march towards securing nuclear arms. The French reticence seemed to indicate that a crack was forming in the Western powers' façade.

Doubts from French leaders were apparently overcome, however, when in November 2013, an interim nuclear deal was struck between Iranian Prime Minister Rouhani and the so-called "P5+1 countries" comprised of the U.S., France, Russia, China, and France plus Germany. The deal gives Iran six months and $7 billion dollars in sanction relief during which time attempts to reach a final agreement on Iran's future nuclear pursuits will be discussed.

Prime Minister Benjamin Netanyahu said of the deal:

> What was reached last night in Geneva is not a historic agreement, it is a historic mistake. Today the world became a much more dangerous place because the most dangerous regime in the world made a significant step in obtaining the most dangerous weapons in the world....I want to clarify that Israel will not let Iran develop nuclear military capability.[134]

Leaders of Muslim countries with largely Sunni populations—Saudi Arabia, Kuwait, the United Arab Emirates, Bahrain,
Qatar, Egypt and Jordan—were coldly silent on the accord reached
in Geneva. Chairman Abdullah al-Askar of Saudi Arabia's Shoura
Council, a group that advises the Saudi government on policy said:

> I am afraid Iran will give up something to get some-
> thing else from the big powers in terms of regional
> politics—and I'm worrying about giving Iran more
> space or a freer hand in the region. The government
> of Iran, month after month, has proven that it has an
> ugly agenda in the region, and in this regard no one
> in the region will sleep and assume things are going
> smoothly.[135]

Why would Iran's leaders, who have no shortage of insolence
and audacity, agree to suspend nuclear enrichment for any period
of time? Simple: the money to keep their program running has been
severely compromised by the sanctions. There is speculation that
the $7 billion in sanction relief will not benefit the Iranian people,
but will go directly into the coffers of Ali Khamenei, the Supreme
Leader's Revolutionary Guard Corps. Such a lofty sum would purchase a lot of equipment for the various centrifuges in the land of the
ayatollahs.

One thing is certain: If the US hopes to be blessed by God
Almighty, her loyalty must be to Israel and not to her enemies; her
willingness to act in support of Israel, unwavering. Sadly, the occu-
pant of the White House, regardless of party affiliation, seems not to
understand that biblical precept.

CHAPTER TWENTY-TWO

THE JERUSALEM PRAYER TEAM

"Pray for the peace of Jerusalem…"

(PSALM 122:6, KJV).

Following Israel's rebirth, organizations in support of the return of the Jewish people to the Holy Land began to spring up—many comprised of Bible-believing Christians. By the late twentieth century, Evangelicals had been infused with ever-growing numbers of those God-fearing people who bless Israel in daily prayer and intercession as well as with monetary support.

Members of today's Christian Zionist organizations have great respect for the Jewish people and for Judaism. They believe it is the very foundation upon which Christianity is based—after all, Jesus was a Jew who kept the entire Mosaic Law.

A Jerusalem Prayer Team–sponsored petition to President Bush in 2003 read in part:

> We support Israel's right to their land spiritu-
> ally and legally. History records that God deals with

nations in accord with how these nations deal with Israel. We rejoice that here in America, for 228 years, we have been committed to the Jewish people. The Jewish people have found refuge here; they have found a people who love them; and we can take pride in saying that Israel is not an exclusively Jewish issue.

Bible-believing Evangelicals consider the support of Israel a biblical mandate. Regardless of contrary opinion, we do not believe Israel has to offer an excuse for its existence. Israel lives today as a right! A right that has been hallowed by the Bible, by history, by sacrifice, by prayer, and by the yearning for peace![136]

Multitudes of Christian Zionists believe God's promise to Abraham: Those who bless His descendants will be blessed of God.

In 1982, I sponsored the first National Prayer Breakfast in honor of Israel. A "Proclamation of Blessing" was introduced in support of the Jewish nation, and read in part:

As Bible-believing Americans, we believe there exists an iron-clad bond between the State of Israel and the United States. We believe that bond to be a moral imperative.

Representing the vast majority of evangelicals in the United States, we have gathered together at this National Prayer Breakfast to reaffirm our support and prayers, that this bond not be weakened or diminished.

But it was in East Texas that I had perhaps the most moving encounter in my life with another Christian Zionist. That meeting changed my life. I was in Texarkana, a town on the Texas/Arkansas border, when I saw an elderly lady carrying her suitcase into a Holiday Inn. As I hurried to open the door for her, I asked if I might carry her bag. She smiled her thanks, and as she did, her eyes lit up. Suddenly I realized I was standing in the presence of one of my heroines: Corrie ten Boom. We enjoyed a bowl of soup together and shared our love for the Jewish people. It was Corrie's vision that her home and the clock shop in Haarlem, Holland, be restored.

After the purchase had been completed, I vowed that no one would ever pay a cent to visit the ten Boom home; that the story of God's love would be available to all. Since its restoration, the shop has been open, free of charge, to thousands of visitors. Many of those leave with tears of remembrance and grateful hearts for the family that gave their lives to help Jewish people escape Hitler's plan from hell. Some of those who have come were relatives of the people whose lives were saved by the courageous ten Boom family. All the work there is done on a volunteer basis. No one, including the board of directors, of which I am chairman, has ever received any compensation for our work, and we each have paid our own expenses.

In 2002, I founded the Jerusalem Prayer Team (JPT) and Churches United with Israel (CUI). The mayor of Jerusalem, Ehud Olmert, traveled to Dallas, Texas, to join me in launching JPT, an outreach of the Corrie ten Boom Fellowship. Through the years JPT has grown from that rally in Dallas to more than a million people worldwide who receive weekly email updates. Churches United with Israel was formed to encourage churches to stand alongside the Jerusalem Prayer Team and encourage their members to actively pray for the Jewish people. It was the first organization of its kind and has some 300 top church leaders on its board of governors.

Evangelicals are not engaged in terrorist attacks *against* their enemies; they are intent upon doing God's work on Earth *for* Him. They are advocates for the State of Israel; they are defenders of God's Word and His children. Many evangelical groups support programs to provide food, clothing, housing, and more for Jews who have returned to Israel and especially those from Russia. They employ whatever political clout that can be utilized in order to stand in strong support of Israel. With over sixty million-plus Christian Zionists in the world, their presence remains a force with which to be reckoned.

Those who support the Jewish people have expended billions of dollars in assistance through aiding orphanages, providing medical supplies, and sponsoring social assistance programs for the poor and needy in Israel. Information is dispensed through conferences in support of Israel, through promoting better understanding between Christians and Jews, by denouncing anti-Semitism and especially through prayer. Various groups have sponsored marches through Jerusalem in support of the nation and the right of the Jewish people to live there. Many have aided Jews from Russia and other countries to immigrate to Israel.

The Jerusalem Prayer Team has been at the forefront of these efforts to provide assistance to the Jewish people. JPT has raised funds and invested millions of humanitarian dollars in Israel by providing food for the hungry, warm hats and coats for thousands of elderly Jews, basic necessities for Russian Jewish refugees, back-packs for school children, medical equipment for terror victims, and the preparation of a bomb shelter/community center in Jerusalem to be used as a safe place during terrorist strikes. It contains a kitchen, televisions, telephones, and much more. The Jerusalem Prayer Team is also helping to fund bomb shelters near schools for children to seek safety during attacks. It continues to invest in the lives and safety of the Jewish people in Israel, and prayers for Israel can be posted on an interactive prayer wall website open not just to JPT members but to people worldwide.

The founding of the Jerusalem Prayer Team has afforded a platform to meet with dozens of heads of state, including President Massoud Barzani of Kurdistan, President Alfredo Cristiani of El Salvador, President Yoweri Musevani of Uganda, President Mahmoud Ahmadinejad of Iran, as well as numerous prime ministers, kings, foreign ministers, secretaries of state, and other world leaders. JPT has become a vehicle to allow me to achieve my life's work among my people, the Jews.[137]

The stated purpose of the Jerusalem Prayer Team is: To guard, defend, and protect the Jewish people and *Eretz Yisrael* until she is secure; to see Christians and Jews standing together to find better understanding of each other; to establish a strong and secure Bible Land; and to benevolently meet the needs of those whom Jesus describes in Matthew, chapter 25:35-36, 40, NKJV:

> *For I was hungry and you gave Me food; I was thirsty and you gave Me drink; I was a stranger and you took Me in; I was naked and you clothed Me; I was sick and you visited Me; I was in prison and you came to Me....*
>
> *And the King will answer and say to them, "Assuredly, I say to you, inasmuch as you did it to one of the least of these My brethren, you did it to Me."*

Today my heart is overflowing with gratitude to God as the dream He placed in my spirit more than thirty years ago has become a reality. When the contract for the purchase of the building that will house the Jerusalem World Center—within walking distance of the Temple Mount in Jerusalem—was signed, I was reminded once again that every promise from God is certain and sure, no matter how long we have to wait for it. Abraham waited for the promised birth of Isaac for some twenty-five years, but in God's perfect timing, the son of promise was born.

When I first met with Prime Minister Menachem Begin more than thirty years ago and we agreed to work together to build a bridge between Christians and Jews, part of that dream was to have a permanent presence in the Holy City. Now we can move forward with this beautiful facility to minister to the Jewish people and to you.

The attitude that pervades the Jerusalem Prayer Team partners is one of determination that the Jewish people will be able to see and hear the stories of Christian Zionists who have provided comfort and aid to them. There is a God-given, biblical—and intimate—connection between Christians and Jews. Based on love and truth, and surrounded by prayer, it can never be broken. The Jewish Messiah and our Lord and Savior sprang from the root of Jesse and will occupy the throne of King David in Jerusalem, Mount Zion, when He returns.

For centuries Christians who understood and believed the promises and prophecies of Scripture shared the dream of the return of the Jewish people to their ancient homeland in Palestine. The stories of Christians who played a crucial role in helping to promote, defend, support and establish the modern state of Israel, and who fulfilled the moral duty to rescue Jewish people from the Holocaust, has been largely untold.

Friends of Zion, an Israeli not-for-profit corporation, have begun the planning phase of the Museum of Christian Zionism. My vision is to celebrate through the Museum the achievements of those most prominent in helping bring about the rebirth of Israel. In this way, their stories will be captured for future generations. The attractive building that will house the Museum sits in the heart of Jerusalem at 20 Rivlin Street, a prominent location overlooking Independence Park and within walking distance to the Old City.

The museum will be a showcase for the many Christian Zionists who have played a key role in the rebirth of the State of Israel. The list of men and women who lobbied for a Jewish homeland long before the rise of Theodor Herzl is long and impressive. William Blackstone, a staunch Christian Zionist, authored a declaration entitled, "Palestine for the Jews" in 1878, five years before the father of modern-day Zionism, Theodor Herzl, published his book, *The Jewish State* and founded the Zionist Movement. Blackstone had written a book which listed hundreds of biblical passages declaring why the Jewish people would be restored to their homeland. He then marked all the prophecies of the Old Testament concerning Israel's rebirth in a Bible and sent it to Herzl. Blackstone so greatly influenced Herzl that the Bible containing those prophecies has been displayed at Herzl's tomb in Israel.

Blackstone's treatise became known as the Blackstone Memorial. He gathered 413 signatures of prominent Americans—among them John D. Rockefeller, J. P. Morgan, William McKinley, Cyrus McCormick, Supreme Court Justice Melville Fuller, and Speaker of the House T. B. Reed. It simply called for a conference to discuss the possibilities of a Jewish homeland.

Laurence Oliphant of Great Britain, assuming the mantle of unauthorized diplomat, was passionate about the restoration of the Jews in their homeland. From a financial point of view, Oliphant thought it would be an easy undertaking. After all, England and America were rife with monetary support to be had. In 1882, Oliphant traveled to Palestine with his secretary Naftali Herz Imber, who later penned the lyrics for the Jewish National Anthem, *Hatikvah*. According to Imber, "Divine providence propelled me in the course of my wanderings into the care of the late Laurence Oliphant. Credit is due him that the Zionists have a national anthem."

Horatio Spafford was another Christian Zionist and the author of one of Christendom's most beloved hymns, *"It is well with my Soul."* In September 1881, Horatio and Anna Spafford left the United States for the Holy Land. Moving into a house in the Old City of Jerusalem, they established the American Colony. Spafford and his friends were determined to simply serve the Jewish people by meeting the needs of the underprivileged, distressed, and exiled.

There were men such as Orde Charles Wingate who sought permission from the Jewish leadership in Palestine to train a defense force. He was granted approval to seek out *Haganah* soldiers and train them especially to protect the Jewish community. The *Haganah* ultimately became the foundation for the modern-day Israeli Defense Forces.

It was said that John Henry Dunant, Swiss-born banker, humanitarian, and founder of the Red Cross, was first labeled a Christian Zionist by Theodor Herzl. Because of their close friendship, Dunant accompanied Herzl to the First World Zionist Congress in 1897, one of only a handful of Gentiles to have been invited. Dunant's belief in his vision of a Jewish homeland in Palestine was so vivid that he worked tirelessly for renewal along the shore of the Mediterranean Sea. He developed large areas of the coast and strived to ensure that Jews immigrated. Although Dunant failed in efforts to enlist the aid of numerous highly-visible public figures, his zeal for bringing the Jews home to Palestine never wavered.

Lieutenant Colonel John Henry Patterson was an Anglo-Irish soldier, hunter, author and Zionist, and among those conservative

Protestants whose Zionist leanings made him the perfect commander for the Zion Mule Corps. His familiarity with the Bible, its stories, laws, geography, prophecies, and morals, stood him in good stead when his army superiors chose him to take over the Corps. Patterson, who later commanded the Jewish Legion, was such an ardent supporter of Zionism he believed that Lloyd George and Sir Arthur Balfour had been elevated to positions of power just as Esther had been in ancient Persia. His excitement was palpable as he watched unprecedented events taking place before his very eyes. Patterson became a close friend of Benzion Netanyahu and was the godfather of his eldest son, Jonathan Netanyahu.

Surprisingly, the vast majority of Zionists today are not Jewish; however, the Christian Zionist movement globally numbers in the millions. Since that momentous announcement of the rebirth of Israel on May 14, 1948, the tiny nation has fought for her very life—not once but multiple times. Joining the Jewish people in the trenches have been sympathetic Gentiles from around the world. With each succeeding battle for existence, new Christian Zionists have sprung up to stand with the Children of Israel in their battle to survive. The new Museum of Christian Zionism will spotlight the many men and women who have staunchly supported the Jewish people before, during, and after the formation of the state of Israel.

During the Jerusalem Prayer Team's inaugural event in 2002, Mayor Ehud Olmert said:

> I wish to thank you on behalf of the people of Jerusalem for your support, for your care, for your love, for your friendship, for your generosity. I will go back... to Jerusalem, and I will tell the people of Jerusalem that we have established here in Dallas something

that will spread across America, and later across the world...the Jerusalem Prayer Summits...the Jerusalem Prayer Team...that I have the honor to inaugurate today. I promised it to my friend, Mike Evans, that I would join him in going from one congregation to the other, from one community to the other to participate in the Jerusalem Prayer Summits. And we will talk, and we will approach people, and we will share with them the responsibility and the love that Christians and Jews have together for the destiny of Jerusalem. For the future of Jerusalem, for the love of God for this city, for the love of God for all of us, thank you, thank you from Jerusalem. God bless all of you!

Franklin Graham wrote in a letter (read at the inaugural Prayer Summit):

...I certainly wish you and all those participating God's blessing and that God will use this to help strengthen the Jewish people. We have all been dismayed at how much positive media attention these fanatic Muslims are getting in this country and we certainly pray for the peace of Jerusalem.

The vision of the Jerusalem Prayer Team is to have ten million intercessors praying daily for national revival according to 2 Chronicles 7:14 as prophesied by King David's son, Solomon. King David declared: *"Pray for the peace of Jerusalem; they shall prosper that love thee,"* (Psalm 122:6.) Praying for the peace of Jerusalem is not praying for stones or dirt; they don't weep or bleed. It is praying for God's protection over the lives of the citizens of Jerusalem. It is praying for revival. It is praying for God's grace to be poured out.

Mother Teresa was one of the first people to tell me when I met her in Rome that she prayed daily for the peace of Jerusalem. She said to me, "Love is not something you say, it's something you do." I believe that with all my heart. That is why I am appealing to you to join me in seeing what King David saw...what Solomon saw...and what our beloved Lord saw as they prayed in Jerusalem. Each experienced the power of God in Jerusalem—God's glory filled the house where they stood!

I speak at conferences and churches across America, and the one question I am repeatedly asked is, "Why should I support Israel—what does Israel have to do with me, with America?"

My friend, Israel has *everything* to do with you, with your family, with your country. The short answer to why you should embrace, uphold, and support Israel is that by blessing Israel, you will be blessed:

> *Now the LORD had said to Abram: "Get out of your country, From your family And from your father's house, To a land that I will show you. I will make you a great nation; I will bless you And make your name great; And you shall be a blessing. I will bless those who bless you, And I will curse him who curses you; And in you all the families of the earth shall be blessed,"* (Genesis 12:1-3.)

As Bible-believing Christians, you and I should support Israel simply because God has ordained it in the pages of His Word.

When we pray for Jerusalem we are saying, "Maranatha, come Messiah!"

For the Lord shall build up Zion; He shall appear in his glory! (Psalm 102:16.)

The Messiah is indeed coming back, and He is coming to Jerusalem! That is something on which both Jews and Christians agree. As Christians, we believe that we know His name, while the Jewish people say they don't. But there is no question that when Messiah comes, everyone will know His name.

Our Lord was asked by His disciples in Matthew 24:3, NASB:

And what will be the sign of Your coming, and of the end of the age?

He clearly gave them the signs beginning with the destruction of the Temple. In verse 2, Jesus prophesied that the Temple would be taken apart stone by stone forty years before it happened. The fig tree has always been a symbol of the Nation of Israel. In verses 32-36, Jesus laid out the key sign of His return, and the end of the age... the sign of the fig tree. That "fig tree" did bloom on May 14, 1948, in fulfillment of Isaiah 66:8.

Jesus warned to not set dates:

But of that day and hour no one knows, not even the angels of heaven, nor the Son, but the Father alone, (Matthew 24:36, NASB.)

He also said that the generation which saw the blooming of the fig tree would not pass away until He came.

It was 597 B.C. in the days of Nebuchadnezzar in Babylon (now modern-day Iraq) that Israel was taken into captivity. Since then,

Israel has changed hands 26 times. Jerusalem has been leveled to the ground five times. But in 1948, the prophecies of Matthew 24:32 began to knock at the door:

> *Now learn this parable from the fig tree: When its branch has already become tender and puts forth leaves, you know that summer is near,* (NKJV.)

A generation is most often defined as seventy to eighty years. Those born in 1948 when this prophecy was fulfilled, would be the same age as the nation of Israel. There is no question that we will not know that day or the hour, but Matthew 24 seems to indicate that we are very, very close to Messiah's return. Events in the Middle East are surely lining up with this prophecy.

Jesus is coming soon! We must be certain that what we are living for is worthy of Christ having died for, and that we ask ourselves this simple question: How will what happens to Israel through apathy or inaction matter in the light of eternity? Like the prophet Isaiah, we must determine:

> *For Zion's sake will I not hold my peace, and for Jerusalem's sake I will not rest, until the righteousness thereof go forth as brightness, and the salvation thereof as a lamp that burneth. And the Gentiles shall see thy righteousness, and all kings thy glory: and thou shalt be called by a new name, which the mouth of the LORD shall name. Thou shalt also be a crown of glory in the hand of the LORD, and a royal diadem in the hand of thy God. Thou shalt no more be termed Forsaken; neither shall thy land any more be termed Desolate: but*

thou shalt be called Hephzibah, and thy land Beulah: for the LORD delighteth in thee, and thy land shall be married. For as a young man marrieth a virgin, so shall thy sons marry thee: and as the bridegroom rejoiceth over the bride, so shall thy God rejoice over thee. I have set watchmen upon thy walls, O Jerusalem, which shall never hold their peace day nor night: ye that make mention of the LORD, keep not silence, And give him no rest, till he establish, and till he make Jerusalem a praise in the earth, (Isaiah 62:1-7, KJV.)

EPILOGUE

Stand with Israel is a treatise on why Christians should provide encourage, assistance, defense and financial aid to the Jewish people in Israel. It provides biblical validation of all the reasons it is important to care for God's Chosen People.

In summary, below are nine reasons why it is vital that you and I *Stand with Israel*:

1. God made a covenant with Abraham that would give the land of Israel to the Jewish people. He cannot violate His covenant. (Genesis 12.God's Word is true, righteous, and unchangeable. (John 17:17.)

2. God promises to bless those who bless Israel and curse him who curses Israel. (Genesis 12:1-3.)

3. God hates anti-Semitism. (I John 4:20.)

4. God's word says we are to comfort the House of Israel. (Isaiah 40:1-2.)

5. God has not revoked His gifts and call to Israel. (Isaiah 49:15.)

6. God has preserved Israel through the ages. (Psalm 121:4-8.)

7. God has written His Name in Jerusalem. (II Chronicles 6:6.)

8. God is preparing the Church for His return. (Psalm 102:16.)

9. God has raised up intercessors to pray for the Jewish people. (Isaiah 62:6-7.)

PRAYERS AND BLESSINGS FOR ISRAEL

I Samuel 12:22, NIV

For the sake of his great name the Lord will not reject his people, because the Lord was pleased to make you his own.

Psalm 17:6-9, NIV

I call on you, my God, for you will answer me;
turn your ear to me and hear my prayer.
Show me the wonders of your great love,
you who save by your right hand
those who take refuge in you from their foes.
Keep me as the apple of your eye;
hide me in the shadow of your wings
from the wicked who are out to destroy me,
from my mortal enemies who surround me.

Psalm 17:16-19, NIV

As for me, I call to God,
and the Lord saves me.
Evening, morning and noon

I cry out in distress,
and he hears my voice.
He rescues me unharmed
from the battle waged against me,
even though many oppose me.
God, who is enthroned from of old,
who does not change—
he will hear them and humble them,
because they have no fear of God.

Psalm 25:22, NIV
Deliver Israel, O God,
from all their troubles!

Psalm 100, NIV
Shout for joy to the Lord, all the earth.
Worship the Lord with gladness;
come before him with joyful songs.
Know that the Lord is God.
It is he who made us, and we are his[a];
we are his people, the sheep of his pasture.
Enter his gates with thanksgiving
and his courts with praise;
give thanks to him and praise his name.
For the Lord is good and his love endures forever;
his faithfulness continues through all generations.

Psalm 102:12-16, NIV
But you, Lord, sit enthroned forever;
your renown endures through all generations.

You will arise and have compassion on Zion,
for it is time to show favor to her;
the appointed time has come.
For her stones are dear to your servants;
her very dust moves them to pity.
The nations will fear the name of the Lord,
all the kings of the earth will revere your glory.
For the Lord will rebuild Zion
and appear in his glory.

Psalm 1226-8, NIV
Pray for the peace of Jerusalem:
"May those who love you be secure.
May there be peace within your walls
and security within your citadels."
For the sake of my family and friends,
I will say, "Peace be within you."

Proverbs 16:7, NIV
When the Lord takes pleasure in anyone's way,
he causes their enemies to make peace with them.

Isaiah 45:3-4, NIV
I will give you hidden treasures,
riches stored in secret places,
so that you may know that I am the Lord,
the God of Israel, who summons you by name.
For the sake of Jacob my servant,
of Israel my chosen,

I summon you by name
and bestow on you a title of honor...

Isaiah 45:17-18, NIV
But Israel will be saved by the Lord
with an everlasting salvation;
you will never be put to shame or disgraced,
to ages everlasting. For this is what the Lord says—
he who created the heavens,
he is God;
he who fashioned and made the earth,
he founded it;
he did not create it to be empty,
but formed it to be inhabited—
he says: "I am the Lord,
and there is no other.

Jeremiah 33:6-11, NIV
"'Nevertheless, I will bring health and healing to it; I
will heal my people and will let them enjoy abundant
peace and security. I will bring Judah and Israel back
from captivityand will rebuild them as they were
before. I will cleanse them from all the sin they have
committed against me and will forgive all their sins
of rebellion against me. Then this city will bring me
renown, joy, praise and honor before all nations on
earth that hear of all the good things I do for it; and
they will be in awe and will tremble at the abundant prosperity and peace I provide for it.' "This is
what the Lord says: 'You say about this place, "It is a

desolate waste, without people or animals." Yet in the towns of Judah and the streets of Jerusalem that are deserted, inhabited by neither people nor animals, there will be heard once more the sounds of joy and gladness, the voices of bride and bridegroom, and the voices of those who bring thank offerings to the house of the Lord, saying, "Give thanks to the Lord Almighty, for the Lord is good; his love endures forever." For I will restore the fortunes of the land as they were before,' says the Lord.

Ezekiel 34:11-15, NIV
"'For this is what the Sovereign Lord says: I myself will search for my sheep and look after them. As a shepherd looks after his scattered flock when he is with them, so will I look after my sheep. I will rescue them from all the places where they were scattered on a day of clouds and darkness. I will bring them out from the nations and gather them from the countries, and I will bring them into their own land. I will pasture them on the mountains of Israel, in the ravines and in all the settlements in the land. I will tend them in a good pasture, and the mountain heights of Israel will be their grazing land. There they will lie down in good grazing land, and there they will feed in a rich pasture on the mountains of Israel. I myself will tend my sheep and have them lie down, declares the Sovereign Lord.

Ezekiel 34:25-31, NIV

"'I will make a covenant of peace with them and rid the land of savage beasts so that they may live in the wilderness and sleep in the forests in safety. I will make them and the places surrounding my hill a blessing.[a] I will send down showers in season; there will be showers of blessing. The trees will yield their fruit and the ground will yield its crops; the people will be secure in their land. They will know that I am the Lord, when I break the bars of their yoke and rescue them from the hands of those who enslaved them. They will no longer be plundered by the nations, nor will wild animals devour them. They will live in safety, and no one will make them afraid. I will provide for them a land renowned for its crops, and they will no longer be victims of famine in the land or bear the scorn of the nations. Then they will know that I, the Lord their God, am with them and that they, the Israelites, are my people, declares the Sovereign Lord. You are my sheep, the sheep of my pasture, and I am your God, declares the Sovereign Lord.'"

Joel 2:19-27, NIV
The Lord replied to them:"I am sending you grain, new wine and olive oil,
enough to satisfy you fully;
never again will I make you
an object of scorn to the nations.
"I will drive the northern horde far from you, pushing it into a parched and barren land;
its eastern ranks will drown in the Dead Sea

and its western ranks in the Mediterranean Sea.
And its stench will go up;
its smell will rise." Surely he has done great things!
Do not be afraid, land of Judah;
be glad and rejoice.
Surely the Lord has done great things!
Do not be afraid, you wild animals,
for the pastures in the wilderness are becoming green.
The trees are bearing their fruit;
the fig tree and the vine yield their riches.
Be glad, people of Zion,
rejoice in the Lord your God,
for he has given you the autumn rains
because he is faithful.
He sends you abundant showers,
both autumn and spring rains, as before.
The threshing floors will be filled with grain;
the vats will overflow with new wine and oil.
"I will repay you for the years the locusts have eaten—
the great locust and the young locust,
the other locusts and the locust swarm—
my great army that I sent among you.
You will have plenty to eat, until you are full,
and you will praise the name of the Lord your God,
who has worked wonders for you;
never again will my people be shamed.
Then you will know that I am in Israel,
that I am the Lord your God,
and that there is no other;
never again will my people be shamed.

Joel 3:16, NIV

The Lord will roar from Zion
and thunder from Jerusalem;
the earth and the heavens will tremble.
But the Lord will be a refuge for his people,
a stronghold for the people of Israel.

REMARKS OF PRESIDENT BARACK OBAMA

A New Beginning

CAIRO, EGYPT / JUNE 4, 2009

I am honored to be in the timeless city of Cairo, and to be hosted by two remarkable institutions. For over a thousand years, Al-Azhar has stood as a beacon of Islamic learning, and for over a century, Cairo University has been a source of Egypt's advancement. Together, you represent the harmony between tradition and progress. I am grateful for your hospitality, and the hospitality of the people of Egypt. I am also proud to carry with me the goodwill of the American people, and a greeting of peace from Muslim communities in my country: *assalaamu alaykum*.

We meet at a time of tension between the United States and Muslims around the world–tension rooted in historical forces that go beyond any current policy debate. The relationship between Islam and the West includes centuries of co-existence and cooperation, but also conflict and religious wars. More recently, tension has been fed by colonialism that denied rights and opportunities to many Muslims, and a Cold War in which Muslim-majority countries were too often treated as proxies without regard to their own aspirations. Moreover, the sweeping change brought by modernity and globalization led many Muslims to view the West as hostile to the traditions of Islam.

Violent extremists have exploited these tensions in a small but potent minority of Muslims. The attacks of September 11th, 2001 and the continued efforts of these extremists to engage in violence against civilians has led some in my country to view Islam as inevitably hostile not only to America and Western countries, but also to human rights. This has bred more fear and mistrust.

So long as our relationship is defined by our differences, we will empower those who sow hatred rather than peace, and who promote conflict rather than the cooperation that can help all of our people achieve justice and prosperity. This cycle of suspicion and discord must end.

I have come here to seek a new beginning between the United States and Muslims around the world; one based upon mutual interest and mutual respect; and one based upon the truth that America and Islam are not exclusive, and need not be in competition. Instead, they overlap, and share common principles—principles of justice and progress; tolerance and the dignity of all human beings.

I do so recognizing that change cannot happen overnight. No single speech can eradicate years of mistrust, nor can I answer in the time that I have all the complex questions that brought us to this point. But I am convinced that in order to move forward, we must say openly the things we hold in our hearts, and that too often are said only behind closed doors. There must be a sustained effort to listen to each other; to learn from each other; to respect one another; and to seek common ground. As the Holy Koran tells us, "Be conscious of God and speak always the truth." That is what I will try to do—to speak the truth as best I can, humbled by the task before us, and firm in my belief that the interests we share as human beings are far more powerful than the forces that drive us apart.

Part of this conviction is rooted in my own experience. I am a

Christian, but my father came from a Kenyan family that includes generations of Muslims. As a boy, I spent several years in Indonesia and heard the call of the *azaan* at the break of dawn and the fall of dusk. As a young man, I worked in Chicago communities where many found dignity and peace in their Muslim faith.

As a student of history, I also know civilization's debt to Islam. It was Islam—at places like Al-Azhar University—that carried the light of learning through so many centuries, paving the way for Europe's Renaissance and Enlightenment. It was innovation in Muslim communities that developed the order of algebra; our magnetic compass and tools of navigation; our mastery of pens and printing; our understanding of how disease spreads and how it can be healed. Islamic culture has given us majestic arches and soaring spires; timeless poetry and cherished music; elegant calligraphy and places of peaceful contemplation. And throughout history, Islam has demonstrated through words and deeds the possibilities of religious tolerance and racial equality.

I know, too, that Islam has always been a part of America's story. The first nation to recognize my country was Morocco. In signing the Treaty of Tripoli in 1796, our second President John Adams wrote, "The United States has in itself no character of enmity against the laws, religion or tranquility of Muslims." And since our founding, American Muslims have enriched the United States. They have fought in our wars, served in government, stood for civil rights, started businesses, taught at our Universities, excelled in our sports arenas, won Nobel Prizes, built our tallest building, and lit the Olympic Torch. And when the first Muslim-American was recently elected to Congress, he took the oath to defend our Constitution using the same Holy Koran that one of our Founding Fathers—Thomas Jefferson—kept in his personal library.

So I have known Islam on three continents before coming to the region where it was first revealed. That experience guides my conviction that partnership between America and Islam must be based on what Islam is, not what it isn't. And I consider it part of my responsibility as President of the United States to fight against negative stereotypes of Islam wherever they appear.

But that same principle must apply to Muslim perceptions of America. Just as Muslims do not fit a crude stereotype, America is not the crude stereotype of a self-interested empire. The United States has been one of the greatest sources of progress that the world has ever known. We were born out of revolution against an empire. We were founded upon the ideal that all are created equal, and we have shed blood and struggled for centuries to give meaning to those words—within our borders, and around the world. We are shaped by every culture, drawn from every end of the Earth, and dedicated to a simple concept: *E pluribus unum*: "Out of many, one."

Much has been made of the fact that an African-American with the name Barack Hussein Obama could be elected President. But my personal story is not so unique. The dream of opportunity for all people has not come true for everyone in America, but its promise exists for all who come to our shores—that includes nearly seven million American Muslims in our country today who enjoy incomes and education that are higher than average.

Moreover, freedom in America is indivisible from the freedom to practice one's religion. That is why there is a mosque in every state of our union, and over 1,200 mosques within our borders. That is why the U.S. government has gone to court to protect the right of women and girls to wear the *hijab*, and to punish those who would deny it.

So let there be no doubt: Islam is a part of America. And I believe that America holds within her the truth that regardless of race, religion, or station in life, all of us share common aspirations—to live in peace and security; to get an education and to work with dignity; to love our families, our communities, and our God. These things we share. This is the hope of all humanity.

Of course, recognizing our common humanity is only the beginning of our task. Words alone cannot meet the needs of our people. These needs will be met only if we act boldly in the years ahead; and if we understand that the challenges we face are shared, and our failure to meet them will hurt us all.

For we have learned from recent experience that when a financial system weakens in one country, prosperity is hurt everywhere. When a new flu infects one human being, all are at risk. When one nation pursues a nuclear weapon, the risk of nuclear attack rises for all nations. When violent extremists operate in one stretch of mountains, people are endangered across an ocean. And when innocents in Bosnia and Darfur are slaughtered, that is a stain on our collective conscience. That is what it means to share this world in the 21st century. That is the responsibility we have to one another as human beings.

This is a difficult responsibility to embrace. For human history has often been a record of nations and tribes subjugating one another to serve their own interests. Yet in this new age, such attitudes are self-defeating. Given our interdependence, any world order that elevates one nation or group of people over another will inevitably fail. So whatever we think of the past, we must not be prisoners of it. Our problems must be dealt with through partnership; progress must be shared.

That does not mean we should ignore sources of tension. Indeed, it suggests the opposite: we must face these tensions squarely. And so in that spirit, let me speak as clearly and plainly as I can about some specific issues that I believe we must finally confront together.

The first issue that we have to confront is violent extremism in all of its forms.

In Ankara, I made clear that America is not—and never will be—at war with Islam. We will, however, relentlessly confront violent extremists who pose a grave threat to our security. Because we reject the same thing that people of all faiths reject: the killing of innocent men, women, and children. And it is my first duty as President to protect the American people.

The situation in Afghanistan demonstrates America's goals, and our need to work together. Over seven years ago, the United States pursued al Qaeda and the Taliban with broad international support. We did not go by choice, we went because of necessity. I am aware that some question or justify the events of 9/11. But let us be clear: al Qaeda killed nearly 3,000 people on that day. The victims were innocent men, women and children from America and many other nations who had done nothing to harm anybody. And yet Al Qaeda chose to ruthlessly murder these people, claimed credit for the attack, and even now states their determination to kill on a massive scale. They have affiliates in many countries and are trying to expand their reach. These are not opinions to be debated; these are facts to be dealt with.

Make no mistake: we do not want to keep our troops in Afghanistan. We seek no military bases there. It is agonizing for America to lose our young men and women. It is costly and politically difficult to continue this conflict. We would gladly bring every single one of our troops home if we could be confident that there were not violent extremists in Afghanistan and Pakistan determined to kill as many Americans as they possibly can. But that is not yet the case.

That's why we're partnering with a coalition of forty-six countries. And despite the costs involved, America's commitment will not weaken. Indeed, none of us should tolerate these extremists. They have killed in many countries. They have killed people of different faiths—more than any other, they have killed Muslims. Their actions are irreconcilable with the rights of human beings, the progress of nations, and with Islam. The Holy Koran teaches that whoever kills an innocent, it is as if he has killed all mankind; and whoever saves a person, it is as if he has saved all mankind. The enduring faith of over a billion people is so much bigger than the narrow hatred of a few. Islam is not part of the problem in combating violent extremism—it is an important part of promoting peace.

We also know that military power alone is not going to solve the problems in Afghanistan and Pakistan. That is why we plan to invest $1.5 billion each year over the next five years to partner with Pakistanis to build schools and hospitals, roads and businesses, and hundreds of millions to help those who have been displaced. And that is why we are providing more than $2.8 billion to help Afghans develop their economy and deliver services that people depend upon.

Let me also address the issue of Iraq. Unlike Afghanistan, Iraq was a war of choice that provoked strong differences in my country and around the world. Although I believe that the Iraqi people are ultimately better off without the tyranny of Saddam Hussein, I also believe that events in Iraq have reminded America of the need to use diplomacy and build international consensus to resolve our problems whenever possible. Indeed, we can recall the words of Thomas Jefferson, who said: "I hope that our wisdom will grow with our power, and teach us that the less we use our power the greater it will be."

Today, America has a dual responsibility: to help Iraq forge a better future—and to leave Iraq to Iraqis. I have made it clear to the Iraqi people that we pursue no bases, and no claim on their territory or resources. Iraq's sovereignty is its own. That is why I ordered the removal of our combat brigades by next August. That is why we will honor our agreement with Iraq's democratically-elected government to remove combat troops from Iraqi cities by July, and to remove all our troops from Iraq by 2012. We will help Iraq train its Security Forces and develop its economy. But we will support a secure and united Iraq as a partner, and never as a patron.

And finally, just as America can never tolerate violence by extremists, we must never alter our principles. 9/11 was an enormous trauma to our country. The fear and anger that it provoked was understandable, but in some cases, it led us to act contrary to our ideals. We are taking concrete actions to change course. I have unequivocally prohibited the use of torture by the United States, and I have ordered the prison at Guantanamo Bay closed by early next year.

So America will defend itself respectful of the sovereignty of nations and the rule of law. And we will do so in partnership with Muslim communities which are also threatened. The sooner the extremists are isolated and unwelcome in Muslim communities, the sooner we will all be safer.

The second major source of tension that we need to discuss is the situation between Israelis, Palestinians and the Arab world.

America's strong bonds with Israel are well known. This bond is unbreakable. It is based upon cultural and historical ties, and the recognition that the aspiration for a Jewish homeland is rooted in a tragic history that cannot be denied.

Around the world, the Jewish people were persecuted for centuries, and anti-Semitism in Europe culminated in an unprecedented Holocaust. Tomorrow, I will visit Buchenwald, which was part of a network of camps where Jews were enslaved, tortured, shot and gassed to death by the Third Reich. Six million Jews were killed—more than the entire Jewish population of Israel today. Denying that fact is baseless, ignorant, and hateful. Threatening Israel with destruction—or repeating vile stereotypes about Jews—is deeply wrong and only serves to evoke in the minds of Israelis this most painful of memories while preventing the peace that the people of this region deserve.

On the other hand, it is also undeniable that the Palestinian people—Muslims and Christians—have suffered in pursuit of a homeland. For more than sixty years they have endured the pain of dislocation. Many wait in refugee camps in the West Bank, Gaza, and neighboring lands for a life of peace and security that they have never been able to lead. They endure the daily humiliations—large and small—that come with occupation. So let there be no doubt: the situation for the Palestinian people is intolerable. America will not turn our backs on the legitimate Palestinian aspiration for dignity, opportunity, and a state of their own.

For decades, there has been a stalemate: two peoples with legitimate aspirations, each with a painful history that makes compromise elusive. It is easy to point fingers—for Palestinians to point to the displacement brought by Israel's founding, and for Israelis to point to the constant hostility and attacks throughout its history from within its borders as well as beyond. But if we see this conflict only from one side or the other, then we will be blind to the truth: the only resolution is for the aspirations of both sides to be met through two states, where Israelis and Palestinians each live in peace and security.

That is in Israel's interest, Palestine's interest, America's interest, and the world's interest. That is why I intend to personally pursue this outcome with all the patience that the task requires. The obligations that the parties have agreed to under the Road Map are clear.

For peace to come, it is time for them—and all of us—to live up to our responsibilities.

Palestinians must abandon violence. Resistance through violence and killing is wrong and does not succeed. For centuries, black people in America suffered the lash of the whip as slaves and the humiliation of segregation. But it was not violence that won full and equal rights. It was a peaceful and determined insistence upon the ideals at the center of America's founding. This same story can be told by people from South Africa to South Asia; from Eastern Europe to Indonesia. It's a story with a simple truth: that violence is a dead end. It is a sign of neither courage nor power to shoot rockets at sleeping children, or to blow up old women on a bus. That is not how moral authority is claimed; that is how it is surrendered.

Now is the time for Palestinians to focus on what they can build. The Palestinian Authority must develop its capacity to govern, with institutions that serve the needs of its people. Hamas does have support among some Palestinians, but they also have responsibilities. To play a role in fulfilling Palestinian aspirations, and to unify the Palestinian people, Hamas must put an end to violence, recognize past agreements, and recognize Israel's right to exist.

At the same time, Israelis must acknowledge that just as Israel's right to exist cannot be denied, neither can Palestine's. The United States does not accept the legitimacy of continued Israeli settlements. This construction violates previous agreements and undermines efforts to achieve peace. It is time for these settlements to stop.

Israel must also live up to its obligations to ensure that Palestinians can live, and work, and develop their society. And just as it devastates Palestinian families, the continuing humanitarian crisis in Gaza does not serve Israel's security; neither does the continuing lack of opportunity in the West Bank. Progress in the daily lives of the Palestinian people must be part of a road to peace, and Israel must take concrete steps to enable such progress.

Finally, the Arab States must recognize that the Arab Peace Initiative was an important beginning, but not the end of their responsibilities. The Arab-Israeli conflict should no longer be used to distract the people of Arab nations from other problems. Instead, it must be a cause for action to help the Palestinian people develop the institutions that will sustain their state; to recognize Israel's legitimacy; and to choose progress over a self-defeating focus on the past.

America will align our policies with those who pursue peace, and say in public what we say in private to Israelis and Palestinians and Arabs. We cannot impose peace. But privately, many Muslims recognize that Israel will not go away. Likewise, many Israelis recognize the need for a Palestinian state. It is time for us to act on what everyone knows to be true.

Too many tears have flowed. Too much blood has been shed. All of us have a responsibility to work for the day when the mothers of Israelis and Palestinians can see their children grow up without fear; when the Holy Land of three great faiths is the place of peace that God intended it to be; when Jerusalem is a secure and lasting home for Jews and Christians and Muslims, and a place for all of the children of Abraham to mingle peacefully together as in the story of Israel, when Moses, Jesus, and Mohammed (peace be upon them) joined in prayer.

The third source of tension is our shared interest in the rights and responsibilities of nations on nuclear weapons.

This issue has been a source of tension between the United States and the Islamic Republic of Iran. For many years, Iran has defined itself in part by its opposition to my country, and there is indeed a tumultuous history between us. In the middle of the Cold War, the

United States played a role in the overthrow of a democratically-elected Iranian government. Since the Islamic Revolution, Iran has played a role in acts of hostage-taking and violence against U.S. troops and civilians. This history is well known. Rather than remain trapped in the past, I have made it clear to Iran's leaders and people that my country is prepared to move forward. The question, now, is not what Iran is against, but rather what future it wants to build.

It will be hard to overcome decades of mistrust, but we will proceed with courage, rectitude and resolve. There will be many issues to discuss between our two countries, and we are willing to move forward without preconditions on the basis of mutual respect. But it is clear to all concerned that when it comes to nuclear weapons, we have reached a decisive point. This is not simply about America's interests. It is about preventing a nuclear arms race in the Middle East that could lead this region and the world down a hugely dangerous path.

I understand those who protest that some countries have weapons that others do not. No single nation should pick and choose which nations hold nuclear weapons. That is why I strongly reaffirmed America's commitment to seek a world in which no nations hold nuclear weapons. And any nation—including Iran—should have the right to access peaceful nuclear power if it complies with its responsibilities under the nuclear Non-Proliferation Treaty. That commitment is at the core of the Treaty, and it must be kept for all who fully abide by it. And I am hopeful that all countries in the region can share in this goal.

The fourth issue that I will address is democracy.

I know there has been controversy about the promotion of democracy in recent years, and much of this controversy is connected to the war in Iraq. So let me be clear: no system of government can or should be imposed upon one nation by any other.

That does not lessen my commitment, however, to governments that reflect the will of the people. Each nation gives life to this principle in its own way, grounded in the traditions of its own people. America does not presume to know what is best for everyone, just as we would not presume to pick the outcome of a peaceful election. But I do have an unyielding belief that all people yearn for certain things: the ability to speak your mind and have a say in how you are governed; confidence in the rule of law and the equal administration of justice; government that is transparent and doesn't steal from the people; the freedom to live as you choose. Those are not just American ideas, they are human rights, and that is why we will support them everywhere.

There is no straight line to realize this promise. But this much is clear: governments that protect these rights are ultimately more stable, successful and secure. Suppressing ideas never succeeds in making them go away. America respects the right of all peaceful and law-abiding voices to be heard around the world, even if we disagree with them. And we will welcome all elected, peaceful governments— provided they govern with respect for all their people.

This last point is important because there are some who advocate for democracy only when they are out of power; once in power, they are ruthless in suppressing the rights of others. No matter where it takes hold, government of the people and by the people sets a single standard for all who hold power: you must maintain your power through consent, not coercion; you must respect the rights of minorities, and participate with a spirit of tolerance and compromise; you must place the interests of your people and the legitimate workings of the political process above your party. Without these ingredients, elections alone do not make true democracy.

The fifth issue that we must address together is religious freedom. Islam has a proud tradition of tolerance. We see it in the history of Andalusia and Cordoba during the Inquisition. I saw it firsthand as a child in Indonesia, where devout Christians worshiped freely in an overwhelmingly Muslim country. That is the spirit we need today. People in every country should be free to choose and live their faith based upon the persuasion of the mind, heart, and soul. This tolerance is essential for religion to thrive, but it is being challenged in many different ways.

Among some Muslims, there is a disturbing tendency to measure one's own faith by the rejection of another's. The richness of religious diversity must be upheld—whether it is for Maronites in Lebanon or the Copts in Egypt. And fault lines must be closed among Muslims as well, as the divisions between Sunni and Shia have led to tragic violence, particularly in Iraq.

Freedom of religion is central to the ability of peoples to live together. We must always examine the ways in which we protect it. For instance, in the United States, rules on charitable giving have made it harder for Muslims to fulfill their religious obligation. That is why I am committed to working with American Muslims to ensure that they can fulfill *zakat*.

Likewise, it is important for Western countries to avoid impeding Muslim citizens from practicing religion as they see fit—for instance, by dictating what clothes a Muslim woman should wear. We cannot disguise hostility towards any religion behind the pretense of liberalism.

Indeed, faith should bring us together. That is why we are forging service projects in America that bring together Christians, Muslims, and Jews. That is why we welcome efforts like Saudi Arabian King Abdullah's Interfaith dialogue and Turkey's leadership in the Alliance of Civilizations. Around the world, we can turn dialogue into Interfaith service, so bridges between peoples lead to action—whether it is combating malaria in Africa, or providing relief after a natural disaster.

The sixth issue that I want to address is women's rights.

I know there is debate about this issue. I reject the view of some in the West that a woman who chooses to cover her hair is somehow less equal, but I do believe that a woman who is denied an education is denied equality. And it is no coincidence that countries where women are well-educated are far more likely to be prosperous.

Now let me be clear: issues of women's equality are by no means simply an issue for Islam. In Turkey, Pakistan, Bangladesh and Indonesia, we have seen Muslim-majority countries elect a woman to lead. Meanwhile, the struggle for women's equality continues in many aspects of American life, and in countries around the world.

Our daughters can contribute just as much to society as our sons, and our common prosperity will be advanced by allowing all humanity—men and women—to reach their full potential. I do not believe that women must make the same choices as men in order to be equal, and I respect those women who choose to live their lives in traditional roles. But it should be their choice. That is why the United States will partner with any Muslim-majority country to support expanded literacy for girls, and to help young women pursue employment through micro-financing that helps people live their dreams.

Finally, I want to discuss economic development and opportunity.

I know that for many, the face of globalization is contradictory. The Internet and television can bring knowledge and information, but also offensive sexuality and mindless violence. Trade can bring new wealth and opportunities, but also huge disruptions and changing communities. In all nations—including my own—this change can bring fear. Fear that because of modernity we will lose of control over our economic choices, our politics, and most importantly our identities—those things we most cherish about our communities, our families, our traditions, and our faith.

But I also know that human progress cannot be denied. There need not be contradiction between development and tradition. Countries like Japan and South Korea grew their economies while maintaining distinct cultures. The same is true for the astonishing progress within Muslim-majority countries from Kuala Lumpur to Dubai. In ancient times and in our times, Muslim communities have been at the forefront of innovation and education.

This is important because no development strategy can be based only upon what comes out of the ground, nor can it be sustained while young people are out of work. Many Gulf States have enjoyed great wealth as a consequence of oil, and some are beginning to focus it on broader development. But all of us must recognize that education and innovation will be the currency of the 21st century and in too many Muslim communities there remains underinvestment in these areas. I am emphasizing such investments within my country. And while America in the past has focused on oil and gas in this part of the world, we now seek a broader engagement.

On education, we will expand exchange programs, and increase scholarships, like the one that brought my father to America, while encouraging more Americans to study in Muslim communities. And we will match promising Muslim students with internships in America; invest in on-line learning for teachers and children around the world; and create a new online network, so a teenager in Kansas can communicate instantly with a teenager in Cairo.

On economic development, we will create a new corps of business volunteers to partner with counterparts in Muslim-majority countries. And I will host a Summit on Entrepreneurship this year to identify how we can deepen ties between business leaders, foundations and social entrepreneurs in the United States and Muslim communities around the world.

On science and technology, we will launch a new fund to support technological development in Muslim-majority countries, and to help transfer ideas to the marketplace so they can create jobs. We will open centers of scientific excellence in Africa, the Middle East and Southeast Asia, and appoint new Science Envoys to collaborate on programs that develop new sources of energy, create green jobs, digitize records, clean water, and grow new crops. And today I am announcing a new global effort with the Organization of the Islamic Conference to eradicate polio. And we will also expand partnerships with Muslim communities to promote child and maternal health.

All these things must be done in partnership. Americans are ready to join with citizens and governments; community organizations, religious leaders, and businesses in Muslim communities around the world to help our people pursue a better life.

The issues that I have described will not be easy to address. But we have a responsibility to join together on behalf of the world we seek—a world where extremists no longer threaten our people, and American troops have come home; a world where Israelis and Palestinians are each secure in a state of their own, and nuclear energy is used for peaceful purposes; a world where governments serve their citizens, and the rights of all God's children are respected. Those are mutual interests. That is the world we seek. But we can only achieve it together.

I know there are many—Muslim and non-Muslim—who question whether we can forge this new beginning. Some are eager to stoke the flames of division, and to stand in the way of progress. Some suggest that it isn't worth the effort—that we are fated to disagree, and civilizations are doomed to clash. Many more are simply skeptical that real change can occur. There is so much fear, so much mistrust. But if we choose to be bound by the past, we will never move forward. And I want to particularly say this to young people of every faith, in every country—you, more than anyone, have the ability to remake this world.

All of us share this world for but a brief moment in time. The question is whether we spend that time focused on what pushes us apart, or whether we commit ourselves to an effort—a sustained effort—to find common ground, to focus on the future we seek for our children, and to respect the dignity of all human beings.

It is easier to start wars than to end them. It is easier to blame others than to look inward; to see what is different about someone than to find the things we share. But we should choose the right path, not just the easy path. There is also one rule that lies at the heart of every religion—that we do unto others as we would have them do unto us. This truth transcends nations and peoples—a belief that isn't new; that isn't black or white or brown; that isn't Christian, or Muslim or Jew. It's a belief that pulsed in the cradle of civilization, and that still beats in the heart of billions. It's a faith in other people, and it's what brought me here today.

We have the power to make the world we seek, but only if we have the courage to make a new beginning, keeping in mind what has been written.

The Holy Koran tells us, "O mankind! We have created you male and a female; and we have made you into nations and tribes so that you may know one another."

The Talmud tells us: "The whole of the Torah is for the purpose of promoting peace."

The Holy Bible tells us, "Blessed are the peacemakers, for they shall be called sons of God."

The people of the world can live together in peace. We know that is God's vision. Now, that must be our work here on Earth. Thank you. And may God's peace be upon you.

APPENDIX B

AMERICA THE TARGET

By: Mike Evans

On a September evening in 1980 in Tel Aviv, I sat with former Mossad chief Isser Harel for a conversation about Arab terrorism. As he handed me a cup of hot tea and a plate of cookies, I asked him, "Do you think terrorism will come to America, and if so, where and why?"

Harel looked at his American visitor and replied, "I fear it will come to you in America. America has the power, but not the will, to fight terrorism. The terrorists have the will, but not the power, to fight America—but all that could change with time. Arab oil money buys more than tents."

As to the where, Harel continued, "New York City is the symbol of freedom and capitalism. It's likely they will strike the Empire State Building, your tallest building [at that time] and a symbol of your power."

With my Western mind-set I replied that America was dedicated to fighting terrorism. Harel smiled and said, "You kill a fly and you celebrate. We live with flies daily. One dies and 100 flies come to the funeral."

"If 'land for peace' happens," Harel continued, "I think it will mean America gets peace for a season, as the West pressures Israel into giving Arafat our land. But once you let the genie of appeasement out of the bottle, he will grow and eventually turn on you. In time America itself will be in the crosshairs."

"Hitler first killed Jews, and then he killed Christians. Our culture and our democracies are the root of [the terrorists'] rage. If we're right, then they are wrong."

Twenty-one years later, the first part of Harel's prediction came true; except, of course, that the twin towers of the World Trade Center were much taller than the Empire State Building. However, it was the second part of his doomsday prediction that came true much earlier.

It was 1982 and Israel had declared its own war on terrorism by invading Lebanon to root out Arafat's terrorist infrastructure. I was summoned to New York by Prime Minister Menachem Begin's aide, Reuven Hecht, for a meeting with Begin prior to his meeting with President Ronald Reagan. Hecht had just met in Washington with secretary of state Alexander Haig, who had told him that America had changed its mind: it would no longer support Israel's war against terrorism in Lebanon.

Begin was in shock. The West—whose planes had been blown out of the sky, its diplomats, soldiers, and civilians murdered by terrorists—was now fighting to save the primary organization responsible for these vile acts. In the end, American pressure prevailed and Arafat's 10,000 PLO terrorists, rifles in hand, were escorted out of Beirut to safe bases in Tunisia and other Arab lands. The cries of Israeli mothers whose sons had died in Lebanon and who stood outside his apartment screaming "Murderer!" were more than Begin could bear. He resigned a depressed and broken man.

Since then hundreds of Israeli civilians have been killed and thousands wounded by terrorists recruited, trained and equipped in territory controlled by Arafat's Palestinian Authority. Osama bin Laden's cells operated in the West Bank and Gaza Strip, as did Hezbollah—all with Arafat's blessing.

After declared its own war against terrorism, Arafat summoned the press to photograph him giving blood ostensibly for the victims of the attacks on America. Meanwhile, his Palestinian Police threatened journalists who filmed Palestinians dancing in the streets to celebrate the 9/11 attacks... all this supposedly in aid of encouraging Islamic states to join the anti-terrorism coalition.

Even Arafat's Hamas successor announced it was willing to suspend suicide attacks inside Israel "unless provoked." Can you imagine someone like the late Osama bin Laden saying, "I will suspend suicide attacks against America unless I am provoked—now let me join the anti-terrorism coalition"?

Israel and America share the same democratic values that terrorists despise and seek to destroy. For Americans to think that Arafat, the godfather of Islamic terrorism, did not continue to support it is absurd. He advocated bringing more terror to America. Arafat's supporters, the Liberal Left in the U.S. believed (and still believes) that some terrorists can be categorized as good and some as bad. This is a guarantee for failure.

APPENDIX C

Abraham's Land Grant from Jehovah God

The countries that would be affected if Israel were to claim the land promised by God in Numbers 34:1-13[138]:

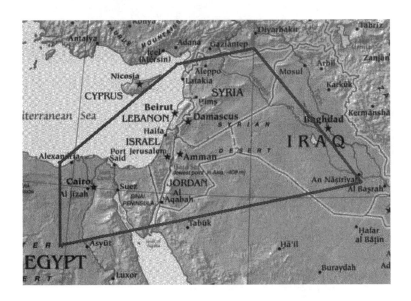

TEXT OF LETTER TO PRIME MINISTER YITZHAK RABIN

Dear Prime Minister Rabin,

I just left the White House with a broken heart. I did not go to be a part of the Arafat celebration. I went as a representative of the 50 million evangelicals in America. My purpose for going, Mr. Prime Minister, was not to express support for Yasser Arafat, nor to get his autograph, but to express support for Israel's Bible Lands.

I did not feel tears running down my face as many did at the White House. Nor did my heart pound from hyped-up media reports of an historic reconciliation with a man who ordered the murders of school children in Avivim, Ma'alot and Antwerp, of eleven Jewish athletes in Munich, Synagogue worshippers in Istanbul, a child and his pregnant mother in Alfeh Menashe, and a mother and her children on a bus in Jericho. This same man who ordered innocent Arabs in Nablus hanged by their chins on butcher's hooks until they died, ordered the bellies of pregnant Arab women split open before the eyes of their husbands, and the hands of Arab children chopped off while their parents watched...simply because these Arabs disagreed.

Mr. Prime Minister, how can the government of Israel commit itself to the withdrawal of armed forces from Gaza and Jericho and provide security for Israeli citizens in the West Negev and in southern Israel? How can the doors opening to the Palestinians, worldwide, into Jericho and Gaza, keep from escalating terrorism and a deepening of hostility? How will foreign international forces insure Israel's security? They didn't do it in Lebanon when the United Nation forces worked with the P.L.O. When the P.L.O. strikes Israel, it will be virtually impossible for Israel to retaliate with the U.N. or international forces in the way.

As Evangelicals, we believe in peace and forgiveness. Indeed, this is the Jewish year 5754 when your nation is in the midst of celebrating its Holy days. During this Holy season, there is a need for repentance, humbling ourselves and asking forgiveness by God Almighty, for any and all sins.

Mr. Prime Minister, the healing and reconciliation must happen in the human heart between Arab and Jew. The basis for it cannot be land or cutting deals with a terrorist who has repented of nothing. God dearly loves the Arab people just as He loves your beloved people. The question is: How will innocent children and even innocent civilians benefit by dealing with shrewd, demon-inspired terrorists and politicians who wish Israel no good...only their destruction. To think that the P.L.O. would take over the administrated territories that God Almighty gave to your beloved people, and that more than 120,000 settlers in these territories will be subject to the P.L.O. is beyond reason. Even if the army succeeds in protecting them against terrorists, no Jew will want to live at the mercy of a dictatorial P.L.O. regime, which will have control of land, water and services.

President Clinton has coined this... "A brave gamble." Mr. Prime Minister, one does not gamble with God's prophetic land or His prophetic plan. Nebuchadnezzar tried that and lived to greatly regret it.

In my 13 meetings with Prime Minister Begin, we talked about building a bridge based upon mutual respect. My greatest fear, Mr. Prime Minister, is that there seems to be a bridge being built between Gaza and Jericho based upon destruction. Can you imagine America inviting a terrorist organization that had terrorized our country and killed our civilians like Arafat has yours to have a state in Virginia... just a few miles from our capital, Washington, D.C.? There is no question that Arafat demands a Palestinian state and not in Jericho and Gaza. He wants it all.

Prime Minister Rabin, we believe that God Almighty promised the land of Israel, in its entirety, to your people, and the promises of God's Word are non-negotiable.

On October 30, 1991, at the Middle East Peace Conference, I boldly confronted Secretary of State, James Baker, and said the following,

"Most of the times that our Presidents have run for election, they have always told us evangelicals that they were going to move the U.S. Embassy to Jerusalem. Obviously, every capital in the world is recognized as a capital, except Jerusalem. Why can't America recognize Jerusalem as Israel's capital as a gesture of peace? Secondly, we are moving our military presence into the Arab world for a sense of security, why can't we have a military presence in Israel to help its security? It has suffered so greatly...especially paying such a dear price during the Persian Gulf War."

You know Mr. Baker's response: "These things must be determined by negotiations."

With whom shall God negotiate? One must be very careful before one begins negotiating on Bible Lands without considering the God who gave these lands. If one determines that they are going to divide what God Almighty has given, then indeed, the judgment of God could very severely fall upon the head of that individual. Either God exists...or He doesn't. Either God's Word is true...or it isn't. If He does, and it is, then one must walk very softly.

At the 43rd Session of the U.N. General Assembly meeting in Geneva on December 13, 1988, Arafat made the statement:

"The only birth certificate for the establishment for the state of Israel is resolution 181 approved by the General Assembly on November 29, 1947...the first and decisive resolution of our Palestine National Council was the proclamation of the establishment of the state of Palestine with the Holy City of Jerusalem-al-Quds ask-Shareef as its capital."

Arafat, on December 13, 1988, stated in his speech: "I condemn terrorism in all its forms."

Only God knows the number of funerals you have had since 1988 when Arafat lied. Prime Minister Rabin, I have written six major books on your nation and hundreds of articles. I have worked very closely with, and have had eighteen meetings with your last four prime ministers. In the last two decades, when Israel has had a crisis, I have always been there. Based upon my experience and knowledge, I do not believe for a second that there is any intention of these players in the peace process, to respect Israel's rights. This is more Arab "rhetoric"... more as we say, "shuck and jive."

Mount Calvary, the Lord's Tomb, the Mount of Olives, the Via Dolorosa, the Garden of Gethsemane and even the Temple site where we believe the Messiah will come back to...are all part of East Jerusalem. We believe in our Bible that it will be in Jewish hands when our Messiah returns. To place it in the hands of an Arab P.L.O. State is paramount to ripping pages of prophecy right out of the Bible and shaking your fist in the face of God Almighty who gave you this land.

I see no indication that America's policy has changed, or that Arafat's policies have changed. When three Palestinians are on trial for attempting to blow up the World Trade Center, when four graves were being dug in Jerusalem because of Palestinians killing Israelis while you were with Arafat at the White House, and when the very man who embraced Saddam Hussein and helped orchestrate a war not only to eliminate Kuwait but to hopefully destroy Israel, has repented of nothing, has refused adamantly to denounce terrorism in his speech at the White House, I cannot understand why you would shake his hand.

Mr. Prime Minister, you and I met recently and I gave you copies of my television specials seen by more than 23 million people in America, "Israel, America's Key to Survival," "Jerusalem, D.C. ," and "Let My People Go." I brought my Bible. We discussed the prophecies of the Bible, and I prayed with you. I urged you to base your decisions on the Bible and not public opinion, because ultimately the blessings of God will be the determining factor upon which nations fall or rise. I have made the same appeal to your predecessors during the last two decades.

Twenty-three nations, which lifted their hands against your nation throughout history, have ceased to exist. But the people of the Book live on. Perseverance based upon faith in God and in His Word will outlast persecution.

I appeal to you to make your decisions based upon God's promise to your land. Israel was not created in 1948, and Jerusalem was not given to you in 1967. It was given by God Almighty 3,000 years ago through the father of your faith, Abraham. If the Bible is not to be considered the basis for your right to the land, then you may as well tell the people of Israel to pack their bags. Life will become so unbearable, the Jews will not want to move to Israel and great numbers there will move out because of the hell they are going through...like a great exodus. The world community will attempt to pressure Israel to give up every inch of land possible...making life absolutely unbearable for your beloved nation.

Prime Minister Rabin, this week I will address the entire nation of the former U.S.S.R. and all of its republics. I will be speaking to them for one hour, prime time, from 7:00-8:00 p.m. on Moscow I, on September 26. This is a message that I spoke at the Kremlin Palace. With all of my heart, I believe that the one million Russian Jews coming to Israel is a fulfillment of prophecy. This prophetic exodus must continue, but it will not, based upon Arafat's present policies.

On Monday, September 13, Yasser Arafat made his pledge and promise to America and Israel that he would accept Jericho and Gaza, but on Sunday, September 19, the P.L.O. Chairman, Yasser Arafat, promised the Arab Foreign Ministers at the Islamic conference in Cairo:

> "The peace accord with Israel is only the first step in an effort to regain lands controlled by Israel, including East Jerusalem. The three million Palestinian refugees outside of Israel will be allowed to return home. Israel must return all territories taken from the '67 war. The agreement we have reached is nothing but a first step. It is the basis for a transitional solution and the broad outline for an ultimate solution that will be based on the ending of the occupation and the total withdrawal from our land...our Holy sites, and our Holy Jerusalem. The most important part of the agreement is not only the withdrawal from Gaza and Jericho, but the recognition of the Palestinian authority and jurisdiction over all the occupied territories."

The basic promise God gave to the Nation of Israel and the Jewish descendants of Abraham is given in Genesis 15:18 with the Covenant God made with Abraham:

"To your descendants I have given this land, from
the river of Egypt as far as the great river, the river
Euphrates."

All this land was what God promised would eventually be under
Jewish control and part of the Nation of Israel. Giving away any of this
land violates the Covenant God made with Israel, with the final fulfillment of the boundaries of Israel to come during the Messianic Age.

In regards to specific land in question that the P.L.O. would control, Jericho is predominantly mentioned in the Bible in regards to
God's promises to the Jewish successors of Abraham. It is believed
that God continued the promise, of inheritance of the land to Moses
and Joshua, at the time of the crossing of the Jordan River into the
Promised Land. This promise was continued in Joshua 1:3-4 where
God spoke to Joshua and said:

"Every place on which the sole of your foot treads,
I have given to you, just as I spoke to Moses. From the
wilderness and from Lebanon as far as the great river,
the river Euphrates as far as the great sea toward the
setting of the sun, will be your territory."

The specific right to the city of Jericho was given to the Nation of
Israel through God's promise to Joshua in Joshua 6:2 where the Lord
said:

"See I have given Jericho into your hand, with its
king and the valiant warriors."

The basic principle was laid forth by Joshua in Joshua 6:26, that anyone that fortified the city of Jericho against the Nation of Israel would be cursed with a curse. The Lord made this oath to Joshua after the city of Jericho had been destroyed and all the people killed as per God's instructions to Joshua. Joshua 6:26 gives the oath that Joshua and the Nation of Israel made:

> "Joshua made them take an oath at that time, saying, 'Cursed before the Lord is the man who rises up and builds the city Jericho; with the loss of his firstborn he shall lay his foundation, and with the loss of his youngest son he shall set up its gates.'"

We see an example of the fulfillment of this oath in I Kings 16:34 where Hiel fortified Jericho, and with its foundation he lost his firstborn son, Abiram, and with its gates, he lost his youngest son, Segub, which the Bible says was according to the Word of the Lord which was spoken by Joshua the son of Nun.

Prime Minister Rabin, as a Bible believing Christian, my face turned red with embarrassment when President Clinton said:

> "The sound we heard today, once again as in ancient Jericho, was of trumpets toppling walls, the walls of anger and suspicion between Israeli and Palestinian, between Arab and Jew. This time, praise God, the trumpets herald not the destruction of that city, but its new beginning."

President Clinton praised God that the "trumpets herald not the destruction of Jericho but its new beginning." The walls of Jericho fell by a mighty act of God because of a glorious miracle. To mock that miracle, or to compare that miracle with what is happening with Jericho today, is an embarrassment to all Bible believing Christians.

It is quite obvious that with autonomy given to the P.L.O. and the Palestinian people of Jericho, that the city will once again be fortified with its own police force and with heavy security if Yasser Arafat establishes his temporary home and headquarters in that city. The curse of God will descend upon anyone who does this.

While the actual city of Jericho lies within the boundaries of the land originally given to the tribe of Benjamin, the area of Judah and Judea are, without question, lands promised by God Almighty to the Jewish people. This land cannot be devoid of Jewish control and Jewish settlement at that time when God, through the Messiah, defends the Nation of Israel in its time of greatest danger.

Zechariah Chapter 12 and 14 indicate that the last battle of the world will center on Jerusalem and that the Lord will stand on the Mount of Olives to defend the inhabitants of Jerusalem. God specifically states that He will watch over the house of Judah and that the inhabitants of Judah will be saved first before the inhabitants of Jerusalem in this great carnage so that the inhabitants of Jerusalem will not be magnified above Judah. Therefore, it is absolutely imperative that before the coming of the Messianic age and the deliverance of the Nation of Israel through the Messiah, that the ancient boundaries of Judah be under control of the Jewish people, and not under Arafat and the P.L.O. terrorist organization.

While he was here in America, Arafat arrogantly boasted that his P.L.O. flag would fly over Jerusalem, and all aspects of U.N. resolution 242 and 338 must be implemented as a basis for peace.

Mr. Prime Minister, please be kind enough to tell me what the basis is for allowing this terrorist to enter the global community as a world diplomat, serving as head of the 20th Arab state. That will be paramount to the P.L.O. serving as dictators over another hostile Arab state, carved out of the back of the Bible Lands, with its headquarters to be in the very door that God Almighty told Joshua would be the entrance to the Promised Land...Jericho.

Surely, you recognize that the Holy Land is the home not only of the Muslim, and the Jewish faiths, but also the Christian faith. We evangelicals have been strong, courageous and uncompromising supporters of your land.

Mr. Prime Minister, your credentials as a famous General and Chief of Staff are extremely commendable. Please enlighten us on why you would trust Yasser Arafat. Did the Arab world rush to give up its territory when six million Jews died in the Holocaust? No, it was the Jewish people themselves who sacrificed and suffered so that the prophecies could be fulfilled and your beloved people could have a homeland.

It is not the fault of Israel that the Palestinians have had difficulty in Gaza. It is the fault of many current, rich, Arab dictators, who refuse to give a crumb of bread, or a small piece of their vast lands to establish a Palestinian state, but would rather slip a knife in the back of their Arab brothers who attempt to build any bridges based upon mutual respect with your beloved land. Prime Minister Rabin, why the great change in Israel's policy?

We love you and your beloved country more than words can express, and pray for Israel daily. Mr. Prime Minister, when does a pig have enough to eat? Will Jericho and Gaza satisfy his appetite? How could that be possible when he is already boasting about having East Jerusalem and much more?

What is the basis for faith in an Islamic religion, which has done everything in its power to boycott and unmercifully eliminate the Jewish people? Why did the Jewish people leave all of the 19 Arab states? It surely wasn't because they were treated well. On the contrary, they were hung, burned alive and tortured unmercifully. For what? For being Jewish. Will it be any different in the 20ᵗʰ Arab state under a terrorist leader? Why give the P.L.O. a state when history records that the Palestinians are Jordanians. Seventy percent of all Palestinians carry Jordanian passports. Even if Arafat was a moderate, is it possible that the P.L.O. terrorist organization will improve after Arafat is gone? And, can you really believe that Arafat will survive if he becomes a moderate? Sadat did not.

History records that the Arab nations have always run their countries off the bullet not the ballot. As you well know, this feud has gone on for 3,000 years...since the days of Ishmael and Isaac. It is much bigger than a handshake and political speeches.

We evangelicals have no hatred in our hearts toward the Arab people. We love them and pray for them. But we have no respect for an unrepentant terrorist who wants to deceive America and the nations of the world. There will be a man born in days to come who will be like Yasser Arafat, but a thousand times worse. In your Jewish Bible, he is prophesied in the Book of Daniel, Chapter 8:23-25:

> "And in the latter time of their kingdom, when the transgressors are come to the full, a king of fierce countenance, and understanding dark sentences, shall stand up. And his power shall be mighty, but not by his power: and he shall destroy wonderfully, and shall prosper, and practice, and shall destroy the mighty and the holy people. And through his policy also he shall cause craft to prosper in his hand; and he shall magnify himself in his heart, and by peace shall destroy many: he shall also stand up against the Prince of princes; but he shall be broken without hand."

Mr. Prime Minister, this prophecy describes a false messiah who will rise up promising peace to the world, and use economic leverage to manipulate the world into that peace. Arafat is a perfect forerunner of that which is to come. The spirit in which Arafat is being influenced by is described in the Book of Revelation 12:9:

"And the great dragon was cast out, that old serpent, called the Devil, and Satan, which deceiveth the whole world: he was cast out into the earth, and his angels were cast out with him."

Our former Speaker of the House, Jim Wright and I talked about this matter. Jim Wright explained that he had met with Sadat in Cairo, had flown to Jerusalem to talk to Begin and was in the Knesset when Sadat made his famous speech. I asked Jim Wright, "How much do you know about Arafat? Have you ever met him?" He answered, "No, but he is a charming fellow, wouldn't you agree?" I told my friend, Jim Wright, "I am sure many thought Hitler was a charming fellow, too."

I had a similar conversation with Rev. Jesse Jackson. He said to me, "This is a wonderful day. It is the beginning of peace. Israel must recognize the golden rule."

I replied, "We live in a day when those who have the gold make the rule on the short term. On the long term, man proposes, but God disposes. God will indeed have the last word when it comes to the Bible Lands and prophecy."

Prime Minister Rabin, we as Bible believing Christians are loyal allies and friends of your beloved land. We have not been consulted concerning the decisions that are being made. Our opinion has not been asked. Are you not interested in our opinions? If you are, I can tell you, specifically, that evangelicals do not believe that God breaks His promises...or that the Bible is negotiable.

I was asked by Prime Minister Shamir's Senior Advisor, Dr.

Reuben Hecht, if I would speak up for Israel at the 43rd General Assembly of the United Nations at Geneva when your Ambassador and Foreign Minister held their specially convened conference. I told him I would be delighted to do so. I boldly expressed the same view that I am expressing in this letter. Your Foreign Minister made a statement saying:

> "No one can be sure of what the Bible says concerning our land, in that we do not determine our foreign policy by the Bible, nor do we know for sure what God says."

There was quite the uproar in Israel over this as I am sure you are aware because of the fact that this was broadcast live to the nation. The truth is that you must determine your foreign policy, and all policies, by the Bible. Your history records leaders upon whom God put His hand, and leaders from whom God removed His hand. David was a man after God's own heart, because he loved God's Word, and he attempted to humble himself, even when he made mistakes. God blessed him. But Saul was rejected by God and cursed. The people in the land experienced a terrible curse because of their disobedience.

We have no intention of seeing the Holy sites that we love so dearly being desecrated as toilets as they were before 1967. How hypocritical for the community of nations to demand that Israel trade land for peace! We did not do it in America with Mexico, nor did we do it with the American Indians. We told the American Indians that they could live in America, but they would have to abide by our rules. What has made our nation great is mutual respect...not trading land for peace.

Can you imagine a Mexican or an Indian terrorist being invited to the White House and applauded by the world community if he proclaimed Washington, DC. as his capital and had killed, proportionately, the number of people the PLO have killed, over the years, in your land?

Please explain to me, Mr. Prime Minister, so I can communicate it to the Evangelical community of America, what the reason is for this festival of hypocrisy and theater of the absurd that I witnessed in Washington, D.C. Is it economic blackmail or is it just a genuine willingness to want peace so desperately that you are willing to take such an enormous risk?

Tom Foley, the Speaker of the House, when asked if he would permit Arafat, in the future, to address the Congress and the Senate in a joint session, he said:

> "Seven days ago, I would have said unequivocally, no. But after seeing Arafat today, I would say that it would be highly probable."

Prime Minister Rabin, what in the world did Arafat do to be granted amnesty for all of his acts of butchery? Can you imagine an American doing what Arafat has done in America, slaughtering innocent civilians, hijacking planes, committing unbelievable atrocities, and then the President of the United States throwing him a multi-million dollar party in the White House promising to raise him over $7 billion? Why, the President would be impeached within 24 hours for attempting to conduct himself in such a way.

I could not believe it when I saw many Senators and Congressmen, that I highly respect, standing in line as if they were at a carnival attempting to get Yasser Arafat's autograph. If I have ever seen a gathering of the most powerful leaders of the world totally deceived by one man, I saw it that day. As an American, and in behalf of our leaders who are more concerned about political expediency and the history books than they are about human lives, I humbly ask your forgiveness for the embarrassing position in which you were placed.

How in the world can a smile and a handshake be the basis for mutual respect? God only knows how many individuals received a smile and a handshake from Hitler before they were shot in the head.

How much land, Mr. Prime Minister, will Israel be forced to give up before the security of your beloved nation is jeopardized? At the present moment, your early warning time is zero.

In the Islamic religion, "Muslims are required to make war on the Jewish 'infidels' and all others who reject Islam, because this is just punishment. The Islamic Resistance Movement must aspire to the realization of Allah's promises, no matter how long it takes."

The Prophet Allah...has said:

"The day of judgment will not come until Muslims fight and kill the Jews."

Mr. Prime Minister, the Arab population in the Middle East is 500 times the size of Israel size, and their armies outnumber you thirteen-to-one. Their combined air force is three times larger than yours, and they have even a greater advantage in the number of tanks. They need more land like they need a hole in their head. The Arabs have plenty of land to give away, and plenty of money to establish a Palestinian state.

Salman Rushdie still fears for his life because of simply writing the book, *Satanic Verses*. In the eyes of Islam, he deserves to die. The entire world, all of its journalists and its appeals have not been able to pacify the wrath of Islam fanatics who want to kill Rushdie.

Prime Minister Rabin, in the last 3,000 years, in spite of the signing of 5,721 major peace treaties, there has only been 268 years of peace. The Arab world is still in a state of war against your great nation. They are still boycotting the land of Israel. America still refuses to recognize Jerusalem as your capital and calls your Bible Land territories occupied.

"Make war upon those who believe not...even if they be people of the book. Make war upon them until idolatry is no more and Allah's religion reigns supreme."

Mr. Prime Minister, as our President forced you to shake Yasser Arafat's hand, the words of the Koran were ringing through my ears. The miracle of the re-birth of Israel in 1948 followed 2,536 years of almost uninterrupted foreign subjugation.

The miracle of the restoration of Jerusalem as your Holy capital is indeed a fulfillment of God's promises. God always keeps His promises. That cannot be said for man. The motto of the British 14th Bomber Squad as they flew over Jerusalem in 1917 was "I spread my wings and keep my promise." The British never kept their promise, but God Almighty has. He has been faithful.

When I confronted Yasser Arafat, face-to-face, at the 43rd General Assembly in Geneva, asking him to recognize Jerusalem as your capital and your biblical rights, he went into a rage telling me,

"Shut up. Shut up." He asked, "What must I do to make you shut up?"

Mr. Prime Minister, I have no intention of shutting up. I believe the Bible, and I, along with Bible believing evangelicals, will courageously stand up for your biblical, historical and humanitarian rights...in spite of weak-kneed politicians or the liberal press.

Prime Minister Rabin, the P.L.O. covenant in Article II denies the possibility of dividing mandatory Palestine into more than one state. Article VI excludes all Jews who arrive in Palestine after 1917 from remaining in the projected Arab Palestine state. Article IX offers armed struggle as the only way to liberate Palestine. Article XIX and XX declares illegal the Balfour Declaration, and the mandate for Palestine, and the 1947 U.N. decision to petition Palestine and establish the state of Israel and which determines the Jews are members of a religion not a nationality or a nation. I do not need to remind you of Article XXII challenging Zionism.

Mr. Prime Minister, I realize that a great number of the Jewish organizations in America are applauding your meeting with Arafat... as are the World Council of Churches. Both of these organizations have a lot in common. They both reject the Bible as the Word of God.

We Evangelicals accept the Bible as non-negotiable. God Almighty exists, and He miraculously gave your beloved people Jericho, how in the world can this same Jericho be given to Arafat as his transitional capital? Has anyone asked God's opinion or even consulted your Eternal Declaration of Independence...the Word of God?

I realize that you do have peace, to some degree, with Egypt because Anwar al-Sadat presented a new type of Islam in which he said: "No religion in politics. No politics in religion...an ecumenical Islam."

But as you well know, Sadat was not quoting from the Koran. This was a new philosophy that he thought he could sell to the Islamic world, but as we say in Texas, "that dog won't hunt." His Muslim brothers assassinated Sadat for being what they considered a traitor to their cause.

I want to remind you of what Yasser Arafat did in 1981 at the Islamic conference in Mecca when he pressed for a swearing of a collective oath by Muslim delegation heads binding them to afford all means to liberate Jerusalem. This time, however, Saudi King Khalid managed to dissuade him. According to Saudi Foreign Minister, Saud al-Faysal:

> "There was a proposal on the liberation of Jerusalem at the opening session of the Islamic conference in the Mecca Mosque. King Khalid asserted to the P.L.O. leader that the meeting of Muslims near the Ka-ba in the house of God, in a conference designated as the Palestinian and Jerusalem conference is already a binding pledge to liberate Holy Jerusalem... 'I believe that the whole conference represents a pledge by Muslims to liberate Jerusalem."

Has anything really changed in the minds of the Arab leaders of the Middle East?

In 1970, Jordan was virtually overthrown by Yasser Arafat because of his terrorist activities. It was your own nation that saved Jordan from this maniac. Why in the world would you want to sandwich him between the Holy City of Jerusalem and Jordan?

The Arab world wants Jerusalem. They have their own version of "next year in Jerusalem," and it is not based upon the desire to pray for the return of the Messiah, but to drive your beloved people out of the land.

But God keeps His promises, and the Word of God proclaims:

> "I will restore the captivity of my people, Israel, and they will rebuild the ruined cities and live in them. They will also plant vineyards and drink their wine, and make gardens, and eat their fruit. I will also plant

them in the land, and they will not again be rooted out from their land...which I have given them...says the Lord your God" (Jeremiah 29:4-10).

Mr. Prime Minister, from the old border, the pre-1967 border, the distance is nine miles, or fifteen kilometers. This is the distance between Kennedy Airport and Queens in New York. From the Jordan River or the Jordanian territory that is east of the Jordan River to Jerusalem...is six minutes. This is with an F5G with a full load of bombs at a low altitude. As a military general, you have to know that in strictly military terms, you have about four minutes of early warning time. Four minutes of early warning time, in practical terms, means zero warning time.

What guarantee do you have that Russia will not ultimately move in the direction of your land in the future? Your Jewish Bible predicts in Ezekiel 38, by the prophet Ezekiel, that indeed she will. And by the way, Mr. Prime Minister, more than two-thirds of the prophecies of your Jewish prophets have already been fulfilled concerning your land. God does keep His promises. General George Keegan, a former head of the U.S. Air Force, mentioned to me in the past that if the West Bank were to fall into Arafat's hands, and two brigades of well-equipped Soviet divisions were introduced into the West Bank, in one night, Israel would cease to exist. I don't believe it will cease to exist because the Bible prophesies a battle called the Battle of Armageddon. But God forbid that the winds of that battle have to blow prematurely because of mistakes made by man...because of a world that wants Israel to give up its territory and lose the security of its nation.

President Clinton referred to the Arab and Palestinian children and said that this decision needed to be made for their safety. What will the Soviet Union be like ten or twenty years from now? High-level Soviet Generals, with whom I have met, have told me that there will ultimately be a revolution and it will be worse than before. If indeed that is the case, could your decision be forcing the children of Israel into a premature Armageddon?

Prime Minister Rabin, when I founded the Prayer Breakfast in honor of Israel in conjunction with the National Religious Broadcasters, I gave a speech, which is in the Congressional Record. (Appendix E.)

Mr. Prime Minister, the land of Palestine belongs to the Jewish people. Millions of evangelicals signed this proclamation. I appeal to you to read Psalm 83:3-5...especially these words:

> "Those who hate thee have exalted themselves. They make shrewd plans against thy people and conspire together against thy treasured ones. They have said come let us wipe them out as a nation. Let the name of Israel be remembered no more. They have conspired together with one mind against thee to make a covenant."

The Chief Rabbi of Jerusalem met with Harry Truman in the White House concerning the re-establishment of your state. He said:

> "President Truman, God put you in your mother's womb to bring about the re-birth of Israel after 2,000 years."

President Truman had the courage to stand up and acknowledge

Israel's biblical rights. As amazing as it might sound, the Soviets did also.

Please Mr. Prime Minister, God did not put you in your mother's womb to bring about the destruction of Israel. The Word of God declares in Isaiah 62:6-7:

> "I have set watchmen upon the walls O Jerusalem which shall never hold their peace...day or night. He that make mention of the Lord keep not silent. Give him no rest until he make Jerusalem a praise in the earth. Comfort ye. Comfort ye my people, saith your God."

The Bible also says:

> "When they shall cry peace and safety, then shall come sudden destruction upon them as travail upon a woman with child."

Jerusalem is facing the greatest threat in its 3,000-year history.

Mr. Prime Minister, call the people of the Book to humble themselves and fast and pray on these your Holy days. God is able to do what no man can do. He has done it before for your beloved land. Let me quote from II Chronicles 7:14:

> *"If my people, which are called by my name, shall humble themselves, and pray, and seek my face, and turn from their wicked ways; then will I hear from heaven, and will forgive their sin, and will heal their land."*

I humbly appeal to you to call your nation to humble itself, fast and pray based upon II Chronicles 7:14 that the God of Heaven will hear and answer your prayers. More than anything else, Israel needs a revival...a spiritual rebirth. That spiritual rebirth, indeed, will bring God's blessings and favor.

You are giving up everything. Yasser Arafat, and his P.L.O. terrorist organization, is giving up nothing. If that is the basis for a marriage, then Yasser Arafat will become delighted to be married to your beloved land.

Mr. Prime Minister, always remember: When you dance with a gorilla, the dance isn't over until the gorilla says so.

With sincere prayers for the peace of Jerusalem and the land of Israel, above all,

Michael David Evans"

CONGRESSIONAL RECORD COPY

WASHINGTON, D.C.,
TUESDAY, MARCH 16, 1982

"Proclamation of Blessing"

As Bible-believing Americans, we believe there exists an iron-clad bond between the State of Israel and the United States. We believe that bond to be a moral imperative.

Representing the vast majority of evangelicals in the United States, we have gathered together at this National Prayer Breakfast to reaffirm our support and prayers, that this bond not be weakened or diminished

We agree with the sentiments or our President:

That a secure, strong Israel is in America's self-interest. Israel is a major strategic asset to America. Israel is not a client, but a very reliable friend. To weaken Israel is to destabilize the Middle East and risk the peace of the world, for the road to world peace runs through the Middle East.

We support Israel's right to their land spiritually and legally. History records that God deals with nations in accordance with how these nations deal with Israel. We rejoice that here in America, for 206 years {now 235 years}, we have been committed to the Jewish people. The Jewish people have found refuge here; they have found a people who love them; and we can take pride in saying that Israel is not an exclusively Jewish issue.

Bible-believing evangelicals consider the support of Israel a biblical mandate. Regardless of contrary opinion, we do not believe Israel has to offer an excuse for its existence. Israel lives today as a right—a right that has been hallowed by the Bible, by history, by sacrifice, by prayer, and by the yearning for peace!

"'I will bring back the captives of My people Israel; They shall build the waste cities and inhabit them; They shall plant vineyards and drink wine from them; They shall also make gardens and eat fruit from them. I will plant them in their land, And no longer shall they be pulled up From the land I have given them,' Says the Lord your God" (Amos 9:14-15).

We believe one of the reasons America has been blessed over the years is because we have stood with Israel. This promise is taken from Genesis 12:3, "I will bless them that bless thee." So, for biblical reasons first and foremost, we support the State of Israel. For humanitarian reasons, we support the Jewish people. For historical reasons, believing that Palestine belongs to the Jewish people, we support the State of Israel. For legal reasons, dating back to 1948, and even further to the establishment of the British Mandate, we believe the land of Palestine belongs to the Jewish people.

Israel and the United States are not separate and distinct—we are one. We share common ideals and common democracy. What unites us across the ocean, and brings Jew and Christian together, is the recognition that Israel is a nation that is a manifestation of what America was and is.

America has a strong interest in the Middle East. We affirm our belief that the nation of Israel is the key to that interest because of our common bonds, our common values, our common belief in social justice, and the Godly principles on which our two countries were founded.

In affirmation of these beliefs, we hereby set our hands this 10th day of February, 1982.

ENDNOTES

1. Operation Entebbe, a hostage-rescue mission, was carried out by commandos of the Israel Defense Forces (IDF) at Entebbe Airport in Uganda on 4 July 1976. On 27 June, an Air France plane with 248 passengers was hijacked, by members of the Popular Front for the Liberation of Palestine and the German Revolutionary Cells, and flown to Entebbe. The hijackers separated the Israelis and Jews from the larger group and forced them into another room. Non-Israeli hostages were allowed to leave the next day. More than 100 Israeli and Jewish passengers, along with the non-Jewish pilot remained as hostages.

   The IDF, acting on intelligence provided by the Israeli intelligence agency Mossad, stormed the airport at night. Israeli transport planes carried 100 commandos over 2,500 miles (4,000 km) to Uganda for the rescue operation which lasted only 90 minutes. One hundred two hostages were rescued. Five Israeli commandos were wounded and one, the unit commander, Lt. Col. Yonatan Netanyahu, was killed. All the hijackers, three hostages and 45 Ugandan soldiers were killed. (http://en.wikipedia.org/wiki/Operation_Entebbe; accessed December 2013.)

2. Charles Krauthammer, *The Weekly Standard*, May 11, 1998, http://www.eternaltreeofpeace.com/; accessed October 2013.

3. Rockwell Lazarus, "Who Are the Palestinians? What and Where is Palestine?" http://www.newswithviews.com/israel/israel14.htm/; accessed October 2013.

4. Christian Assemblies International; http://www.cai.org/bible-studies/bible-prophecy-0; accessed May 2012.

5. *"Lawrence of Arabia"* was a 1962 British-American film based on the life of T. E. Lawrence. The film starred Peter O'Toole in the title role. O'Toole died in December 2013.

6. Colonel C. G. Powles, "The History of the Canterbury Mounted Rifles, 1914–1919," New Zealand Electronic Text Center, p. 195; http://www.nzetc.org/tm/scholarly/tei-WH1CMRi-t1-body-d14.html; accessed June 2010.

7. Elli Wohlgelernteri, "One Day that Shook the World," *The Jerusalem Post*, 30 April 1998; accessed October 2013.

8. George Gilder, *The Israel Test* (Minneapolis, MN: Richard Vigilante Books, 2009), pp. 234-235.

9. David Naggar, "The Case for a Larger Israel," http://alargerisrael.blogspot.com/; accessed October 2013.

10. Israel Matzav, "I will bless those who bless you, and I will curse him that curses you," Thursday, April 22, 2010, http://israelmatzav.blogspot.com/search?q=I+will+bless+them+that+bless+you; accessed June 2013.

11. Daniel 4

12. Martin Gilbert, *Churchill and the Jews* (Toronto: McClelland & Steward, 2007), pp. 160-161.

13. Alfred Lord Tennyson, http://thinkexist.com/quotation/more_things_are_wrought_by_prayer_than_this_world/12679.html; accessed October 2013.

14. Carino Casas, "Why the Church Should Stand with Israel," http://roamingchile.com/2013/06/why-the-church-should-stand-with-israel/; accessed October 2013.

15. George Bakalav, "10 Reasons Why Christians Should Support Israel—whether it's Popular or Not," January 20, 2009, http://voices.yahoo.com/10-reasons-why-christians-support-israel-whether-2498811.html; accessed November 2013.

16. Senator James Inhofe (R-OK), "Seven Reasons Why Israel has the Right to Her Land," http://www.senate.gov/~inhofe/fl030402.html; accessed September 2013.

17. Fuel for Truth; http://www.fuelfortruth.org/thetruth/truth_10.asp; accessed April 2010.

18. Michael D. Evans, *Save Jerusalem* (Euless, TX: Bedford Books, 1995), p. 94.

19. Moshe Dayan, Address in the General Assembly by Foreign Minister Dayan, September 27, 1979; http://www.mfa.gov.il/MFA/Foreign%20Relations/Israels%20Foreign%20Relations%20since%201947/1979-1980/46%20Address%20in%20the%20General%20Assembly%20by%20Foreign%20Mini; accessed April 2010.

20. Christopher Wise, *Derrida, Africa and the Middle East* (New York, NY: St. Martin's Press, 2009), p. 59.

21. Phillip Misselwitz and Tim Rieniets, *City of Collision: Jerusalem and the Principles of Conflict Urbanism;* (Germany: Die Deutsche Bibliothek, 2006), p. 49.

22. "The Mists of Antiquity 2000-1000 BC, Teddy Kollek and Moshe Pearlman, *Jerusalem: Sacred City of Mankind*, Steimatzky Ltd., Jerusalem, 1991, http://cojs.org/cojswiki/The_Mists_of_Antiquity_2000-1000_BC%2C_Teddy_Kollek_and_Moshe_Pearlman%2C_Jerusalem:_Sacred_City_of_Mankind%2C_Steimatzky_Ltd.%2C_Jerusalem%2C_1991; accessed November 2013.

23. Amikam Elad, "Why did 'Abd al-Malik Build the Dome of the Rock?" Bayt-al-Maqdis: 'Abd al-Malik's Jerusalem, ed. Julian Raby and Jeremy Johns (Oxford: Oxford University Press, 1992), vol. 1, p. 48.

24. Rod Dreher, "Evangelicals and Jews Together, *National Review*, April 5, 2002, http://old.nationalreview.com/dreher/dreher040502.asp; accessed September 2013.

25. Dr. Billy Graham, "Jesus Willingly Gave His Life for Us," *Chicago Tribune*, April 5, 2012, http://articles.chicagotribune.com/2012-04-05/features/sns-201203130000--tms--bgrahamctnym-a20120405apr05_1_sins-eternal-life-god; accessed October 2013.

26. Allen Webster, "Salvation is of the Jews, Part I," http://www.housetohouse.com/HTHPubPage.aspx?cid=3360; accessed October 2013.

27. Judaism Now," http://judaism-now.blogspot.com/2009/09/is-god-man.html; accessed October 2013.

28. Peter Wehner, "Israel and Evangelical Christians, *Commentary Magazine*, October 28, 2013, http://www.commentarymagazine.com/2013/10/28/israel-and-evangelical-christians/#more-835429; accessed October 2013.

29. Martin Luther King, Letter to a friend on Anti-Semitism, http://www.internationalwallofprayer.org/A-022-Martin-Luther-King-Zionism.html; accessed October 2013.

30. Cohn, Norman (1966), *Warrant for Genocide: The Myth of the Jewish World-Conspiracy and the Protocols of the Elder of Zion* (New York: Harper & Row, 2006), pp. 32–36.

31. "Hamas Covenant," Yale, 1988: "Today it is Palestine, tomorrow it will be one country or another. The Zionist plan is limitless. After Palestine, the Zionists aspire to expand from the Nile to the Euphrates. When they will have digested the region they overtook, they will aspire to further expansion, and so on. Their plan is embodied in the 'Protocols of the Elders of Zion', and their present conduct is the best proof of what we are saying."; accessed May 2013

32. Islamic Antisemitism in Historical Perspective (PDF), Anti-Defamation League, 276 kB; accessed October 2013.

33. As quoted in footnote 220 of *Left in Dark Times: A Stand against the New Barbarism* (NY: Random House, 2008).

34. Omri Ceren, "O Beloved Belgium, Sacred Land of Anti-Semitism," *Commentary Magazine*, May 17, 2011, http://www.commentarymagazine.com/2011/05/17/belgian-minister-says-to-forget-about-nazis/; accessed October 2013.

35. Benzion Netanyahu, *The Origins of the Inquisition in Fifteenth-Century Spain*, second edition (New York: New York Review Books, 2001), p. 3.

36. "The Inquisition," http://www.simpletoremember.com/articles/a/the_inquisition/; accessed October 2013.

37. Ibid.

38. "Judaism," Wikipedia: John Adams, in a letter to F. A. van der Kemp (February 16, 1809) as quoted in The Roots of American Order (1974) by Russel Kirk; http://en.wikiquote.org/wiki/Jews; accessed October 2011.

39. Reuben Finkh, Excerpting from an address by Woodrow Wilson on May 7, 1911, titled "The Bible and Progress"; http://www.sweetliberty.org/perspective/jewishpersecution12.htm; accessed October 2011.

40. "National Affairs: Abraham, Isaac, Jacob," *Time Magazine US*, May 11, 1925; http://www.time.com/time/magazine/article/0,9171,728422,00.html; accessed October 2011.

41. Ibid.

42. Charles Spencer Hart, *George Washington's Son of Israel* (Freeport, NY: Books for Libraries Press, 1937), p. 5.

43. Walter Brueggemann, *Isaiah 40-66* (Louisville, KY: Westminster John Knox Press, 1998), p18.

44. Corrie ten Boom, with John and Elizabeth Sherrill, *The Hiding Place* (Old Tappan, NJ: Spire Books, 1971), p. 61.

45. Ibid. p. 63

46. Ibid. p. 101

47. Ibid. p. 196

48. Msgr. John Oesterreicher, "Auschwitz, the Christian, and the Council," *CatholicCulture.org*; http://www.catholicculture.org/culture/library/view.cfm?id=609&repos=1&subrepos=0&searchid=527089; accessed June 2010.

49. Corrie ten Boom with John and Elizabeth Sherrill, *The Hiding Place*, p. 212.

50. Corrie ten Boom with John and Elizabeth Sherrill, *The Hiding Place*, p. 238.

51. Barry Rubin, "The Region: All Israel, all the Time," *The Jerusalem Post*, August 23, 2010, http://www.jpost.com/Opinion/Op-Ed-Contributors/The-Region-All-Israel-all-the-time; accessed October 2013.

52. Bernard Avishai, *The Hebrew Republic: How Secular Democracy and Global Enterprise will Bring Israel Peace at Last* (New York: Harcourt, 2008), pp. 198-201.

53. Giulio Meotti, "The Churches against Israel," YNet News.com; July 3, 2011; http://www.ynetnews.com/articles/0,7340,L-4090528,00.html; accessed August 2011.

54. Paul C. Merkley, "Christian Attitudes: A Bird's Eye View," *Arutz Sheva*, March 14, 2004; http://www.israelnationalnews.com/Articles/Article.aspx/3444; accessed August 2011. (NOTE: WCC Press Releases issued July 1997, October 4, 1997, November 1997; March 1998; September 21, 2001.)

55. Global Ministries of the United Methodist Church; http://gbgm-umc.org/global_news/full_article.cfm?articleid=694; accessed January 2012.

56. Ibid.

57. Quoted by George Gilder in *The Israel Test* (Minneapolis, MN: Richard Vigilante Books, 2009), p. 22.

58. Arthur W. Pink, "The Death of the Firstborn," Old Testament Study: Exodus 11:1-10, http://www.scripturestudies.com/Vol11/K10/ot.html; accessed November 2013.

59. William L. Shirer, *The Rise and Fall of the Third Reich*, pp. 10–11.

60. "Lloyd George and Hitler. . . Comments on His Visit to Germany and Meeting with Hitler in 1936," *Daily Express,* September 17, 1936; http://www.ww2hc.org/articles/lloyd_george_and_hitler.htm; accessed August 2011.

61. Robert Solomon Wistrich, *Who's Who in Nazi Germany* (Hove, East Sussex, UK: Psychology Press, 2002), p. 118.

62. John Toland, *Adolf Hitler* (London: Book Club Associates, 1977), p. 116.

63. Houston Stewart Chamberlain, *Letters* (1882–1924 and correspondence with Emperor Wilhelm II) (Munich: F. Bruckmann, 1928), p. 124. (Translated from the German by Alexander Jacob.)

64. "Adolf Hitler," *Deutsche Presse,* April 20–21, 1944, p. 1.

65. Deborah E. Lipstadt, *Beyond Belief: The American Press and the Coming of the Holocaust, 1933–1945* (New York: Simon and Schuster, 1993), pp. 79–80.

66. "Wannsee Conference, Jewish Virtual Library; http://www.jewishvirtuallibrary.org/jsource/judaica/ejud_0002_0020_0_20606.html; accessed March 2012.

67. Ibid. p. 44

68. Ibid. pp. 47–48

69. "*SS Exodus*"; http://en.wikipedia.org/wiki/SS_Exodus; accessed October 2011.

70. Norman Bentwich, *For Zion's Sake: A Biography of Judah L. Magnes* (Philadelphia: Jewish Publication Society, 1954), p. 267.

71. Ibid. p. 90

72. "The Little Known Story of a Christian Minister who helped make Israel Possible," *The Jewish Magazine,* June 2008, http://www.jewishmag.com/134mag/exodus_grauel/exodus_grauel.htm; accessed May 2103.

73. http://www.mideastweb.org/trusteeship.htm; United States Proposal for Temporary United Nations Trusteeship for Palestine Source: Department of State Bulletin, vol. 18, No. 457, 4 April 1948, p. 451; accessed December 2013.

74. Ibid.

75. Arab League Declaration on the Intervention in Palestine, 15 May 1948, http://en.wikisource.org/wiki/Cablegram_from_the_Secretary-General_of_the_League_of_Arab_States_to_the_Secretary-General_of_the_United_Nations; accessed December 2913; accessed December 2013.

76. The Palestine National Charter, July 17, 1968, Article 22, http://www.jewishvirtuallibrary.org/jsource/Peace/PLO_Covenant.html; accessed December 2013.

77. "Oslo II Agreement," December 28, 1995, http://www.acpr.org.il/resources/oslo2.html; accessed December 2013.

78. Yoram Hazony, The Jewish State: The Struggle for Israel's Soul (New York, NY: Basic Books, 2001), p. 333.

79. Arthur A. Goren, *Dissenter in Zion: From the Writings of Judah L. Magnes* (Cambridge, MA: Harvard University Press, 1982), p. 472.

80. Paul C. Merkley, *American Presidents, Religion, and Israel: the Heirs of Cyrus* (Westport, CT: Greenwood Publishing Group, 2004), p. 58.

81. Zalmi Unsdorfer, "Young Winston Churchill—a true friend of our people," *The Jerusalem Post,* June 4, 2010; http://www.jpost.com/Opinion/Op-EdContributors/Article.aspx?id=172525; accessed March 2010.

82. "The Six-Day War," *Committee for Accuracy in Middle East Reporting in America*; http://www.sixdaywar.org/content/ReunificationJerusalem.asp; accessed January 2012.

83. "Golda Meir on peace," http://www.jewishvirtuallibrary.org/jsource/Quote/MeironPeace.html; accessed December 2013.

84. Seymour Hersh, The Samson Option: Israel's Nuclear Arsenal & American Foreign Policy (New York, NY: Random House, 1991), pp. 224-226.

85. Seymour M. Hersh, The Samson Option: Israel's Nuclear Arsenal and American Foreign Policy (New York: Vintage Books, 1991), p. 223.

86. Seymour M. Hersh, The Price of Power: Kissinger in the Nixon White House (New York: Summit Books, 1983), p. 234.

87. Jerry Klinger, "Richard Nixon, the anti-Semite who Saved Israel",http://www.jewishmag. com/167mag/kissinger-nixon-war-watergate/kissinger-nixon-war-watergate.htm

88. "Zionism, Nixon-style," The Jerusalem Post editorial, December 12, 2010; http://www.jpost. com/Opinion/Editorials/Article.aspx?id=199133&R=R6; accessed January 2012.

89. Jason Maoz, "Nixon: The Anti-Semite who Saved Israel," The Jewish Press, August 5, 2005.

90. Yitzhak Rabin, The Rabin Memoirs (Boston: Little, Brown and Company, Inc., 1979), p. 100; in Schoenbaum, The United States and the State of Israel, p. 167.

91. Thomas F. Kranz, "Robert F. Kennedy Assassination (Summary)," for the Federal Bureau of Investigation and made available by the Freedom of Information Act (March 1977), p. 17.

92. Ibid. p. 10

93. Ibid. p. 15

94. Ibid. p. 6

95. "Robert Kennedy and Israel," http://robertkennedyandisrael.blogspot.com/; accessed May 2012.

96. Jay Newton-Small, "Ted Kennedy's Wake: Farewell to 'Captain Ahab'", Time, August 29, 2009, http://www.time.com/time/nation/article/0,8599,1919470,00.html#ixzz2MtXckazY; accessed January 2012.

97. Irwin Abrams, The Words of Peace: Selections from the Speeches of Winners of the Nobel Peace Prize (New York: Newmarket Press, 2008) p. 11.

98. Menachem Begin, The Revolt (NY: Nash Publishing, 1977), p. 224.

99. Benjamin Netanyahu, ed., "International Terrorism: Challenge and Response," Proceedings of the Jerusalem Conference on International Terrorism, July 2-5, 1979 (Jerusalem: The Jonathan Institute, 1980), p. 45.

100. Dr. Evans' personal interview with Menachem Begin in Jerusalem, 1980.

101. Ibid.

102. Ibid.

103. Personal interview with Shimon Peres, January 2007.

104. Ibid.

105. "Sabena Flight 571", http://en.wikipedia.org/wiki/Sabena_Flight_571_hijacking; accessed December 2013.

106. See Footnote 121.

107. Tal Silberstein, an interview with Amnon Lord, Nov.2, 2003.

108. Yossef Bodansky, The High Cost of Peace: How Washington's Middle East Policy Left America Vulnerable to Terrorism (Roseville, CA: Forum, 2002), p. 223.

109. Tal Silberstein, an interview with Amnon Lord, Nov.2, 2003.

110. Joseph Klein, "Obama, Sarkozy's Contempt for Netanyahu Exposed," *Front Page Magazine*, November 9, 2011; http://frontpagemag.com/2011/11/09/obama-sarkozys-contempt-for-netanyahu-exposed/; accessed January 2012.

111. "Bad to Worse: Iran Deal Strains Obama-Netanyahu Relationship," NPR, November 27, 2013, http://www.npr.org/blogs/itsallpolitics/2013/12/02/247520449/bad-to-worse-iran-deal-strains-obama-netanyahu-relationship; accessed December 2013.

112. Ibid.

113. Barak: Arab parts of Jerusalem could become Palestinian capital," Haaretz.com, March 8, 2008; http://www.haaretz.com/news/barak-arab-parts-of-jerusalem-could-become-palestinian-capital-1.253169; accessed September 2010.

114. "Barak: Israel ready to cede parts of Jerusalem in peace deal," Haaretz.com, September 1, 2010; http://www.haaretz.com/news/diplomacy-defense/barak-israel-ready-to-cede-parts-of-jerusalem-in-peace-deal-1.311450; accessed September 2010.

115. Etgar Lefkovits, "Jerusalem will never be divided," *The Israel Report*, May/June 2000; http://christianactionforisrael.org/isreport/mayjun00/never.html; accessed September 2010.

116. Ehud Barak, http://www.jewishvirtuallibrary.org/jsource/biography/barak.html; accessed December 2013.

117. Jerusalem Issue Brief, Volume 1, No. 16, January 24, 2002,http://www.jcpa.org/art/brief1-16.htm, accessed December 2013.

118. "The Mitchell Report", Jewish Virtual Library, May 4, 2001; accessed December 2013.

119. Sheryl Gay Stolberg, "Bush and Israel—Unlike his father," *The New York Times*; February 8, 2006; http://www.nytimes.com/2006/08/02/world/americas/02iht-bush.2363483.html?pagewanted=all; accessed January 2012.

120. "Ehud Olmert, ex-Israeli leader, gets light sentence for corruption," *Los Angeles Times*, September 24, 2012, http://latimesblogs.latimes.com/world_now/2012/09/israel-ehud-olmert-sentence-corruption.html; accessed December 2013.

121. Kenneth R. Timmerman, *Insight on the News*, "The Truth About Mahmoud Abbas," July 8, 2003; http://findarticles.com/p/articles/mi_m1571/is_2003_July_8/ai_104842031;a; accessed July 2008.)

122. "On October 29, hijackers of a German Lufthansa passenger jet demanded the release of the three surviving terrorists...being held for trial. [Two] were immediately released by Germany, receiving a tumultuous welcome when they touched down in Libya and giving their own firsthand account of their operation at a press conference broadcast worldwide. In both ESPN/ABC's documentary The Tragedy of the Munich Games and in Kevin Macdonald's Academy Award-winning documentary One Day in September, it is claimed that the whole Lufthansa hijacking episode was a sham, concocted by the West Germans and Black September so that the Germans could be rid of the three Munich perpetrators. The view is that the Germans were fearful that their mishandling of the rescue attempt would be exposed to the world if the three Fürstenfeldbruck survivors had ever stood trial." http://en.wikipedia.org/wiki/Munich_massacre; accessed July 2008.)

123. Irwin N. Graulich, "Why America Supports Israel," FrontPageMag.com, December 20, 2002; http://archive.frontpagemag.com/readArticle.aspx?ARTID=20579; accessed January 2012.

124. Paul Goldman, "Dying 4-year old girl finds life-savers in the land of the enemy," http://worldnews.nbcnews.com/_news/2013/05/26/18445610-dying-4-year-old-girl-finds-life-savers-in-land-of-the-enemy?lite, May 2013; accessed June 2013.

125. David Miller, "Intelligent 'Wrapping Paper' Heals Broken Bones in Half the Time," December 31, 2013; http://news.yahoo.com/blogs/this-could-be-big-abc-news/intelligent-wrapping-paper-heals-broken-bones-half-time-190710297.html?vp=1; accessed January 1, 2014.

126. Marcella Rosen, "65 years of innovations from Israel," May 9, 2013, *The Jewish Observer*, http://jewishobservernashville.org/2013/05/09/65-years-of-innovations-from-israel/; accessed June 2013.

127. See the full list of innovations and inventions at http://jewishobservernashville.org/2013/05/09/65-years-of-innovations-from-israel/.

128. "Nobel Prize in Literature 2002," Nobel Foundation; accessed June 2013.

129. "The Nobel Peace Prize for 1986: Elie Wiesel," Nobelprize.org, 14 October 1986; accessed June 2013.

130. "Professor Robert Aumann: He's Got Game," *The Jerusalem Post*, November 1, 2005, www.jpost.com/servlet/Satellite?cid=1129540643006&pagename= JPost%2FJPArticle%2FShowFull; accessed June 2013.

131. Robert Aumann, http://en.wikipedia.org/wiki/Robert_Aumann, accessed June 2013.

132. http://www.quotationcollection.com/author/Ernest-Hemingway/quotes; accessed June 2013.

133. Reza Kahlili, "Ayatollah: Kill all Jews, Annihilate Israel," *World Net Daily*, February 5, 2012, http://www.wnd.com/2012/02/ayatollah-kill-all-jews-annihilate-israel/#dUomRSFSddGwcqWP.99; accessed November 2013.

134. Josep Federman, "Netanyahu: Iran Nuclear Deal a 'historic mistake'," *Huffington Post*, November 25, 2013, http://www.huffingtonpost.com/2013/11/24/netanyahu-iran-deal-israel-nuclear_n_4332906.html; accessed November 2013.

135. "Arabs not allied with Iran not quiet over nuclear deal," *USAToday*, November 24, 2013, http://www.usatoday.com/story/news/world/2013/11/24/iran-nuclear-deal-arab-reactions/3691289/; accessed November 2013.

136. Jerusalem Prayer Team Petition to President George W. Bush, JPT archives, used by permission.

137. Dr. Evans was born in Springfield, Massachusetts, in 1947, to a non-practicing Jewish mother whose grandparents were immigrants from the Soviet Union. He is Jewish by birthright.

138. http://www.biblicalheritage.org/BHR/BHR-43.pdf; accessed December 2013.

BOOKS BY: MIKE EVANS

Israel: America's Key to Survival

Save Jerusalem

The Return

Jerusalem D.C.

Purity and Peace of Mind

Who Cries for the Hurting?

Living Fear Free

I Shall Not Want

Let My People Go

Jerusalem Betrayed

Seven Years of Shaking: A Vision

The Nuclear Bomb of Islam

Jerusalem Prophecies

Pray For Peace of Jerusalem

America's War: The Beginning of the End

The Jerusalem Scroll

The Prayer of David

The Unanswered Prayers of Jesus

God Wrestling

Why Christians Should Support Israel

The American Prophecies

Beyond Iraq: The Next Move

The Final Move beyond Iraq

Showdown with Nuclear Iran

Jimmy Carter: The Liberal Left
and World Chaos

Atomic Iran

Cursed

Betrayed

The Light

Corrie's Reflections & Meditations
(booklet)

GAMECHANGER SERIES:
　GameChanger
　Samson Option
　The Four Horsemen

THE PROTOCOLS SERIES:
　The Protocols
　The Candidate

The Revolution

The Final Generation

Seven Days

The Locket

Living in the F.O.G.

Persia: The Final Jihad

Jerusalem

The History of Christian Zionism

Countdown

Ten Boom: Betsie, Promise of God

Commanded Blessing

Born Again: 1948

Presidents in Prophecy

Stand with Israel: Friends of Zion

COMING SOON:

Born Again: 1967

Christopher Columbus

To purchase, contact: orders@timeworthybooks.com
P. O. Box 30000, Phoenix, AZ 85046